Sharing the Word
through the
Liturgical Year

Sharing the Word through the Liturgical Year

Gustavo Gutiérrez

*Translated from the Spanish
by Colette Joly Dees*

ORBIS BOOKS
Maryknoll, New York

E. J. DWYER

GEOFFREY
CHAPMAN

Originally published as *Compartir la Palabra: A lo largo del Año Litúrgico* by the Instituto Bartolomé de Las Casas-Rimac, Belisario Flores 687, Lima 14, Apdo. 3090, Lima, Peru, and the Centro de Estudios y Publicaciones (CEP), Camilo Carrillo 479, Lima 11, Apdo. 11-0107, Lima, Peru, copyright © 1995.

Translation copyright © 1997 by Orbis Books

Published in the United States of America by Orbis Books, Maryknoll, NY 10545-0308

Published in Great Britain by Geoffrey Chapman, a Cassell imprint, Wellington House, 125 Strand, London WC2R 0BB, England

Published in Australia and New Zealand by E. J. Dwyer (Australia) Pty Ltd, Unit 13, Perry Park, 33 Maddox Street, Alexandria NSW 2015, Australia

Blockprint from *Clip Art: Blockprints for Sundays Cycles A, B, C* (Revised Edition) by Helen Siegl. Copyright © 1990 (Pueblo Publ. Co.) by The Order of St. Benedict, Inc. Published by The Liturgical Press, Collegeville, Minnesota. Used with permission.

Cover design: Jerry Braatz

Library of Congress Catalog Card No: 97-19495

British Library Cataloguing-in-Publication Data
A catalogue record for this book is available from the British Library.

National Library of Australia Cataloguing-in-Publication Data
A catalogue record for this book is available from the National Library of Australia.

ORBIS/ISBN – 1-57075-138-2
CASSELL/ISBN – 0-225-66858-0
DWYER/ISBN – 0-85574-119-8

To the Community of Christ the Redeemer,
who inspired my journey
and with whom I have shared these reflections first.

To Rolando López,
a friend always present,
who welcomed these pages as a brother.

Contents

Introduction

The characteristic mission of Christians is proclaiming the gospel, the good news of the gratuitous love of God for every person but preferentially for the poor and the excluded. This proclamation takes place in terms of deeds and words embodied in human history, which is also the way God's self-revelation comes to us through the life and message of Jesus Christ (see *Dei Verbum*, no. 2).

The church reads the scriptures in the course of the liturgical year which, centered on the "great solemnity of Easter" (*Sacrosanctum Concilium*, no. 102), presents "all the mysteries of Christ" as the theme for our meditation and as the example of Christian practice. Each week, on Sunday, the Lord's day, the ecclesial assembly remembers and makes present the resurrection of Christ in the here and now of history. Communicating the gospel is, in fact, announcing the fullness of life in Jesus. Our vital and communitarian reference to the biblical text is essential. As the second letter to Timothy states, scripture "is useful for teaching, for reproof, for correction, and for training in righteousness" (3:16).

The homily is part of the liturgy. It serves as a bridge between the two parts of the eucharistic celebration: the word and the rite. This familiar conversation, which is what the term "homily" means, prolongs the reading of scripture and seeks to bring the word close to us: a word which liberates and calls us to friendship, banishing a world of injustice and selfishness. The homily makes no sense outside of the biblical texts on which it is supposed to shed light. The homily may speak of many things but in the final analysis, it is to proclaim only one thing: the message of the good news.

Our greatest wish is that these pages will be useful to those who seek to meditate on the Lord's word and to share it with others by following the subject matter of the liturgical year. The different cycles invite us to follow in the footsteps of the Galilean preacher, the Son of God, the one who by his explanation of the scriptures to his disciples on the way to Emmaus "opened their eyes and made their hearts burn" (Lk 24).

This book is a compilation of articles published over several years in the biweekly publication *Signos* (CEP, IBC, Lima). I am grateful to the editorial team for their encouragement. We have omitted some references to circumstances which are not currently relevant and, on the other hand, we have added quite a few commentaries which were never published. To avoid lengthening the text, the quotations from the biblical passages which we explain are short. Therefore, it is important to have the texts at hand.

Advent

*"Come, let us walk
in the light of the Lord!"*
(Is 2:5)

First Sunday of Advent

A. Walking in the Light of the Lord
Is 2:1–5; Rom 13:11–14; Mt 24:37–44

Advent is a time of vigilance as we wait for God's coming in our history. Through conversion we prepare ourselves to welcome God who is born among us.

Keeping Awake

Advent is a time for strengthening hope, a period of preparation for Christmas but also a time to underscore an attitude toward life, toward history, and toward God, the God of hope and of the promise. The history of humanity is a great advent, a journey toward the future: God and his reign become incarnate in our history.

Paul tells us, "Let us lay aside the works of darkness and put on the armor of light" (v. 12), not the armor which creates violence, lies, and despair but rather the armor which secures peace, establishes justice, and creates solidarity among peoples. The face and model of this armor is the one who came to us as the light of the world. Hence, Paul's invitation to put on "the Lord Jesus Christ" (v. 14).

When we have put on his spirit, we will be alert and ready for his coming. The Son of Man comes and surprises us at the least expected hour (Mt 24:44), especially in our daily encounter with human beings he has made his brothers and sisters. Thus the need to keep awake (v. 42) translates into listening to the clamor for liberation, supporting and empowering our peoples' deepest hopes. Waiting for the Lord does not bring us out of history; it involves us with it since we are hoping for the God who has come and is in our midst. Such a hope is ambitious but it is worthwhile. It will help us see what is inconsistent in our behavior, what is deceptive and underhanded in our personal lives but also what is hopeful in our efforts to defend life and justice.

From Swords to Plowshares

Today's liturgy recalls the beautiful utopia of humankind found in the text of Isaiah (and also in Micah, see 4:1–3). The text refers to the house and the temple of the Lord, places and symbols of his presence (vv. 2–3). The Lord is at the center of history attracting and energizing the path of his people. We should ask ourselves: In what direction are we going? Hopefully, our answer will be: toward peace and solidarity for everyone, a desire we all share. But the path presented to us is perplexing. Because we are used to the saying: "If you wish for peace, prepare for war," this path does not correspond to our expectations. If peoples decide to choose God as judge and arbitrator among nations, the prerequisite is "not to learn war any more" (v. 4). Instead, a political, economic and reconciling program is proposed in the evocative expression of "beating swords into plowshares." We dedicate huge amounts of resources to the industry of war, destruction, and death. Isaiah's text suggests total disarmament, from our hearts where unjust violence begins to the structures preparing for war. A wise and enlightened decision-making people exclaim: "O house of Jacob, come, let us walk in the light of the Lord" (v. 5). For our particularly dark time both at the national and international level, this expression is highly significant.

B. Doing Right Gladly
Is 63:16–17, 19, 64:2–7; 1 Cor 1:3–9; Mk 13:33–37

Let us start preparing ourselves for the Lord's coming. Mark's text urges us to pay attention to the signs of the times, to history.

Encounter at an Unknown Time

Mark warns us at the beginning of his gospel: "The time is fulfilled" (1:15). He is speaking of the *kairos,* the propitious time, the quality time — without a specific date — when something important will take place. Here again, Mark uses this term (*kairos*) to tell us that we must be alert and know how to discern the occasion the Lord has chosen to come to our encounter: "for you do not know when the time will come" (13:33).

But on the basis of what we might be tempted to consider common sense, we could object: Don't we always celebrate Christmas on the same day of the year? On this first Sunday of Advent, Mark's text seeks precisely to get us out of our humdrum, static, chronological perspective. In fact, December 25 can come and go without our encountering the Lord in the now of our lives and of our history. Because of the advertising pounding for useless things out of reach for most Peruvians, because of one more or one less festive cake, our Christmas may not be what Paul calls "the day of our Lord Jesus Christ" (1 Cor 3:8). In other words, Christmas may come and go without changing our lives, without "the testimony of Christ" (v. 6) being strengthened in us.

Raising Hope

For that to happen, we have to stay alert, as the Markan text repeats again and again — staying awake, not stagnating in a Christian life we think we have acquired once and for all. The liturgy loves vigils, the paschal vigil, for example, with its profound theological meaning. Like the doorkeeper in Mark's passage (v. 34), Christians have to be attentive to what the Lord wants to reveal to them in events. In Latin America and in Peru, we experience a situation of increasing deterioration in the daily lives of the poor, economic and social differences are becoming increasingly more abysmal, new — or rather old — siren songs announce old tunes, promoting deceit and passivity before the real causes of those unjust situations and of the deaths which they cause.

At times, we feel that a people's hope is also dying. Preparing to receive Jesus means refusing to accept that situation. Vigilance implies there is a commitment in our actions. Raising the hope — not the illusions — of the poor is situating ourselves at the time of the advent of the "faithful God" (1 Cor 1:9) coming to us. The time of this encounter is God's design but it is also our task. It is not some type of chronological fatality because, as we hear in the first reading, God "meets those who gladly do right and remember God's ways" (Is 64:5).

In fact, justice must be practiced with joy and hope (Is 64:3), not with bitterness and discouragement. Thus will the Lord meet us and the feast of Christmas will have meaning for our lives and for the history of the people to whom we belong.

C. Be on Your Guard
Jer 33:14–16; 1 Thes 3:12–4:2; Lk 21:25–28, 34–36

We are starting Advent. Something will happen: the Lord's coming. Expectation means being alert; this is the call of today's texts.

Liberation Is Approaching

This is a difficult gospel text. Shortly before, Luke was telling us about the siege and the destruction of Jerusalem (Lk 21:20–23). Now he is referring to Jesus' second coming, namely, what we call the Parousia. At times, the Parousia is not very present in the awareness of average Christians, but it is part of our faith. The scene is apocalyptic; however, the Apocalypse does not mean catastrophe, as we tend to think, but rather revelation. The Lord's second coming will reveal history to itself. The truth which was hidden will appear in full light. We will all know ourselves better.

Therefore, the Parousia does not suggest terror but courage "because redemption is drawing near" (v. 28). Besides, attention to the future does not eliminate today's demands. This is not passive but vigilant waiting, being attentive to the signs of the times (Lk 21:29–33) in which the Lord manifests himself. We must pray "at all times" (v. 36) because prayer is a gesture and an experience of gratuity, of the gratuity of God's love which gives full meaning to the demand making hope authentic.

Love and Justice

The first two readings tell us about love and justice. Vigilance before the Lord's coming presupposes the practice of "justice and righteousness in the land" (Jer 33:15). This is part of the mission of the "son of David" whose first coming into the world we celebrate at Christmas. Justice and righteousness are two essential aspects of the Lord's promise (v. 14). When the promise is fulfilled "Judah will be saved and Jerusalem will live in safety and it will be called: the Lord is our righteousness" (v. 16). Prophets often give Jerusalem names expressing the fulfillment of God's will. For example, Isaiah calls Jerusalem "joy" (65:18) because in it everyone will be able to live fully.

Luke's text makes us think of the Lord's second coming on the Sunday we begin preparing for Christmas. One advent leads to another. Between the two lies the time of the Christian community, the time when it has to strive to build up "justice and righteousness." This implies concrete commitments with the "daily via crucis" lived by the poor people of the world. That solidarity must be concretized in our decision to build a different society in which justice, love, and peace are possible, a society in which God's gift, God's kingdom is expressed in history so that the poor and every human being may call their countries "justice" and "joy."

This will not be achieved unless "love abounds" (1 Thes 3:12), that is to say, unless everything is permeated with generous and gratuitous surrender, "in love for one another and for all" (ibid.). This is not a question of superficial feelings. It is a way of being vigilant as we await "the coming of our Lord Jesus Christ" (v. 13).

Second Sunday of Advent

A. The Ax at the Root of the Tree
Is 11:1–10; Rom 15:4–9; Mt 3:1–12

During these days, we are renewing our hope in the Lord who continues to come into our lives.

The Ways of the Lord

According to Matthew, Mark, and Luke, the gospel, the good news, starts with John the Baptizer. He is the first to proclaim God's kingdom. He announces it in the desert, the place where our faith is tested and the place of encounter with God. The Jewish people were called to cross the desert to come into the promised land. And so are we now. This implies a change of attitude since without conversion it is impossible to welcome Christ. Baptism is a sign of this change. Those who reject Christ do not have access to baptism. John the Baptizer refuses to accept them despite their appearing — and prestige — as religious people (Mt 3:7). John does not find in them (who are economically and politically powerful) the will to change. In the tone that the Lord will use later on, John reminds them that the change which he is asking for is not something formal, something done by complying with external rituals. John demands they "bear fruit worthy of repentance" (3:8).

Our lives are determined on the basis of our actions. The ax is already at the root of the tree that does not bear fruit. In response to the Lord's teaching that there is either wheat or chaff (3:12), acceptance or rejection, there is no middle path. Later on (Mt 25:31–45), Jesus will say, they gave me food, they did not give me food. John the Baptizer precedes Christ in time. Yet, we who come after him must also have something of the forerunner. Bearing witness to the reign of God consists in preparing the Lord's coming. Our welcoming our neighbors is the condition and the expression of Christ's welcoming us (Rom 15:7).

Judging with Righteousness

Isaiah, the prophet quoted by John the Baptizer, reminds us that the Messiah "will judge the poor with righteousness" (11:4). The practice of justice is part of John's proclamation which opposed him to the powerful of his time, who asked for his head. According to the prophet, God's kingdom expresses a world of profound peace and harmony. The beautiful images taken from a rural context simply reinforce this proclamation (11:6–9). But, as a result of it, the establishment of justice emerges as an indispensable condition.

This has been the understanding of many Christians of this continent. Their struggle for peace implies fighting for justice. Many have paid for this with their own lives. In these years, with pain and horror, we have endured the murders — in El Salvador — of six Jesuit priests and of two other people (mother and daughter) who were working with them. Their commitment was clear. They wanted peace for the people that one of them, Ignacio Ellacuría, called "a crucified people." They did a great deal to attain that peace. But those who murdered Archbishop Romero could not allow that either. Those who have given their lives are also precursors of Jesus in some way. They are calling us to convert and to prepare the way for the advent of the Lord.

B. John the Baptizer
Is 40:1–5, 9–11; 2 Pet 3:8–14; Mk 1:1–8

The good news begins with the sending of someone to prepare the way.

Conversion

In Mark, John the Baptizer seems to emerge suddenly; he "appeared" (v. 4). He is an envoy, a messenger. What John announces prepares what Jesus is going to proclaim. John baptizes in the desert as a sign of life, and he calls for repentance (v. 4), namely, to change what must be changed, to straighten what is crooked, to seek justice and to prepare earnestly for the encounter with the Lord who comes daily in the midst of what is insignificant in this world. John the Baptizer represents the function which God, who reveals his love and presence, fulfills in what we call the Old Testament. This revelation reaches its fullness with Jesus.

The Lord comes because he loves his own and he hears their sorrows and their clamor. God does not come by chance but out of love. This joyful encounter is what Christians have been expecting from the start of their faith, and for that to happen they have to give up their idols (objects of a trust which is due to God alone) and turn to the living God who comes to their encounter. We are dealing with a radical change since the Spirit will pour upon us the life and the love of the Father and of the Son. Baptism in water prepares us for baptism in the Holy Spirit (v. 8).

An austere man clothed with camel's hair, eating what he finds in the desert (v. 6), brings this anticipatory message. The people wishing to prepare themselves flock to him; they do not go to the temple but to the desert at the edge of the promised land, and they are baptized in the river Jordan (v. 5).

Speaking to the Heart

"Comfort my people," says the Lord (Is 40:1). In Isaiah, comforting means liberating. This is what John the Baptizer has started to do. He "speaks tenderly" (Is 40:1) to the people of Jerusalem. It is necessary to change the root of personal behavior, but the results have to be substantial: the valleys will be lifted up and the mountains made low (v. 4). This is not something superficial. With the Lord's coming into history and into our lives, the panorama will be different with the advent of God's kingdom.

John the Baptizer gives a testimony of humility. He does not obstruct the Lord's way, but he points it out. He provides a guideline for Jesus' followers, for us who must bear witness to him, to him, not to ourselves. A Christian community which proclaims and affirms itself is hiding the presence of the Lord. By living friendship and understanding and by serving without seeking privileges within the Christian community, we will make God's love known.

Advent is the time to prepare for the Lord's nativity to the extent that it is a time to prepare for our encounter with Jesus. The Lord will fulfill his promise, and he invites us to a radical change in terms of accepting him by accepting the little ones and the marginalized (2 Pet 3:9–10).

C. Peace with Justice
Bar 5:1–9; Phil 1:4–6, 8–11; Lk 3:1–6

Advent, a time of hope and of openness to change: change of clothing, change of name (Baruch), and change of ways (Isaiah) — changing so that all may see the salvation of God.

God Remembers You

Echoing the prophets of the exile, Baruch speaks comforting words to a people in trouble: "The Lord remembers you" (5:5). Second Isaiah had already asked: "Can a woman forget her nursing child?...even if she forgets, yet I will not forget you" (Is 49:15). God who is faithful does not forget Jerusalem, his bride, who is invited to take off her mourning clothes and to put on "forever the beauty of the glory from God" (Bar 5:1). This change produced by God's mercy for the people is also expressed in terms of a change of clothing and a change of name given to this city: "Righteous peace" (Bar 5:4) or the salvation that God offers to those he loves, to those God remembers in his love.

In the gospel, when the fullness of time comes, God himself announces the proximity of the kingdom through John and confirms with Isaiah that "all will see the salvation of God" (Lk 3:6). With his usual meticulousness, Luke (Lk 1:1–4) provides us with the historical framework of John's preaching (3:1–3). In the now-ness of our own history, we must prepare the way for the God who comes with the gift of salvation.

Preparing the Way

Isaiah's call, reiterated by John the Baptizer and corroborated by Baruch, invites us to enter into the dynamism of conversion, to start on the way, to change — changing from within, growing in what is fundamental, namely, in love to determine what is best (Phil 1:10). With the insight and sensitivity of love, we will hear the Lord's demands better and "having produced the harvest of righteousness" (1:11) we will go out to meet him.

This renewal from within has its external manifestation because "mountains are made low," valleys are filled up, what is crooked is straightened, and what is rough is leveled (Bar 5:7). Asperities are smoothed, inequalities are suppressed, and distances are shortened so that salvation may come to all. A transformed humanity is a reconciled, equal humanity, integrated into the family with its "children gathered from east and west" (Bar 5:5). Converting then means opening up our hearts, expanding hope to make it worldwide and God-like. Men and women who are more equal and more respectful of other people's dignity are the best way for God's salvation to come. All of us have to determine what straightening what is crooked or leveling mountains or filling up valleys imposes in terms of renunciation. Yet, for God to come, our paths have to be straightened.

United in hope, we journey together to meet our God. But at the same time, God is walking with us, indicating the path because "God will lead Israel with joy, in the light of his glory, with the mercy and righteousness that come from him" (Bar 5:9).

Third Sunday of Advent

A. Evangelizing the Poor
Is 35:1–6, 10; Jas 5:7–10; Mt 11:2–11

In spite of poverty, wars, the exclusion of so many people, the season of Advent continues to stir our hope, and it calls us to incarnate it in our daily lives.

Jesus Is the Christ

The things John the Baptizer has heard about Jesus have caused him to wonder and also to have hope. John sends two of his disciples (see also Jn 1:39–45) to find out if Jesus is the Messiah (the Christ) or if they have to wait for another (Mt 11:3). Jesus' answer deals with a very concrete testimony. The disciples are to relate

what they have seen and heard (v. 4). The question concerning
Jesus' identity will be answered by his deeds, which correspond
to what was announced by Is 61:1–2 (and Is 35:5–6), a text which
is very present in the gospels in terms of Jesus' mission. All of
his actions consist in giving life.

Works for the sake of the poor and the needy identify Jesus as
the Messiah. The Son of Man who has no place to lay his head
lives in these works which mark the irruption of God's kingdom into the present, a kingdom which is preferentially destined
to the poor and through them to every human being. The healings mentioned in Matthew's text are the anticipation and the
pledge of that kingdom. Gestures of love toward others nourish
the hope of the final coming of the Lord, and they make it near
and dynamic (Jas 5:7–8).

A Testimony of Life

Relieving the suffering of a few poor in Jesus' days is a sign, a
sign of the strong promise that the good news of God's kingdom
is for all the world's poor. It is a proclamation through liberating
words and deeds. The gospel is proclaimed to the poor by way
of concrete actions: enabling people to see, walk, hear, in other
words, giving life. In his own days, Jesus gives the example in
order for us to understand that it is a commandment for all his
followers in the course of history. Today, our gestures of solidarity
in the presence of the hunger and poverty of so many in the world
have to communicate that God's kingdom is among us.

Jesus' cures give full meaning to the good news to the poor
promised in Isaiah. Now before the very eyes of John's disciples, the good news is accomplished by Jesus' messianic action.
They have seen and heard him, but it is not easy to understand
him. Thus, the text concludes with a beatitude: "Blessed is anyone who takes no offense at me" (v. 6). John the Baptist takes no
offense when he receives the testimony of his disciples, and this
is why Jesus praises him (vv. 7–11). Like John, all of us have to be
messengers of the Lord.

B. In Joyful Expectation
Is 61:1–2, 10–11; 1 Thes 5:16–24; Jn 1:6–8, 19–28

Advent is a time of preparation for the coming of the Lord and therefore a time to be vigilant, as the texts of the first Sunday of this season remind us. We have to clarify the meaning of this expectation.

Rejoice

In the liturgy, every attitude of vigilance has a penitential side to express our being detached from what binds us now and our being available for what will come. In the midst of this taut bow with Christmas at one end of it, today's texts break in with a burst of joy: "Rejoice in the Lord always; again I will say, rejoice" (Phil 4:4–5) as we have in the entrance antiphon and again in these same terms in the second reading (1 Thes 5:16).

In fact, while vigilance supposes our being alert and ready to respond, we should not respond as if we were suffering and downcast. Our waiting for the Lord can only be lived with the anticipatory joy of the forthcoming encounter. The letter to the Thessalonians adds something very important: "Do not quench the Spirit" (5:19). Mediocrity and sadness make us lose the spark of creativity which the Spirit breathes into us — tension in waiting but joy in "the God of peace" (1 Thes 5:23).

Making Way for Liberation

The reason for living the Advent season in this way is that the Lord comes to liberate us. Isaiah's text is the source of important gospel passages. Jesus refers to Isaiah on various occasions when defining his own mission (Lk 4:16–20; 7:18–28; Mt 11:2–6). Anointed by the Spirit, he is sent "to bring good news to the oppressed, to bind up the brokenhearted, to proclaim liberty to the captives and release to the prisoners" (61:1): a message of life and liberation to sustain every believer's hope.

We have to make way for this proclamation with profound humility. Everything seems to indicate that John the Evangelist was a disciple of his namesake, the Baptist. He knew him well, and this is the reason why he can propose him as an example of modesty and discernment with regard to his task. During the severe examination to which he is submitted by the authorities of his people (this is what the term "the Jews" means in John's gospel), the precursor answers with simplicity and moderation. He does not put himself first but behind the Lord (Jn 1:27). His function is merely to break the furrows in which the only sower, Jesus, will place his word. John rejects all ambiguity: he is not replacing the Messiah.

Even though we come after Jesus, as Christians we are precursors like John. Therefore, the Christian community, the church does not replace Christ. In a certain sense, it has to retreat before Christ because it is not worthy "to untie the thong of his sandal" (Jn 1:27). The whole church must have the same spirituality as the precursor, especially in the case of those who, in one way or another, are its representatives. What matters is that the Lord is coming. This is the source of our joy.

C. Joy in Justice
Zep 3:14–18; Phil 4:4–7; Lk 3:10–18

Today's texts invite us to rejoice. This is the way to wait for the coming of the Lord, but vigilance presupposes being attentive to the signs of the times.

Discernment

The passage from Luke speaks of the testimony of the precursor, John the Baptist. His preaching impresses the people who ask him: "What then should we do?" (v. 10). It proves that they understand what they have been told. They do not merely hear or give their assent, but rather they sense that the baptism of John demands involvement. The answer comes quickly: share what you have, clothes, food (vv. 10–11). In these difficult times for the poor, John's demand takes on a new urgency. Now is the time to invite others to share our own food. This is the way to wait for Jesus.

John tells the most difficult people (tax collectors, soldiers) that they must first observe what is just: do not overcharge, do not abuse the power you have, do not accuse falsely, do not seek bribes (Lk 3:13–14). But, according to the Bible, the basic requirement of justice consists in sharing. Accepting the good news of the Lord's coming requires such a conversion. By our actions, we distinguish what brings us close from what takes us away from the Lord's coming. On that day, God will distinguish the wheat from the chaff in our behavior.

A Day of Festival

In the Bible, joy accompanies the fulfillment of God's promises. This time, there will be profound joy: "The Lord is near" (Phil 4:5). Every prayer to God will have to be presented with thanksgiving (v. 6). The practice of justice and the experience of joy will bring us to the authentic peace, to the *shalom* (life, integrity) of God.

In these days of hunger and destitution in Peru, is it possible to experience the joy of waiting for Christmas? First of all, let us admit that it is a difficult question. We cannot answer with a superficial yes, forgetting that human beings do not live by prayers alone. On the other hand, we cannot forget that the sources of joy are profound and they constitute reserves of hope and of transformation of human life. Joy persists obstinately in the midst of suffering, preventing it from becoming sadness, bitterness, and closing in on ourselves. This would be tragic at a time when great solidarity is needed among the poor themselves. Because of all this, we have to be firmly rooted in history to confront the present adversity with the conviction inspired from Zephaniah: "Do not fear; the Lord your God is in your midst; he will rejoice over you with gladness, he will renew you in his love, he will exult over you with loud singing as on a day of festival" (vv. 16–18).

Fourth Sunday of Advent

A. God with Us
Is 7:10–14; Rom 1:1–7; Mt 1:18–24

Our waiting for the fulfillment of the promise is coming to an end. The Lord is about to come.

Bewilderment

In comparison with Luke, Matthew brings us a brief gospel of Jesus' infancy. God fulfills his promise and he does it in a bewildering way. It comes through a young Jewish girl who accepts the work of the Spirit in her (v. 18). Her husband, Joseph, is confused (v. 19) and this perplexity prepares him to understand God's action. When we think that everything is occurring "normally," we are not capable of perceiving what is new. The unexpected interrupts our plans.

The child about to be born will be named Jesus, which means "God saves," because "he will save his people from their sins" (v. 21). "His people" goes beyond the Hebrew world; it encompasses all of humankind becoming the people of God. The one who reestablishes our friendship with God is coming — discreetly — to a humble home in Nazareth, in a young girl's womb.

A Presence

The sign that God gives is to abide forever with those he loves. This sign is not going to be a thing but instead someone who will be named Emmanuel, God with us (v. 14). With this name given to Jesus (mentioned only by Matthew) we are reminded that Matthew's text refers to Isaiah, the most frequently quoted prophet in the gospels. It is a very beautiful text which sets the tone for the final phase of Advent. God dwells in our midst. As John says in his gospel: God "pitched his tent in the midst of history." It is in history that we will encounter the God of our faith and of our hope.

The epistle to the Romans starts as a hymn outlining the testimony of that child, Jesus, Emmanuel who is to be born in a humble home of Nazareth. He comes from God and enters into history according to the flesh (vv. 2–3). His power will be life, victory over death (v. 4). He is the source of our own mission as his witnesses (v. 5). In this mission, we continue the presence of God in history and, in his mission, Paul is recognized as the apostle to the Gentiles (v. 5).

Mary's humility, Joseph's bewilderment, Paul's faith, their simplicity are the attitudes of the followers of Jesus.

B. Mary
2 Sam 7:1–5, 8–11, 16; Rom 16:25–27; Lk 1:26–38

This Sunday is dominated by the presence of Mary, who places herself before God in her condition as a lowly one, someone who believes God simply because he is God.

Rejoice!

In Galilee, a maiden is listening to the messenger telling her: "Rejoice" (Lk 1:28). Joy is one of the characteristics of the fulfillment of a promise of God. Mary receives the grace of God. This is the meaning of the expression "favored one" (v. 28). The Lord is on her side and everything takes place in the presence of God's free and gratuitous love. Faith is the gift which inaugurates dialogue. The Lord trusts Mary and, in turn, she places all her trust in God, who converts her into a person of faith. There is no reason to fear; surrender is the response to the call. The Lord looks upon Mary asking for her faith, and thanks to her free and humble response, the young Jewish girl participates in God's work.

What the messenger announces will be the work of the Holy Spirit (v. 35) and of Mary's faith. Her first words are: "Here I am, the servant of the Lord; let it be with me according to your word" (v. 38). The term "servant" means belonging to God. Those who are sent by God are God's servants. Being a servant is expressed in terms of being available, accepting God's will. The word of God is a gift which has to be accepted by human freedom.

A Dialogue

Mary's trust and humility do not prevent her from initiating a dialogue with God's messenger. She does not simply listen and accept the announcement. Her faith is a free act, and this is why she inquires and wishes to know how what she is told will come about. The power of the Spirit prompts her active participation. It is the collaboration of someone who knows she is in God's hands. Mary's *yes* to motherhood communicates the Messiah to us. Thus, Mary has her place in the history of salvation.

The incarnation takes place in the synthesis of the power of the Holy Spirit and of Mary's lowliness. Her son has a historical function: "He will reign over the house of Jacob and of his kingdom there will be no end" (v. 33). The prophet Nathan announced this about David (2 Sm 7:16) and the definitive reign of the Messiah is foreshadowed in this historical event. Thus, Mary's motherhood is more than a personal gift; it is a gift to humankind in Mary. We have a charism in the strict sense of the term, namely, a gift bestowed on a person for the benefit of the community. This is the mystery "that was kept secret for long ages but is now disclosed" (Rom 16:25).

C. Blessed among Women
Mi 5:1–4; Heb 10:5–10; Lk 1:39–45

Approaching the celebration of Jesus' birth means remembering the condition of Mary as a woman and her faith.

Two Pregnancies

The episode called the visitation relates the encounter of two pregnant women. Mary, the Galilean, goes to Judea, the place where the son she is carrying in her womb will one day be rejected and condemned to die (Lk 1:39). At Mary's greeting, the child to whom Elizabeth was going to give birth "leaped for joy" (vv. 41 and 44). Shortly after that, the mother alludes to what she is experiencing, the joy of the child — the future John the Baptizer — who is the focus of all the events related so far in this first chapter of Luke. Now, John is making room for Jesus. Joy is the first response to the coming of the Messiah. Preparing for Christmas means experiencing the joy of knowing that God loves us.

Then Elizabeth speaks a double blessing. As is often the case in important manifestations, Luke emphasizes that Elizabeth does this "filled with the Holy Spirit" (v. 41). She declares Mary to be "blessed among women" (v. 42). Her condition as a woman is singled out, and as a woman she is loved and favored by God. This is confirmed by the second motive of the praise: "blessed is the fruit of your womb" (v. 42).

Faith and Motherhood

The fruit in question is Jesus, yet the text underlines the fact that for the time he is in the body of a woman, in her womb, flesh of her flesh. And so Mary's body becomes the holy ark harboring the Spirit and manifests the greatness of her condition as a woman. In her visitor, Elizabeth recognizes the "mother of the Lord" (v. 43), the one who will give birth to the One who was to liberate his people as the prophet Micah had announced (5:2–5).

Luke undoubtedly puts on Elizabeth's lips the insight which the Christian community would gain only after the resurrection. However, what is important is that this confession of faith (what it truly is) underscores Mary's motherhood, and this is why it is an unexpected gift for Elizabeth.

Luke's insistence on Mary being a woman shows that, according to him, the essential question consists in discerning what the Lord wants to communicate to us. John the Baptizer's birth is announced to his father, the birth of Jesus to his mother. In addition, another woman, Elizabeth, acknowledges Mary as a woman and a mother. At the end of the text, Elizabeth declares that Mary is blessed because of her faith (v. 45) and because she accepts God's will (Heb 10:5–10) — a faith which is incarnated in Mary's body. In a similar way, our faith has to become present in daily life as a message of hope in the midst of discouragement, of life in the midst of violent and unjust deaths. This is what believing in the child born of Mary means.

Christmas Season

*"And the Word became flesh
and lived among us."*

(Jn 1:14)

The Celebration of Christmas

Joy for All the People
Midnight Mass
Is 9:1–6; Ti 2:11–14; Lk 2:1–14

Christmas is a celebration of joy and hope. However, we have to admit that it is not always easy to experience this in today's world. Overwhelmed by the ever-increasing poverty of so many men and women, our shouts of joy at the birth of the Lord seem to choke up in our throats. For many people, bewildered by the difficulty of finding a solution to this predicament, discouragement destroys the energy needed to face this situation.

The Smell of a Stable

Yet, the presence of the Lord in our history is a permanent call to return to the sources of our faith. Jesus was born in Bethlehem, surrounded by shepherds and animals. His parents had come to a stable because they had not found a place in the inn. There, in marginality, the Son of God entered history, the Word became flesh.

"In those days a decree went out from Emperor Augustus that all the world should be registered. This was the first registration and it was taken while Quirinius was governor of Syria" (Lk 2:1–2). In its simplicity, the text conveys an important message: Jesus was born in a determined place and time: under Augustus and Quirinius and at the time of King Herod, a traitor to his people. Jesus was born at that moment, insignificant in the eyes of arrogant and cynical power and in the eyes of cowardice disguised as peace and political realism.

During this period of Christmas, people often say that Jesus is born in every family and every Christian heart. But these "births" must not bypass the primary and undeniable reality: Jesus was born of Mary in the midst of a people dominated at the time by the greatest empire of those days. If we forget this, Jesus' coming into the world can become an abstraction. For Christians, Christmas manifests God's irruption into human history — a Christmas of lowliness and of service in the midst of the power of domination and the predominance of the powerful of this world, an irruption with the smell of a stable.

God is revealed in Jesus Christ, in him "the grace of God has appeared, bringing salvation to all" (Ti 2:11). We have to learn to believe from the point of departure of our present historical situation: in the midst of the constant deterioration of the conditions of life of a poor and excluded people, the lack of work and opportunities for so many, the lies and manipulations of the powerful to place a smoke screen over their unjust privileges. From the first Christmas on, we cannot separate Christian faith from human history.

Rachel's Wailing

What we know as the Christmas cycle includes a commemoration which runs the risk of being neglected or misinterpreted: the day of the Holy Innocents. The birth of a child in the outskirts of a small town disturbs the traitor. The odor of the stable reaches Herod's palace. The child Jesus escapes the massacre as did the child Moses, the liberator of his people. The assassin's will did not reach him in Egypt. The fear inspired by the newborn would lead to the killing of many innocents. Premature and unjust deaths cruelly accompany this newborn life. Tragedy haunts the joy of the nativity.

The loud wailing of Rachel weeping for her children (Mt 2:18) continues to be heard today. It is the clamor of the mothers of the hundred children dying for every thousand born; it is the lament of the mothers of the thousands of "disappeared" (a cruel current phenomenon in several countries of Latin America); it is the complaint of mothers seeing their children grow up in the midst of malnutrition and sickness.

The incarnation of the Son of God is the heart of a message of solidarity with everyone, especially with the marginalized and the oppressed. As in Jesus' case, the solidarity of so many of his witnesses in Latin America leads to death, yet it is primarily a proclamation of hope — a hope which may appear insignificant to us historically, like the birth of the child we celebrate at Christmas. But this hope is the seed of life and therefore the good news "of great joy for all the people" (Lk 2:10).

One More Christmas, One Less Christmas
Midnight Mass
Is 9:1–6; Ti 2:11–14; Lk 2:1–14

Christmas is a time marked by hope, a hope that has become flesh in human history. This is what we are celebrating on that feast, what we Christians call the incarnation, using a term which paradoxically seems abstract even though it designates a very concrete event.

Reserves of Solidarity

The great Christmas prophet, Isaiah, reminds us that "the people who walked in darkness have seen a great light" (9:2). Perhaps in our own time this darkness is found in the enormous poverty afflicting most of humankind, in the growing gap between nations and persons who use most of the planet's resources and the peoples and persons whom the international economic order increasingly excludes from having access to the most basic goods of this world.

But, to tell the truth, real darkness is not found there but rather in what causes it. This situation is the outcome of a deeper darkness. Its root — not the only cause — lies in forgetting the human dignity of the poor and their status as daughters and sons of God. It is that simple and that horrendous. Of course, this is also true for those who live in poor countries and turn their backs on their own peoples. To speak of poverty is to describe how things are; to speak of injustice is to evaluate this state of affairs morally. In fact, injustice constitutes the nucleus — if we can express it thus — of the darkness of which we were speaking.

Like Fireflies

In the thick of darkness, a lighted match, a spark, a firefly have an unusual reach, and they can get us out of trouble. For a few seconds, they enable us to see faces, to know that we are there, to glimpse at faces less depressed and fearful than what darkness might have made us think, to sense glances inviting us to dialogue and to collaborate. This animates us to turn on other lights and to break up the lack of communication. This is what many have done in these past years during which we have come to a greater conscientization of the marginalization and exclusion of so many persons. These efforts have awakened (or disclosed, which comes to be the same thing) the enormous reserves of solidarity and courage which exist in countless parts of the world.

In rich as well as in poor countries, countless people seek to give a Christian witness by creating organizations of solidarity and groups in defense of human rights. They confront economic systems that exclude the weakest members of society and make gestures of friendship toward this world's forgotten people: they are signs of light in the depth of darkness.

By their commitment and generosity, they are small but contagious lights which bring a ray of light in the thick of the night. The light is not at the end of the tunnel; it is in the tunnel itself, in the people journeying through it. Their role is to bring light in the tunnel and even more to bring down its walls and ceiling, so that it may cease to be an obligatory hemmed-in path and become a wide, open, luminous, and free avenue leading us to "righteousness and justice" and preparing us to welcome the "prince of peace" (Is 9:5–6): Jesus of Nazareth, "joy for all the people" (Lk 2:10).

If during these days the coming of the Lord sets our hearts on fire and if we respond by our commitment and solidarity to the gift of love which God gives us in his Son, we will become the fireflies who will gradually transform the threatening darkness into a human, peaceful, and luminous night. In this way, through us the hope of seeing "a great light" will start to become a reality in an incarnate hope, like Jesus who is reborn in us. In this case, it will have been one more Christmas in which our hope and joy will grow. If we withdraw out of selfishness or simply out of fear, it will have been one less Christmas in our lives.

The Coming of the Lord
Daytime Mass
Is 52:7–10; Heb 1:1–6; Jn 1:1–18

God's presence in history is a central biblical theme which reaches its fullness in the incarnation. This is what we are celebrating at Christmas. John relates this event to us in a different though not less precise tone than the one used in the synoptic gospels.

In the Word Was Life

John presents the great themes of his gospel in the prologue, which is like the overture of a lyrical composition announcing what will be developed later. In fact, in these initial eighteen verses, we find the dialectics of death-life, light-darkness, truth-lie, grace-sin, the theme of testimony, and the relation of freedom-slavery.

The beginning calls our attention first: "In the beginning was the Word and the Word was with God" (v. 1). It is a way of expressing that the Word is divine. Verse 2 takes up the idea of the divine origin of the Word: "He was in the beginning with God." Verse 3 strongly underscores this dimension of the Word: "All things came into being through him and without him not one thing came into being." The Word is not created; it is creating.

The following verse adds an important theme: "In him was life." The God who reveals himself in the Word is fundamentally life. Jesus communicates the life of the Father to us. Life is the purpose of creation and of salvation. "And the life was the light of all people" (v. 4). The Word is life and light. Embracing the perspective of life enlightens us to understand the message. All that implies giving life in various ways is characteristic of the Lord's disciples. On the contrary, all that involves rejection, poverty, exploitation, disregard for life is a pact with death and the negation of the God of Jesus.

Life is light and darkness is the obstacle. The light-darkness opposition is a theme which runs through John's entire gospel. The thickness of darkness is to light what death is to life. In John, darkness is associated with the world of the lie which, as we know, is the other major theme of his gospel. Darkness expresses sin, opposition, and hostility. Light, on the contrary, is the atmosphere of love. There is antagonism between light and darkness, but John tells us that "the light shines in the darkness and the darkness did not overcome it" (v. 5).

In this context of creation, life and light, a prophet appears, John the Baptist, "a man sent from God" (v. 6). With him, we are beginning to sense the history of a people. The precursor comes to testify to the light, but we can be witnesses only of what we have experienced. John the Baptizer is introduced as a witness; his light is a reflection. He has received the necessary clarity to help others enlighten the path which leads to the Lord.

Starting with verse 11, the author introduces us to the central theme of the prologue: the coming into history and the acceptance of the Word: "He came to what was his own and his own people did not accept him." Those who accept the Word receive the gift of being children of God. This gift signifies power and strength; God is making us his sons and daughters. We correspond to this grace by becoming brothers and sisters to one another.

He Made His Dwelling among Us

"He came to his own home" (v. 11) and "the Word became flesh" (v. 14) are expressions manifesting this entering into history. In biblical language, "flesh" means the human being, with at times a touch of weakness. The Word enters into history, taking on our human condition including its most fragile aspect. The Word comes "with the feet of the messenger who announces peace" (Is 52:7).

"The Word made his dwelling among us" (v. 14). This beautiful image has its origin in the Old Testament. In the desert, on the way to the promised land, the shade of the tent provided rest, meaning, and courage for the long march ahead. The presence of this tent changes the aridity of the experience, transforming it into an incipient encounter with God. As Saint Exupéry said, in the middle of the desert the existence of a well transforms it into a place of life and friendship and at the same time it spurs on our search.

For John, the flesh assumed by the Word is the tent of the new encounter. Being disciples of Jesus means living, believing and hoping under this tent. The Word "made his dwelling" among us from Mary's body, and being thus charged with humanity, the Word returns to the Father: "and we have seen his glory, the glory as of a father's only son" (v. 14). John describes a suggestive rhythm: the Word was with God in the beginning, he *enters* into history to bring life, and he *returns* to the Father. This is why in verse 16 John says: "From his fullness we have all received, grace upon grace."

The prologue ends with a reaffirmation of God's transcendence: "No one has ever seen God" (v. 18). The incarnation does not take away God's holiness and transcendence. God is utterly different, not of this world. But the Son has seen God and can therefore reveal him: "the only Son, who is close to the Father's heart, has made him known" (v. 18). Being face to face with the Father, the Son alone can manifest God.

Christmas invites us to celebrate the Lord's involvement with human history, with its most insignificant and poorest people. The Lord is neither intimidated by the hostile darkness nor by the fact that his own people do not accept him. His light is more powerful than all the shadows. Entering into the hereness and nowness of our own history, nourishing our hope with the will to live of our country's poor, these are unavoidable conditions to dwell in the tent which the Son pitched among us. In this way, we will experience in our own flesh, in the flesh of so many brothers and sisters, the encounter with the Word who announces the reign of life.

The Holy Family

A. The Figure of Joseph
Sir 3:3–7, 14–17; Col 3:12–21; Mt 2:13–15, 19–23

We are in the midst of the Christmas season. Jesus' human family is a part of it. Today we are remembering the discreet and just Joseph in a special way.

Out of Egypt, Once More
Matthew's gospel has special connections with the Jewish mentality. For example, Matthew is the only one to mention this episode of the flight into Egypt of Joseph with his family. The history of Israel forms the backdrop. The event occurs immediately after the adoration of the child by those mysterious people designated as the "wise men" (2:1–12). Herod is threatening the newborn's life and his parents receive a signal to take refuge in Egypt (v. 14). The Jewish people had been there too, and they were called by God out of that place. Matthew quotes Hosea's text: "Out of Egypt I have called my son" (Hos 11:1; see also Mt 2:15). As his people had done, Jesus also spends time in Egypt. Like Moses who liberated his people and led them to the promised land, Jesus will come out of Egypt for the salvation of all people and to call them to enter into the kingdom of heaven.

There is a clear and significant parallel, a frequently used procedure in the gospels and other New Testament texts. Their authors were filled with passages, accounts, and biblical reminiscences. In addition, they assumed that their eventual readers would also be familiar with what Christians call the Old Testament (or the First Testament as we are beginning to say now). In this context, these writings attain all their significance.

The Nazarene

The final part of our text brings up an important detail. Herod had died, but his impact was still being felt in Judea. So Joseph decides prudently not to return to the province where Jerusalem is situated because it is a dangerous area for the child Jesus. The family withdraws to Galilee, to the town of Nazareth, a region which was marginal and suspected of not having a national and religious identity (2:19–23). The Nazarene would also face marginalization and suspicion.

We should note that Joseph, the father, the head of the family, is the central person of these verses. The signs are presented to him and he is the one who makes the decision. The passage shows us the concern of Joseph, who strives to protect Jesus, the liberator, and it makes us see his place in salvation history. Joseph's love reaches us through Jesus. We are also reminded that we have to look after one another, especially those who require all our attention because of their frailness.

B. A Sign of Contradiction
Sir 3:3–7, 14–17; Col 3:12–21; Lk 2:22–40

As we know, Luke provides us with a detailed gospel of Jesus' infancy. The perplexity and the promises, the concerns and joys which the annunciation and the nativity of the Lord aroused, form the material of a narrative interwoven with reminiscences from the Old Testament.

Now, Master

Luke insists on the fact that Jesus' family belongs to the people, the religion and the hopes of the Jewish people. Today's text presents us with the episode known as the presentation of Jesus in the temple. Luke speaks of "their purification" (v. 23), when in reality according to the law of Moses (Lv 12:8), it is something which affects only Mary as a woman. In fact, a mother has to offer a sacrifice, in accordance with Leviticus; if she "cannot afford a sheep, she shall take two turtledoves or two pigeons" (12:8; see also 5:7). This is what Mary does (Lk 2:24). It is also what Vatican II calls "the offering of the poor" (*Lumen Gentium*, no. 57). This is the situation of Jesus' family as the evangelist specifies.

In the temple, "a man whose name was Simeon" (v. 25) recognizes the Messiah in Jesus, the hope of Israel beginning to be fulfilled. Simeon is neither an eminent member of the people nor a priest of the temple. He utters a beautiful canticle, and then he can die in peace: "Master, now you are dismissing your servant in peace" (v. 29). But Simeon, a humble member of the Jewish people, also addresses Jesus' mother. This is the last prophecy announced in the Jerusalem temple itself about Jesus, and it also concerns Mary. Jesus will upset the current order; some will be raised and others will fall. The testimony of the Messiah will sift through the inner thoughts of his people, and that will make him a sign of contradiction, the object of resistance and even of rejection (v. 34).

A brief sentence indicates that the implications of this proclamation also involve Mary. The messianic perspective will pierce through her inmost being, her own soul (v. 35). Mary belongs to Israel. Faith is a process, and it can be painful. The suffering in the life of the mother of the Lord will be another way of sharing the work of the Messiah.

Growing in Wisdom and Grace

Then another person, Anna, a "prophetess" as Luke calls her (v. 36), comes forth. She too represents the hope of the "small remnant," the poor of Yahweh. Simeon's age is not mentioned; tradition has considered him as a man in the last years of his life although there are no explicit references to this in the text. Anna, on the other hand, is presented as an elderly woman. She also gives thanks for the coming of the child and speaks about him "to all who were looking for the redemption of Jerusalem" (v. 38).

These presages speak of hope and suffering. However, that does not prevent the child, protected by his parents' love, from growing in favor and in wisdom (vv. 39–40). The child responds to this love in the midst of family life. This is the theme of the text from Sirach in the first reading. The passage from Paul also deals with family relationships. Although some of his considerations are undoubtedly a tribute paid to the mentality of the time, what really matters is the foundation Paul gives for those bonds: in Christ we all form "the one body" (Col 3:15).

C. My Father's Interests
Sir 3:3-7, 14-17; Col 3:12-21; Lk 2:41-52

However strong family unity may be and should be (see the first reading), it does not put an end to the personality and responsibility of its members. On the contrary, family bonds are meant to reinforce the tasks and the mission of each member.

Clothing Ourselves with Love

Paul offers advice for convivial living. We have to be humble and patient and to bear with one another. If necessary, we must also be forgiving. This is the way God is with us, and this attitude has to be a model for ours (vv. 12–13). But, "above all," we have to clothe ourselves with love, Paul says in a metaphor often used in his letters (v. 14). In this way, "the peace of Christ" will rule in our hearts (v. 15).

Peace is the absence of conflicts, though not necessarily the absence of differences and temporary misunderstandings among people. When love is the bond uniting us, peace will be built up step by step, negative encounters will disappear (confrontations as well), and relationships will become more transparent. In the text from Sirach (3:3–17), those bonds are specified in the framework of the human family.

Treasuring in Our Hearts

Once again, Luke presents Jesus' parents fulfilling their religious obligations (vv. 41–42). The child bewilders them by staying behind in the city of Jerusalem, where he will be crucified later. They find him three days later, a period of time laden with symbolic significance. Then we have a difficult dialogue which sounds like a negative encounter starting with a reproach: "Why have you treated us like this?" This question is prompted by the anguish they have just experienced (v. 48). The answer is surprising: "Why were you searching for me?" (v. 49). It is surprising because the reason seems obvious. But the second question is far-reaching: "Did you not know that I must be in my Father's house?"

No, they did not really know; they were learning, and Luke tells us, "They did not understand" (v. 50). Faith and trust always entail a journey. As believers, Mary and Joseph grow in faith in the midst of perplexity, anguish, and joy. Things will gradually become clearer. Luke points out that Mary "treasured all these things in her heart" (v. 51; see the same expression in 2:19). The Greek term (*rhema*) that we translate as "things," also means "word" (like the Hebrew *dabar,* which expresses a prophetic word that is also an event). Mary's contemplation allows her to probe the significance of Jesus' mission. Her special closeness to him does not exempt her from the occasionally difficult process leading to our understanding God's plans. As a disciple, Mary is the first person to be evangelized by Jesus. She must also recognize the signs of the Messiah. Like Jesus, Joseph and Mary have to grow in grace and wisdom (v. 52). And of course, so do we.

Holy Mary, Mother of God

The Mother of Jesus
Nm 6:22–27; Gal 4:4–7; Lk 2:16–21

The texts of the Christmas season call our attention to the place of Mary in salvation history and to the testimony she is giving us as the first believer.

Born of a Woman

Paul is concise but forceful regarding Mary. He emphasizes the human condition of the Son of God, a key element of our faith, reminding us that "God sent his Son, born of a woman" (Gal 4:4). With this, he enters into human history, and from the heart of history he proclaims the love of God. The entry of the Son of God into the historical course of humanity passes through the yes of a young Jewish girl called Mary and through her body.

The Bethlehem shepherds find the child Jesus humbly lying in a manger next to his mother and Joseph. They had gone to look for him because of "what they had been told about the child"

(v. 17), and then they become witnesses of the newborn. All these reactions about the child are important to his mother, who "treasured all these things and pondered them in her heart" (v. 19; see also 2:51). The somewhat general term "things" designates God's prophetic word which is also an event. Mary's trust in God leads her to accept to be the mother of the Messiah. However, this does not in any way mean that her understanding of Jesus' mission is over.

Believing implies a journey and an in-depth searching. Mary also has to make her own journey, and this is why she ponders in her heart what is happening and what is being said in the milieu in which her family and friends are living. Thus, along with the physical closeness to the son of her womb, there is also a deepening communion with the mission Jesus is to accomplish. For us too faith is a process in which we will have ups and downs, periods of light and of darkness, but the testimony of Mary shows us how to move forward on the path to the God of our hope.

His Name Is Jesus

Jesus is born "under the law" (Gal 4:4), and eight days after his birth he receives the mark of his belonging to the Jewish people. And he also receives his name, Jesus, which means "the one who saves," the one who earns for us the power to call God "Abba, Father." This is what makes us free, and for Paul as well as for John being children is synonymous with being free (vv. 6–7).

Thanks to Mary, through the human face of Jesus of Nazareth, the Lord "makes his face known to us and gives us peace," as disclosed in the blessing the Lord wants passed on to the people (Nm 6:26). By becoming human, the Son of God transforms every human face into the expression of God's presence and exigency. In a beautiful text, the Latin American bishops at their conference in Puebla, Mexico, invited us to discover Christ's face in the suffering faces of the poor (nos. 31–39). And at Santo Domingo they called us to lengthen the list of those faces to include those "disfigured by hunger" and other abuses and deprivation (no. 179). Those faces are all present to question and to summon us to be more faithful to the gospel. By pondering Jesus' deeds and words in our hearts as Mary does, the insignificant and the excluded of this world will become an epiphany (a revelation) of God for us.

Second Sunday after Christmas

Before the Creation of the World
Sir 24:1–4, 12–16; Eph 1:3–6, 15–18; Jn 1:1–8

The texts of the Christmas season have presented us with the episodes of the birth of Jesus and its repercussions nearby and far away. Today's passages bring us a theological reflection on these events. On the basis of history, they tell us about the universal significance of what happened.

All Things Came into Being through the Word

The foundation of all that exists is Christ Jesus, the Son who became a human being. He expresses the love of the Father: "all things came into being" through him (Jn 1:3). This marks the meaning of all that exists; the key word is "life." Biblical revelation states this from the initial accounts of Genesis, "God saw everything that he had made and it was very good" (1:31), to the book of Revelation telling us about the "tree of life" (22:19) and in John's own gospel: "I came that they may have life and have it abundantly" (10:10). That is life in all its dimensions.

John underscores one of these dimensions: the Word is life and it is therefore the "light of all people" (v. 4), a light which drives away darkness. In John's gospel, darkness is the world of death, the world which resists God's will for life. Life, light, darkness: are these terms abstract and without historical content? Not at all. The person who inspired these lines (exegetes differentiate between the author and the writer — or writers — of this gospel) was a disciple of a great spiritual master, but "he himself was not the light" (v. 8). But thanks to the Baptist, he encounters Jesus, "the Lamb of God" (Jn 1:36), and this changes his life. Thus, when John tells us about life and light and their opposites, death and darkness, he is referring to his own experiences: for him, Jesus is life and light. He shares with us what he has lived, and his text is filled with the experiences that have transformed his life. He has discovered that the Word was in the beginning and in the end.

If we do not live our encounter with the Lord in depth, our

proclamation of the gospel may be literally faithful, but it will lack the breath of life, the Spirit, characteristic of genuine communication between persons. Let us discover what John was able to discover.

In the Beginning Was Gratuitous Love

The epistle to the Ephesians starts with a beautiful and impressive hymn echoing John's text that we have just cited. We have been chosen in Christ "before the foundation of the world" (v. 4). Someone with short-sighted logic might ask: how can what does not exist yet be chosen? But the text is clear and repeats the idea (v. 5). The point of the affirmation is to make us see the in-depth meaning and the goal of creation. Human persons exist *because* they are destined to be daughters and sons of God (v. 5). Filiation is a gift, a grace, it is not something added on to complete creation but is rather its original significance. Everything has its origin in God's gratuitous love, a love based on God's own goodness, not on our own merits. This is the "word of truth" (v. 13): in the beginning was gratuitous love; the Word is the full expression of God's love.

This selfless love perfumes our lives like cinnamon and lavender, "spreading fragrance like choice myrrh, like the odor of incense in the tent" (Sir 24:15). When we love others unselfishly, as God loves us, we give fragrance and joy to their lives and to ours.

Epiphany

A Light for All
Is 60:1–6; Eph 3:2–3, 5–6; Mt 2:12

Epiphany means manifestation. In some way, it draws us away from the temptation to confine the Christmas celebration to our privacy and it puts it at the crossroads of the paths of history. For men and women traveling these roads, Epiphany is a call and a challenge. Epiphany topples barriers and reiterates that Jesus came for everyone.

Bethlehem, the Least of the Cities

Matthew's account is very colorful. After Jesus was born, the wise men came. The text does not say that there were three of them or that they were kings or that they were of different races (colors). This lack of information was filled in by the imagination of Christian tradition, thus making the text more colorful. The term "magi" should suggest wise men, priests, perhaps astrologers. They are looking for the child, "king of the Jews" (v. 2). The arrival of those unexpected visitors worries those in power. Herod summons his scribes, who remind him that the Messiah was to be born in Bethlehem. Quoting the prophet Micah, Matthew affirms that for that reason and in spite of appearances, Bethlehem is by no means "the least" of the cities of Israel. The evangelist replaces the term meaning least in the Greek version of Micah by another, the term Matthew himself will use in the twenty-fifth chapter to speak of the "least" (vv. 40 and 45) in whom we encounter Jesus. Like Bethlehem, at first sight, the poor and the forgotten are insignificant, yet they are great because through them the Lord is coming to us.

The wise men find the child and pay him homage. The account concludes in a beautiful way. Having learned of Herod's wicked intentions, the magi "left for their own country by another road" (v. 12). We can assume that their having found Jesus has transformed their lives, because in the Bible a change of path symbolizes conversion. This must also be the outcome of our encountering the Lord: a transformation of our lives, the capacity to take another road.

Revelation of the Mystery

In the biblical perspective, mystery does not mean enigma, and still less an unsolvable problem. Instead, it is a reality which surrounds us and therefore escapes our full understanding. But in this context the mystery is not reserved to a select few; it has to be communicated to everyone. Paul speaks to the Ephesians of what has just been revealed in Christ: "the Gentiles have become heirs, members of the same body and sharers in the promise in Christ Jesus through the gospel" (3:6). This is the heart of Epiphany; the revelation to the magi from the east is the manifestation to the Gentiles. In this sense, Christian tradition was on the right track when it made them representatives of different nations and ethnic groups.

Isaiah's text reminds us of a symbol which is essential to the feast of Epiphany: "Arise, shine, for your light has come and the glory of the Lord has risen upon you" (60:1). The light which the Word of the Lord is bringing to us makes the "darkness which covers the earth" (v. 2) withdraw. All the nations will come to this light (v. 3); all are called to become disciples of Jesus Christ (Mt 28:19). This is why Epiphany is the great missionary feast. A church which is not missionary is a contradiction as the community of Christ's followers. This is also true for all Christians, for faith is not a private and interior matter; rather it impels communication and life in community.

The Baptism of the Lord

A. To Fulfill All Righteousness
Is 42:1–4, 6–7; Acts 10:34–38; Mt 3:13–17

The three synoptic gospels relate the baptism of Jesus (John highlights the figure of the Baptizer but he does not narrate this episode). It is a very significant event. In Matthew, the text becomes a program.

From Galilee to the Jordan

Matthew underlines that Jesus goes "from Galilee to John at the Jordan, to be baptized by him" (v. 13). Here the purpose of the journey is clearly expressed, more than what we have in the other gospels. Shortly before, Matthew had stated that many people were coming to be baptized by John (v. 6). From Nazareth in Galilee, Jesus joins them before initiating his mission. John, who had said he was not worthy "to carry his sandals" (v. 11), humbly declines to baptize Jesus (v. 14). The evangelist wants to emphasize the difference between the two men. John had made a profound impression on his people as a spiritual leader (see, for example, Mt 16:14). Therefore, the early Christian community felt the need to assert Jesus' uniqueness. It was imperative to recall and clarify the purpose of his mission: John the Baptist prepared the way for the coming of the Son of God.

In Matthew, John the Baptist is the first person to start a dialogue with Jesus. His narrative provides us with Jesus' first words
in this gospel, words which take on the aspect of a proclamation.
He challenges John's refusal to baptize him; this must be done.
"Let it be so now," says the Lord; do not raise objections (v. 15).
Jesus immediately gives the reason for his insistence: "it is proper
for us in this way to fulfill all righteousness" (v. 16). The term
used by Matthew indicates that it is more than proper; it is urgent. It is not just Jesus' obligation but the plural form "for us"
involves John in the same task: both have to fulfill it.

In his gospel, Matthew frequently uses the term "righteousness." It occupies a central place in the sermon on the mount,
especially in the beatitudes, where it is closely related to the
theme of the kingdom (see Mt 6:33). Of the seven times this term
is used in the gospel, five of them occur in the sermon on the
mount and the other two are associated with the figure of John
the Baptist (see 21:32 in addition to our text).

Called in Righteousness

Matthew maintains the richness and the complexity of the biblical term "righteousness." It is the work of God, and for that
very reason it has to be preached by those who believe in God.
It implies a relationship with the Lord, that is to say, holiness
and at the same time relationships with human beings: acknowledging the rights of everyone, especially the defenseless and
mistreated, in other words, social justice. Thus, righteousness
has both meanings: love of God and love of others, indissolubly
united. Fulfilling righteousness presupposes striving first for the
kingdom of God and his justice (see Mt 6:33). This is the program Matthew places before us as of the first words of Jesus in
his gospel.

To establish righteousness, God presents his servant (Is 42:1).
This is the first song of the servant of the Lord. From the early
days, Christian tradition has considered him as a figure of Christ.
Misunderstood and beaten, the servant of the Lord will console
(that is, liberate) his people. Being "called in righteousness" (v. 6)
means receiving the responsibility to "open the eyes that are
blind, to bring out the prisoners from the prison" (v. 7). Such a
behavior is the essential element of the good news "of peace by
Jesus Christ" (Acts 10:36).

Jesus associates John the Baptist in the fulfillment of righteous-

ness with all that the term implies. In this gesture, we too are
incorporated into that task. We all receive the same call (see Acts
10:34–35). In a continent marked by injustice as in the case of
Latin America, this is an urgent mission. But to make it a really
fruitful way in the perspective of the kingdom, we must carry
it out by keeping in mind the other dimension of righteousness:
holiness.

B. Bringing Forth Justice
Is 42:1–4, 6–7; Acts 10:34–38; Mk 1:6–11

In the gospels, the baptism of the Lord is more than a ritual
gesture. It is the start of the public life of Jesus.

The Beloved Son

Mark is always concise. The text begins with John's austerity, de-
scribing the Baptizer's clothing in terms similar to those used in
the second book of Kings to refer to Elijah, Israel's great prophet
(1:8). John is baptizing in the same place where Elijah was taken
up into heaven by a chariot of fire (2 Kgs 2:11). Mark also mentions the humility of John, who does not consider himself worthy
"to untie the thong of the sandals" of the one who is coming
after him (v. 7). This is not a servile expression but rather the
expression of the clear conscience of one who knows he has to
prepare the way for another. The baptisms are also different: it
is one thing to baptize "with water" and another "with the Holy
Spirit" (v. 8) and the power of God. The gift of the final days is
the Holy Spirit who will put a new heart in every believer (see Jer
31:33 and Ez 36:26).

Then we are given the name of the person to whom John was
referring: Jesus who came "from Nazareth of Galilee and was
baptized by John" (v. 9). The purpose of Jesus' journey is less emphasized than in Matthew, but the fundamental statement is the
same: Jesus accepts being baptized by the man to whom many
members of his people are coming. We have no dialogue between
Jesus and John, as we do in Matthew. But we do have the expression of the Father who is well pleased in "the Son, the Beloved"
(v. 11), who came to this world to proclaim the kingdom of God.

Light of the Nations

An ancient and persistent interpretation understood this myste-rious personage (individual or corporate) of the servant of the Lord to prefigure the Messiah. Upon him, "my chosen, I have put my spirit," Yahweh says. His mission is to "bring forth justice to the nations" (Is 42:1). A few verses below, the author states that the servant has been "called in righteousness" (v. 6). Establishing righteousness and justice is a great prophetic theme to manifest God's will for the people and for the "nations." Second Isaiah has a clear universal vocation: it is necessary "to establish justice in the earth" (v. 4). The practice of justice can bring about suffer-ing like that of the servant; this is not the objective but the price to pay. Such practice points to the liberation from every type of captivity.

This universal perspective is taken up again by Peter, who is able to see it in Jesus. He understands that God rejects no one, "but in every nation anyone who fears him and does what is right is acceptable to him" (Acts 10:35). What matters is to do the will of God; this is the meaning of fearing God. A great expression of this is "to do what is right." All those who do that, from whatever nation, are acceptable to God. Living in the presence of the God of our faith means walking shoulder to shoulder with our brothers and sisters, especially with those who are denied their most basic rights.

C. A People's Expectation
Is 42:1–4, 6–7; Acts 10:34–38; Lk 3:15–16, 21–22

In what is known as the infancy narrative, Luke has established a parallel between John and Jesus (chapters 1 and 2). Then he devotes a long paragraph to John the Baptist as an adult, and he summarizes his preaching in the verses preceding today's passage (3:1–14).

John and Jesus

John calls for conversion in very strong terms. He even confronts the powerful and corrupt people of his day. His basic theme is the practice of justice and love (3:7–14). His preaching seems to have had a strong impact on the people, and he appears as a great spir-itual leader. "The people were filled with expectation and all were questioning in their hearts concerning John, whether he might be the Messiah" (v. 15). The Baptist seems to have the characteristics of the Messiah. But he himself sets things straight: "one who is more powerful than I is coming," he says "to all of them" (v. 16). His calling for penance and his baptism are simply the preparation for the witness of Jesus. Luke stresses this, in the second case, with texts like those found in Matthew and Mark. In the Old Testament, fire (v. 16) is the symbol of God's judgment.

Luke's short version of Jesus' baptism is also similar. He does not say that Jesus had come from Nazareth to be baptized (cf. Mt and Mk). He merely says that Jesus accepts the baptism "when all the people were baptized" (v. 21). There is no dialogue between Jesus and John either, as was the case in Matthew. For Luke, John belongs to a past which is over. Yet we, the disciples of Jesus coming after him, have to keep a dimension of John the Baptist. In other words, in some way, we are all precursors of Jesus for those who do not know his message at all or do not know it well.

Doing What Is Right

Following his experience with the pagan Cornelius (Acts 10:1–33), Peter understands this very well. Peter finds him to be an honest man, ready to listen to the gospel message brought by the apostle. The episode makes Peter understand that "God shows no partiality" (v. 34); all nations are called (v. 35), but for that to happen, Christ's followers have to assume their responsibilities. They are the witnesses of the message "spread throughout Judea, beginning in Galilee after the baptism that John announced" (v. 37). In the phase following John, Jesus appears and his message forms the central substance of the disciples' proclamation.

Proclaiming the "message of peace" (v. 36) implies "doing what is right" (v. 35), whose full meaning is liberation. This is what the Lord says in Isaiah's text: "to open the eyes that are blind, to bring out the prisoners from the dungeon, from the prison those who sit in darkness" (Is 42:7). This familiar and inspiring text will be used shortly by Luke himself (4:16–20) to present what has been called Jesus' "messianic plan." Being faithful to Jesus means carrying out this plan of liberation vis-à-vis today's oppressions.

Lent

*"The kingdom of God
has come near;
repent and believe
in the good news."*
(Mk 1:15)

First Sunday of Lent

A. Service, Not Privileges
Gn 2:7–9, 3:1–7; Rom 5:12–19; Mt 4:1–11

We are beginning Lent, forty days of preparation for the great Christian mysteries: the death and resurrection of Jesus.

Jesus' Fidelity

The three synoptic evangelists place the experience of the desert in relation with the baptism of Jesus presented shortly before. All three also say that Jesus is led by the Spirit. This marks the beginning of his mission, "to be tempted" (4:1), Matthew writes. The forty days refer to the experience of Israel wandering for forty years in the wilderness on the way to the promised land. Jesus' determination in the face of the temptations corroborates the commitment of his baptism and opens paths for his own task. In all three temptations, Jesus responds by using texts from Deuteronomy, the book which is a theological reflection on the experience of the Jewish people liberated from Egypt.

The three temptations are gradually arranged. Jesus refuses to use his condition of Son of God unduly, thereby giving a guideline to his disciples not to use the grace received for their own benefit. Following Jesus is not a privilege placing us above others but rather a service (vv. 3–4). Jesus will show this when he shares the loaves with the crowds (Mt 14:17ff.). Then the Lord refuses to put God to the test, and later he will always reject those who demand a miracle in order to believe. Jesus never works miracles to impress people. His healings are signs of life, not displays of power (vv. 5–7), life against all forms of death, like sin present in humankind (Gn 3:1–7). Jesus is the new Adam (Gn 2:7–9) who conquers the "sin in the world and death through sin" (Rom 5:12).

The Temptation of Power

The third temptation reveals what is at stake in history and the proclamation of the kingdom. In the Bible, the mountain is the place of God's revelation. Jesus is offered power over "all the kingdoms of the world" (v. 8). In return, he is to pay homage to one whose plan is contrary to God's (v. 8). Such is also the temptation of the Christian community: understanding its power to serve as a power to dominate. We are constantly threatened by this perversion. But we cannot confuse a historical reality, whether political or religious, with the kingdom of God. The reign of God must be made present in history now, but it must also impel us toward realities which are beyond history. The identification which we are rejecting would transform the leaders of those historical accomplishments into dominating lords. Instead of that, today, Jesus also reminds us that we are to serve only God (v. 10).

B. A Covenant for Life
Gn 9:8–15; 1 Pet 3:18–22; Mk 1:12–15

This is the first Sunday of Lent, a time when we prepare to celebrate the heart of our faith: Jesus' death and resurrection. This is a time for penance (perhaps easier to see in the northern hemisphere with its winter cold than in the middle of the summer heat, vacation — and the beach — of the countries south of the Equator) and for hope.

The Wilderness: A Place of Testing and Encounter

The gospel of Mark brings us the first proclamation of the kingdom. In the two preceding verses, Mark has spoken with great conciseness of the forty days Jesus spent in the wilderness. We have in mind Matthew's long text on this theme. Mark is sparing in words as usual. The Spirit becomes present at the beginning of Jesus' ministry: driving him into the wilderness where Jesus prepares for his mission (vv. 12–13).

In the Bible, the desert is a place both of testing and of encounter with God. There, our human needs are barely met, the harshness of the situation makes us fight for life, the will is weakened, and we are more prone to give in to the possibility of some relief. Faced with the inclemency of the desert on their way to the promised land, the Israelites were tempted to go back to their oppression in Egypt. But the desert with its profound silence is also a privileged place to encounter God. Freed from the daily turmoil, we are in better condition to hear God's word, which can become firmly rooted in us.

Every mission of proclaiming and witnessing the kingdom must be prepared in the desert, where the proximity of death stirs up our will to live and makes us experience the isolation which leads us to hunger for communion. Today, on our continent, the spirit of many witnesses of the kingdom is being shaped by following the Lord in troubles, difficulties, and hostility. These witnesses know that Christ's death gave them new life (1 Pet 3:18–19).

Communion with All of Life

The text from Genesis shows us the meaning of the covenant. After the destruction caused by the flood, God affirms his covenant for life, including animal life (Mark's text also mentions animals). The covenant is made with every living creature (9:9). This is worth emphasizing because an excessively anthropocentric view does not appear to value other forms of life in God's plan. Paradoxically, our viewing human beings as masters of creation has made us forget the significance of creation and the respect we should have for it. What is not human seems to be outside of the history of salvation. This approach has many repercussions. From our contempt for animal life, we have moved to a religious underestimating of our own physical or material life, as is often said. Thus, the human body also turns out to be outside of God's plan. Reducing ourselves to a disincarnate spiritualism, we easily lose interest in so many other people's daily needs for food, health, and housing. These needs cease to challenge us because these imperatives come precisely from aspects shared with animal life, considered to be of so little value. In destroying creation — for supposedly religious reasons — we are destroying ourselves, and we fail to understand the meaning of our incorporation in the risen body of Christ through baptism (1 Pet 3:21).

This is not the perspective of our text. Not only human beings were saved in Noah's ark but, at the divine request, animals accompanied them in their survival (9:10–12). It is hard for us to integrate this perspective, but it does make us see that the God in whom we believe has a universal and radical will for life. For this reason, in a famous passage Paul tells us that creation itself is also expecting to be set free (Rom 8:21–22).

C. Believing with Our Hearts
Dt 26:4–10; Rom 10:8–13; Lk 4:1–13

Lent is a dynamic time. The liturgy of the church does its best to give us texts which are to lead us to reflect deeply on our Christian lives.

God Is God

Jesus, "full of the Holy Spirit," is led into the wilderness, Luke tells us in this passage as he insists on one of his favorite themes: the power of the Holy Spirit is with Jesus (Lk 4:1, Lk 3:22, and 4:18). In the Bible, the wilderness is the classic place of encounter with ourselves and the place where we are put to the test (see Dt 8:1–4). For forty years, the Jewish people made their way (in the wilderness there are no roads drawn up in advance) toward the promised land. That long march enabled them to know God better and to have a clearer awareness of themselves (see Dt 8:4–10).

Symbolically, Jesus will also spend forty days in the wilderness before starting his mission. There, being hungry, he will be tempted to use his power to satisfy his own needs. But according to the text from Deuteronomy, "one does not live by bread alone but by every word that comes from the mouth of the Lord" (8:3). Everything comes from God, who gives it for the service of others. Jesus will also be asked to forget the meaning of the kingdom of God to put himself in first place. But only God is to be worshiped. Jesus also overcomes the temptation of arrogance subtly presented to him in words from scripture. But the God of Jesus is not the God who works miracles to amaze and to crush but instead he is the God of love and service.

The lesson is clear: in the task that is beginning, Jesus proclaims the primacy of God and of God's kingdom. We cannot use them for our own personal prestige or to dominate others politically or spiritually. The attitude of Jesus must be our own and that of the church. Its message and its power are not to serve itself but to serve God and his chosen ones: the poor.

The Historical Creed

The experience in the wilderness leads the Jewish people to deepen their faith. The first reading brings us a beautiful text. Biblical faith is historical faith. Our belief in God is rooted in the presence of his liberating love in history (Dt 26:4–10). This love is opposed to every form of humiliation and exploitation. The word of faith must be proclaimed (Rom 10:8–13). We have to tell others what we experience with a profound conviction. Communicating faith means telling a story: a story etched in our hearts. We take it from there and retell it. "One believes with the heart and so is justified, and one confesses with the mouth and so is saved" (Rom 10:10). Referring to the liberation from Egypt means affirming that even today the Lord continues to liberate us from oppression and sin.

From the first Sunday of Lent we are called to believe with our hearts, to recall what we will celebrate during Holy Week: that Jesus has risen. Although it is so neglected in so many parts of the world, human life is a gift from God. In some way, it must also be our gift to one another. Proclaiming the kingdom is giving life.

Second Sunday of Lent

A. Go from Your Country
Gn 12:1–4, 2 Tm 1:8–10; Mt 17:1–9

Forty years through the desert to the promised land. Forty days in an inhospitable place before starting the task of proclaiming the kingdom. These experiences of the Jewish people and of Jesus are the framework of Lent.

There Is No Parenthesis

Jesus is approaching the definitive moment. His death will not put an end to his mission; it has to be read in the light of the resurrection. This is what the so-called episode of the transfiguration invites us to do. Jesus' radiant face and his dazzling white clothes (Mt 17:2) anticipate the paschal light. The Lord's death will not be the triumph of darkness, which is already overcome.

We run the risk of losing the paschal perspective, that is to say, the necessary passage through death. In such a case, the anticipation can be construed as something permanent, as a break, a parenthesis. This explains the enthusiasm of Peter who wants to stay in that place (v. 4). In reality, this anticipation is to serve as an impulse, a way to avoid fear (v. 7), to reinforce faith and to face the difficulties involved in communicating it. The transfiguration experience has to encourage the disciples to follow the Master and not hold them back on the way.

The Radicalness of Faith

The first reading presents Abraham, our father in the faith, as Paul will call him. His vocation is marked by a rupture. "Go from your country and your father's house" (Gn 12:1). Let go of all that is yours, your known world, to go "to the land that I will show you" (v. 1). This is the beginning of the promise: "I will make of you a great nation" (v. 2). This implies total faith in the Lord at whose call any other type of security must be abandoned.

Abraham does just that: he leaves his land, his own world, and sets out for the unknown, inspired by his faith in the Lord. The text reminds us of a fundamental aspect of this attitude. It is impossible to believe in God and at the same time to hold on decisively to other securities and references. Faith demands a radical posture. Only thus are we available to serve God and be in solidarity with others. This is the indispensable condition for communicating life "through the gospel" (2 Tm 1:10). Clinging to comfortable situations and social or ecclesiastical privileges makes us useless instruments for conveying the message of Jesus who gave up all his prerogatives and who gave his life. Welcoming the kingdom means believing in the God who rejects all injustice and spoliation of others, especially the most defenseless.

B. A Preview
Gn 22:1–2, 9, 15–18; Rom 8:31–34; Mk 9:1–9

Vigilance always implies austerity. Lent is a time of preparation and expectancy that is situated in a context of austerity and exigency. The texts for this Sunday seem to contradict this frame of reference.

Let Us Stay Here

In Mark's gospel, the preceding scene related the profession of faith of Peter, eager to acknowledge Jesus as the Messiah and slow to understand all that was involved in practice. Jesus avails himself of the opportunity to point out the necessary conditions for discipleship.

Jesus takes Peter, James, and John, who had witnessed the healing of the child whom everyone thought to be dead (Mk 5:37–43), and leads them to a high mountain, the classic place of an important revelation. There the Lord is transfigured. The white of his clothes, which "no one on earth" (Mk 9:3) could bleach, expresses that new condition. The prophets of the law, Elijah and Moses, represent history and the significance of the people of Jesus. In the Lord, this history reaches its total fulfillment.

This episode is filled with light, which foreshadows the resurrection of Jesus. He has spoken about his death and resurrection to his disciples (Mk 8:31), but they, in Peter's words, do not seem to understand what Jesus is telling them. Surprised, Peter himself speaks up and proposes to stay: "It is good for us to be here" (9:5). Implacable, Mark adds: "he did not know what to say" (v. 6); in addition, he points out that the disciples "were terrified" (v. 6). This explains how inopportune Peter's suggestion is. But history cannot be stopped, and we must grasp its significance. The light of the resurrection enables us to see it with hope. The death of Jesus is not the victory of darkness, which is already overcome. This is the meaning of the transfiguration.

Abraham's Faith

The hope which the resurrection infuses in us is a manifestation of God's gratuitous love. If God is with us (Rom 8:31), we have nothing to fear. Fear leads Peter to want to interrupt the course of history and to take refuge in a kind of parenthesis from it. However, belief in God is not an escape from history, however harsh it may be. At the heart of Lent, the resurrection of Jesus must be the cause of profound joy and stimulating hope. It is from God's love that his justice, that is to say, his saving work, comes to us. What it demands, in exchange, is our own surrender, without deceit or holding back, as in the difficult account of the sacrifice of Isaac, which did not take place (Gn 22).

Abraham's faith is absolute; it inspires his life. Encouraged by the hope of the resurrection, our surrender to the Lord has to be a testimony of the love of God. It deals with an affirmation of life in the face of the many unjust deaths we see in various places of the world.

C. Standing Firm in the Lord
Gn 15:5–12, 17–18; Phil 3:17–4:1; Lk 9:28–36

Lent is a time when we prepare ourselves to celebrate the resurrection. The scene of the transfiguration seems to be a high point on the way, but is it really?

An Exodus

The context of Luke's passage is the same as the one we find in Matthew and Mark. According to Paul, those who are considered as "acknowledged pillars" of the church (Gal 2:9) accompany Jesus: Peter, John, and James (Lk 9:28). Matthew and Mark do not specify the content of the conversation of Jesus with Moses and Elijah. Luke, on the other hand, tells us that they were speaking of the "departure" of Jesus, of his death which was about to take place in Jerusalem (v. 31). Significantly, Luke uses the term "exodus" to refer to Jesus' departure. The word is filled with meaning; it is a departure which allows coming to life, to the resurrection. This exodus is the Passover, the passage to the promised land, a sign of the kingdom. Calling death an exodus means that death is not the end of Jesus' plan. This is the conviction which has to sustain the hope of his disciples and of us.

As Jesus' followers, we must proclaim a kingdom of life which encompasses every aspect of human existence. But it also implies an exodus for us, a departure from everything which prevents us from living in full communion with God and with others. This exodus is going to involve painful and unavoidable aspects from which, in his fascination for the moment he is living, Peter wants to escape (v. 33).

Our Citizenship Is in Heaven

Peter is mistaken. We cannot stop on the way as we follow Jesus. We must not seek refuge in a tent (v. 33). The text from Genesis also deals with an exodus. God is asking Abraham to leave the safe world he knows. The faith rooted in Abraham's heart makes him accept the adventure. He leaves in order to enter. God promises him that he will be the father of countless descendants (v. 5) who will live in the land which God will give them (v. 18).

"Our citizenship is in heaven" (Phil 3:20) means that we have to know the ultimate criterion of our daily behavior on earth. Saint Paul reproaches his friends of Philippi precisely because they are not living as he has instructed them (vv. 17–18) in accordance with the testimony of Jesus and of Paul himself. Thus, he is asking them to be "standing firm in the Lord" (4:1).

The episode of the transfiguration reminds us that our being Christians has to be lived in the midst of the ups and downs and the difficulties of history. We welcome the gift of the kingdom in history and we become citizens of heaven, of the kingdom which is coming to us now.

Third Sunday of Lent

A. Jacob's Well
Ex 17:3–7; Rom 5:1–2, 5–8; Jn 4:5–42

Jesus' mission goes beyond the confines of the Jewish people and the ideas and prejudices of his day.

The Living Water

Here we have a wonderful text from John. It reveals an extremely important facet of Jesus' mission. The Samaritans were people despised by good Jews because their religion and their customs were mixed with pagan elements. In the full heat of the day (at noon, the sixth hour), Jesus is alone "near Jacob's well" (v. 6). He asks the Samaritan woman for a drink. She is surprised because she knows that Jews do not speak to Samaritans. But the Lord has asked her precisely for a gesture of elementary human solidarity which is over and beyond religious differences among people. The Lord proceeds boldly as the circumstances allow him to refer to the "living water" of his message. The Samaritan woman is entitled to it too, and Jesus not only speaks to her but he offers life to her. Once again, the attitude of the Lord goes beyond political and religious boundaries. But the woman does not understand; her perspective has to be broadened. Jesus methodically proceeds with his offer: the water he is offering will definitely quench the human thirst for fullness and life (vv. 13–14). He is speaking of the power of the Spirit (v. 24). The resistance of the Samaritan woman begins to weaken. She may not understand everything, but she does ask for that living water (v. 15).

Then Jesus reads the heart of the Samaritan woman, causing her to exclaim: "you are a prophet" (v. 19). Jesus puts the final touch to his proclamation: the Father must be worshiped "in spirit and truth" (v. 24). The worship at stake reaches far beyond the worship of Jews and Samaritans; it is addressed to a God who is close and loving, a Father.

Could It Be the Christ?

The Samaritans were also expecting the Messiah (v. 25). The Lord reveals who he is: "I am he" (v. 26). Encountering Jesus leads to a sharing of that experience, and this woman from a despised people becomes therefore a messenger (vv. 28–29). She goes back to her own people, telling them what she believes she has discovered. On their part, out of respect, the disciples, members of the Jewish people, do not address any reproach to Jesus, but they are surprised. The Lord spends a few days with the Samaritans; he gives them his own direct testimony (vv. 40–42). Through this episode, John may have wanted to indicate the presence of Samaritans in the early Christian communities. The Spirit pours God's love into our hearts (Rom 5:5) regardless of our human condition.

In a religious milieu there is a frequent tendency to withdraw among believers, into an intraecclesial world. But the love of Jesus knows no limits, and the God he proclaims does not fit into the spaces we build for him or into the concepts through which we attempt to understand him. Today in Latin America, we have to announce the good news at the top of our lungs so that God's message of peace and justice may reach every corner of a continent which is bleeding to death and becoming poorer every day. The water which comes out of the rock (Ex 17:6), from Jacob's well, from the heart of Jesus has to flood everything.

B. True Worship
Ex 20:1–7; 1 Cor 1:22–25; Jn 2:13–25

In the rich content of this Sunday's texts, a powerful theme stands out: believing in God means putting all our trust in him. The idolatry of money is contrary to faith in God, who demands genuine worship.

Idolatry and Oppression

John has just presented the start of Jesus' mission in Cana of Galilee (2:1–12). Here, we have the first confrontation with the authorities of the Jewish people. This takes place in Jerusalem and, more specifically, in the temple (the synoptics put this event toward the end of Jesus' ministry). Passover is the celebration of liberation. What the Lord finds in the temple is a new form of oppression of the people, which perverts the worship due the "jealous God" (Ex 20:5). The people are entering into a relationship with God by way of money. As a result, they are finding an oppressing God, not the Father who liberates them from slavery. The house of the Father who loves and liberates his people has become "a market place" (v. 16) which is exploiting and degrading.

The high priests who are behind the trading taking place in the temple are getting richer. The people selling animals and the money changers who receive Roman money (which cannot be offered because it is pagan) and give the coins for the temple are merely intermediaries. Jesus' protest and rejection affect powerful interests: the interests of those who have replaced God (without denying God openly) by greed, which Paul calls "idolatry." Paradoxically, this subtle, incipient substitution is often justified by religious arguments. Not one of us is immune from this. Today's gospel invites us to examine our consciences both at the personal and ecclesial level.

Doves and the Poor

Jesus' harshness with those selling doves (v. 16) calls our attention. But the reason for this is clear: doves were used by the poorest people for the purification sacrifices. As a result, in a special way those selling them represented the exploitation of the poor through worship. This explains why Jesus is very annoyed. The attitude of a true believer toward the poor has to be the very opposite. In his encyclical *Centesimus Annus* (no. 58), John Paul II underscores this by asking us to sell what is luxurious which we attempt to justify as necessary for ourselves or God's worship in order to change it into food, drink, clothing, and housing for the poor (see Mt 25:31–45).

The Lord died for that. We are committed to this type of detachment by our proclaiming "Christ crucified" (1 Cor 1:23), even though it causes scandal. We can conceal our greed behind reasons and even religious motives, but the Lord who knows what is in the human heart (Jn 2:25) will not allow us "to misuse his name" (Ex 20:7).

C. Liberation from Fear
Ex 3:1–8, 13–15; 1 Cor 10:1–6, 10–12; Lk 13:1–9

Lent is usually considered to be a time for penance. However, the gospel liberates us from a narrow and oppressive view of sin and its consequences.

Sinning Is Not Bearing Fruit

Luke's text is referring to historical events that we do not know. However, Jesus' dialogue about them makes us see the extent to which his teaching is related to various events in the life of his people. Proclaiming the good news cannot be done without paying close attention to what is happening. The kingdom is not separate from history: it questions it and interprets it. In turn, the events of our lives enable us to have a better understanding of the scope of the message.

Here, the Lord uses these two events to underscore an important aspect of his message: there are no connections between sin and the misfortunes which may happen to us, whether their cause is human (Pilate, Lk 13:1) or accidental (v. 4). By this statement, Jesus goes against a very common concept of his time, according to which diseases, misfortunes, and poverty are the consequences of the sins committed by the people in those situations. Remnants of this mentality are still present today. Thus, in addition to their harsh lives, the poor and the sick are burdened by a painful sense of guilt.

The Lord frees us from this concept which prevents us, on one hand, from facing the real causes of the evils befalling us by attributing them to some type of fatality which plunges us into passivity. On the other hand, this presents an erroneous image of the God of love and life. Sinning is failing to bear fruit, as Jesus states in the parable immediately following (vv. 6–9). Moreover, we are told that God is patiently waiting for our deeds. He is the God of love, not of punishment.

I Am the Life

Paul gives us an important principle for interpreting the Old Testament: what is narrated here is not merely something belonging to the past; instead it conveys a message to us now (1 Cor 10:11). The text from Exodus describes the moment when the Lord entrusts Moses with the liberation of his people. God gives him that mission because he has heard the clamor of the oppressed and he wants to bring the people to a land where they can build a just society (3:7–8).

This is the immediate context of the revelation of God's name: Yahweh, often translated by "I Am Who I Am." There is another possible meaning of this term, which is particularly interesting. In biblical thinking, life implies "living with," "living for," and "being present to others," in other words, it means communion. Death is the exact opposite: absolute isolation. The term "Yahweh" may follow this line and it may mean precisely: "I am the one who is with you, I am the life." God's presence is creative and liberating.

Fourth Sunday of Lent

A. The Beggar Rises to His Feet
1 Sm 16:1, 6–7, 10–13; Eph 5:8–14; Jn 9:1–41

We are approaching Holy Week, the celebration of the death and, above all, the resurrection of the Lord of life.

Jesus Is Liberating

The ninth chapter brings us one of the most important and best constructed chapters of the gospel of John. Facing a man blind from birth and, as a result, used to beg to live, Jesus' disciples ask who is responsible for the man's misfortune. Job and Ezekiel notwithstanding, this was the predominant view of the time: poverty and disease were punishment for sin. The Lord frees them from such a concept that ties up their hands and prevents them from facing reality: neither this man nor his parents are responsible for his blindness (v. 3). Blaming those who are ill or poor means pushing them deeper into their plight. Moreover, it prevents them from taking appropriate means to get out of those situations.

This approach is by no means over. We find it among our people who live their suffering as a divine punishment. Sin is a human reality, but we Christians believe in a God eager to forgive. Our God is a God of love, not of punishment which may justify what he rejects: the inhuman conditions in which most of our people are living. By liberating us from this narrow and self-serving interpretation, Jesus reveals to us the God of life and love.

The Really Blind

Jesus restores the sight of the blind man who used to sit to beg (v. 8). To the liberation from a distorted religious perspective Jesus adds the elimination of blindness. John gives us a masterful presentation of the harsh polemics that this event brings about. In the course of the discussion, the former blind man affirms himself as a person, and he opens up to believe in the Lord. The leaders of the people try to deny the events by every possible means (vv. 13–21). Besides, since the cure takes place on the sabbath, they claim that the law is not observed. Therefore, what has happened does not come from God and Jesus is a sinner.

The beneficiary of Jesus' gesture approaches the matter differently. He starts with his own experience: "I was blind and now I see" (v. 25). The opponents become hardened and aggressively interrogate the man who has been healed. Seeing them so preoccupied by what has happened, the former blind man sarcastically asks them: "Do you also want to become his disciples?" (v. 27).

A change has occurred in this blind beggar who used to spend his days sitting and holding his hand out for alms. Now he is standing up and, as their equal, he argues with the people's leaders who are blind to the manifestation of the Messiah (vv. 30–33). Gradually he understands Jesus better. First he speaks of him as "the man" (v. 11); then he begins to see and says that Jesus is "a prophet" (v. 17; see also Eph 5:8–14). The Lord appears on the scene and brings him to full faith. The man whom everyone, except Jesus, has treated as being insignificant exclaims: "Lord, I believe" (v. 38). God chooses this man, as he had chosen young David (1 Sm 16:10–13), to manifest the divine deeds. The blind man and those around him are liberated from the concept of a punishing God. Freed from blindness, he grows as a human being, and finally he receives the gift of faith. Reducing the liberation of Jesus to one of those aspects would be cutting it short and impoverishing it. Nothing at all escapes Jesus' love.

B. Grace and Demands

2 Chr 36:14–16, 19–21; Eph 2:4–10; Jn 3:14–21

This Sunday's texts remind us that we cannot separate faith and works, grace and demands.

Doing What Is True

The love of God is fundamentally expressed in sending the Son among us. His presence is the measure of God's love for "the world" (Jn 3:16). Every gesture, every word of Jesus manifests the friendship of God. Faith means welcoming this love which saves us and gives us eternal life (v. 16) as of now. God's salvific will excludes no one; it reaches out to every human being (v. 17). However, this plan must be freely accepted. In some way, rejecting it is condemning oneself (v. 18); it is preferring the darkness to the light (v. 19). This is one of the images most often used by John in speaking of Christ. He is the light, and darkness is the world rejecting God's love.

John makes it clear: people refuse the light "because their deeds are evil" (v. 19). Deeds are essential in matters of faith. In the final analysis, this is how accepting or rejecting Christ is played out. Hating the light and doing evil deeds are synonymous (v. 20). Moreover, some refuse to come to the light so that their deeds may not be exposed (v. 20). The text concludes with a decisive statement: "those who do what is true come to the light" (v. 21). The truth involves not only thinking, accepting, but also doing. It has to be translated into concrete gestures, commitment, and solidarity.

Rich in Mercy

That is the way it is because Christian faith means believing in the One who made a concrete gesture: God sent his own Son. Thus, a solidarity which gives meaning to all of human history is established. In view of this, how are we to express our faith in a God who manifests his love through his deeds, if it is not also by our own deeds?

Saint Paul expresses God's involvement in a beautiful phrase: "God is rich in mercy" (Eph 2:4). This is why God saves us. The gift of life is the result of God's gratuitous love. Salvation, namely, communion, friendship with God and one another, is not of our own doing (v. 8); it is grace. We should not boast of our deeds

(v. 2). This is a major theme in Paul. But God's love is also demanding. We have just seen that in John: our deeds reveal our love of the light, our faith in Christ. Doing what is true means looking at our reality face to face, without lies or subterfuges. It means that in it we discover our brothers and sisters who need us and, by our solidarity, we communicate to them the God who is rich in mercy, the One who feels compassion for his people and, therefore, sends messengers to them (1 Chr 36:15).

C. The Kind Father
Jos 5:9–12; 2 Cor 5:17–21; Lk 15:1–3, 11–32

Lent cannot allow us to forget that every Christian celebration is marked by joy and also by forgiveness.

From Death to Life

As usual, the Pharisees and the scribes are on the lookout. They condemn the welcome that Jesus extends to those considered as public sinners, people who, for that reason, are marginalized and despised by them (Lk 15:1). This allows Luke to convey three beautiful parables expressing the motive of the Lord's attitude. The last two parables are found only in Luke. The one we are reading today is the third parable. It is traditionally known as the parable of the prodigal son. A better name for it might be the parable of the kind father.

In fact, the father is the central character. After having wasted his inheritance and having been reduced to misery, the younger son regrets his behavior. Knowing his father, he is sure that he can go back and ask for forgiveness (vv. 11–19). It is important to emphasize that the son knows his father's love from experience. Yet his father's response will overwhelm him. The son had mentally prepared his formula of repentance. But not letting him speak, the father runs to meet his son, taking the initiative to embrace him. The son recites the phrase he had prepared for a long time, but in the presence of the father's love it becomes a formality (vv. 20–21). Forgiveness comes from the welcoming person rather than from the repenting sinner. Forgiving is giving life.

Loving and Celebrating

Like all authentic joy, the father's joy needs to be shared; it cannot be contained. Therefore, the father organizes a banquet so that others may also rejoice over rekindled friendship (vv. 21–24). The older son, who had always behaved correctly, does not understand what is happening. Moreover, he gets angry with his father and demands what he considers to be owed him (vv. 25–30). His attitude echoes the attitude depicted by Matthew in the parable of the laborers of the eleventh hour (20:1–16). Those who have been working since the early hours do not accept that the workers who arrive late be paid the same wage as they. Jesus tells them that they have "an evil eye," that is to say, they are incapable of understanding the gratuitousness of love. The same happens with the older son. The father's joy comes from the fact that the son who has returned home has come back to life.

Failing to see the gratuitousness of love is failing to understand the gospel. By converting the gospel into a mere set of obligations, external rules or a guarantee of authorities without moral worth, we make a caricature out of it. The gratuitousness of love alone guarantees its being creative of ways to express it, and therefore we can say with Paul: "Everything old has passed away; everything has become new" (2 Cor 5:17). Newness comes from the permanent love of God who always renews our love for others (vv. 18–19). We are "ambassadors" of that newness which Jesus Christ reveals to us (v. 20).

Fifth Sunday of Lent

A. I Am the Resurrection and the Life
Ez 37:12–14; Rom 8:8–11; Jn 11:1–45

Death is present in the journey through the desert and in many ways it is also present on our daily path. The Lord liberates us from it.

Jesus' Friends

This Bethany family forms part of the followers of Jesus, disciples and friends (personal friends, we might say in a redundant way). Jesus is informed of Lazarus's health without being explicitly asked to come. He is simply told: "He whom you love is ill" (Jn 11:3). And so it was, Jesus loved that family (v. 5). The Lord goes back to Judea, risking his life. The disciples are afraid, but the master reminds them that his mission is carried out in broad daylight and the darkness in which those who reject him live does not make him stumble (vv. 7–9). In that light and without fears, the disciples will have to continue the task. Fear kills.

Jesus calls Lazarus a friend (v. 11). Going to see him involves dangers. In Judea, death is threatening Jesus and his followers. Thomas senses this and says firmly: "Let us also go, that we might die with him" (v. 16). This is the same Thomas who will later want to know if Jesus has really risen (Jn 20:25, 27). The grave is a sign of death but it is not closed to God whose action opens it and brings forth life (Ez 37:12). Conquering death, they will know that "I am the Lord" (v. 13), God says. Martha's reproach indicates that friendship can be persistent, and she obtains a similar response from Jesus: "I am the resurrection" (Jn 11:17–25). Jesus embodies life; believing in him means eternal life.

The Presence of the Spirit

Jesus is conscious of his mission, but he is also one of us, and as a friend he shares his friends' pain and weeps with them (vv. 33–36). The sisters think that Lazarus's death is definitive, and they tell Jesus: "Already there is a stench" (v. 39). Jesus remains steadfast and, knowing that the Father is listening to him, he gives thanks and cries out loud: "Lazarus, come out" (v. 43). He lifts up the one who was lying down, loosens what was bound, and gives life to the man who was dead.

This is the work of the Spirit in us (see Ez 37:14). We too are called to bring life to a reality so cruelly marked by death which the poor of the world are experiencing. In this situation, we have to defend this primordial human right which is the right to life violated by the growing impoverishment of the dispossessed and the marginalized in terms of the violence they endure. We must defend them without fearing the risks involved and today's frequent blackmail. The "Spirit is life because of righteousness" (Rom 8:10). The Spirit dwells in us, and death is already overcome. This presence must eliminate the fear paralyzing us, closing in on ourselves and preventing us from seeing what is new in our lives and from perceiving that God is challenging us right there. Jesus liberates us from the mediocrity of a Christian life without vitality.

B. The Hour of Jesus
Jer 31:31–34; Heb 5:7–9; Jn 12:20–33

The "hour" is a biblical term which is repeatedly mentioned in John's gospel. It is the time of the new covenant (see Jer 31:31–34).

To See Jesus

"Some Greeks" who had gone up "to worship at the festival" want to see Jesus. The Lord responds to this request with a long and profound meditation on "the hour." John's gospel is written as a drama in which everything is oriented to the final outcome, namely, the encounter of the power of Jesus based on love with the unjust power rejecting him. This crossroad ends on the cross and finally in the victory over the cross and death: the resurrection.

The "hour" is the moment in which God's gratuitous and universal love at the root of his preference for the poor comes face to face with the social and religious dynamics which reject him, namely, with sin. That conflict is expressed on the cross. This is why it will have to be lifted up (Jn 12:32) to denounce what leads Jesus to death and in witness of his loving surrender. Through his own death, Jesus is revealing the God of life. This is the Jesus whom the Greeks addressing Philip will see (v. 21).

A Free Decision

Death on the cross is not a question of fatality. It is the result of an option. "No one takes my life from me but I lay it down on my own accord" (Jn 10:18). Jesus journeys to his "hour" with the consistency of his life. His words are in accordance with his deeds and his deeds in accordance with his words. This is what makes him dangerous for the powers of this world.

Jesus' death seals the new covenant announced by the prophet Jeremiah in our first reading. This pact means both the belonging of the people to God and of God to the people. Its purpose is knowing God, and we know that in the Bible knowledge means love. This is, therefore, a covenant of love. This is what the cross represents: the free and total surrender of love, the "hour" in which that message is revealed to us, the grain of wheat which dies but bears "much fruit" (Jn 12:24).

These "hours" also occur in the lives of persons and of nations. What is at stake in them is our condition as disciples in the here and now. These "hours" are shaped by our own consistency. If the latter is affirmed, the "hour" will come. In the specific crossroads we face we have to be grains of wheat bearing fruit. In the face of the struggle of the poor to survive, we must find ways to behave with the consistency of Jesus. At that hour, we have to respond to his call, even though it may be painful as it was for Jesus (Heb 5:7–9), by bearing witness to life for all in the midst of a situation which marginalizes and asphyxiates the poor.

C. Forgiveness and Tenderness
Is 43:16–21; Phil 3:8–14; Jn 8:1–11

Without love, there is no forgiveness. Reconciliation is not the result of the sinner's humiliation but of the encounter of two persons.

The Accusation of Inconsistency

According to scholars of these themes, this passage appears foreign to the gospel of John. His references to the Mount of Olives, to the scribes, for example, his vocabulary and style do not correspond to those of the fourth gospel. This is not the place for delving into the subject. Besides, all acknowledge its historical value and the fidelity with which this wonderful episode expresses Jesus' behavior.

The scene highlights something totally new in the attitude of Jesus in the presence of someone who has sinned but also in the presence of a woman. The law prescribed the death penalty for the sin of adultery in the case of the woman. Those who bring the matter to the Lord are aware of it, but they want Jesus to make a mistake so that they can declare him guilty (Jn 8:4–6). Jesus transforms the accusers into the accused by starting to write mysteriously on the ground and by telling them: "Let anyone among you who is without sin be the first to throw a stone at her" (v. 7). This challenge is still perfectly valid in terms of our constant tendency to criticize others while ignoring our own behavior. The Lord rejects the inconsistency of people who say one thing and do another. The accusation and even the forgiveness must be accompanied by a self-examination of conscience.

Woman, Where Are They?

If the adulterous person is a man, the punishment is not death. Jesus' authority makes the accusers, all men, go away one by one (v. 9). Jesus' gesture is one of forgiveness of the sinner but also one of rejection of the cruelty toward the woman and the double standards toward women and men — another form of inconsistency. The woman, because she is a woman, sins seriously, while the man's sin is less serious. For what reason? Jesus rejects this alleged justice with its double standards, and, tenderly, he tells the woman caught in adultery: "Neither do I condemn you. Go your way and from now on do not sin again" (v. 11).

The Lord does not focus on the past. What is evil ("do not sin again") must be rejected, but above all we must be oriented to what lies ahead. God is always accomplishing something new in us (Is 43:19) and like God, we must be attentive to what is springing forth. The past does not matter, and, as Paul says, "forgetting what lies behind, I strain forward to what lies ahead" (Phil 3:13).

Forgiveness presupposes our trusting the person who has sinned. Without love, there is no forgiveness. Jesus' attitude with the adulteress reveals his sensitivity and tenderness, his ability to trust another person and his rejection of any form of Pharisaism.

Holy Week

*"He emptied himself,
taking the form of a slave."*
(Phil 2:7)

Palm Sunday

A. The Tongue of a Disciple
Is 50:4–7; Phil 2:6–11; Mt 26:14–27, 66

We are entering Holy Week. The paschal mystery, the passage from death to life, is the heart of our faith.

The Core of Faith

The account of the passion, death, and resurrection of Jesus forms the oldest part of the gospels. It is what the disciples recorded first. For them, this was the nucleus of the Lord's witness. Gradually, the deeds and words of Jesus were added, as in the case of the infancy narratives. All of this becomes meaningful in the light of the Master's surrender of his life and the action of the Father making him victorious over death by raising him up.

Matthew's version goes into details. The betrayal, the fear, and the denial of the disciples are openly pointed out. The Master bewilders them. The same thing happens to those who seek to condemn him to death, either the Roman or the Jewish leaders. The confrontation presented in the gospel takes away their security; hypocritically, they wash their hands of the matter. Their lack of consistency becomes evident. They accuse Jesus of wanting to become king. Christ does accept his kingship, but his kingdom differs from that of the Roman Caesar or Herod's. His kingdom is one of service, not of domination. It is the kingdom of a God who "emptied himself and took the form of a slave" (Phil 4:6) and surrendered to "death on a cross" (v. 8) to bear witness to the Father's love. The cross, which for us may immediately evoke the theme of suffering, is the expression of total surrender.

Ears to Hear

This humiliation (*kenosis* is the Greek term used by Paul, Phil 2:7) is the obligatory path to serve others. It was also the path followed by the Master and the one which the disciples and the church as a whole have to follow. A church which does not let go of the privileges that history or its place in society have given it is in no position to tell us how to go to God who is love.

This is what the text of Isaiah calls "the tongue of a disciple" (Is 50:4), of someone who has begun to follow the Lord. Our proximity to the sufferings of the poor opens our ears so that we may listen to all the demands of the gospel. If we do not, we are resisting and turning our backs (v. 5) on the challenges of the Lord. Nowadays, being in solidarity with the poor may cause "insults and spitting" (v. 6) on a church striving to be faithful to Christ. But by experiencing them, the church will share what is endured by the poor, victims of diseases already conquered by medicine, living in precarious dwellings and mistreated when they ask for a decent salary. There may be ambiguities (unavoidable in any human situation) in the historical development of such realities, but that does not make them less painful and unjust.

Like the suffering servant of Isaiah, we must be convinced that the Lord is helping us and will not allow us to become cowards. We know that we will not be disgraced (v. 7) if what impels us in our commitment is giving witness that God loves everyone, especially the weakest and the marginalized. The Lord died on the cross for each and every one of us to whom he gives his life in his resurrection. It is a life which overcomes death, sin, injustice and the neglect of our sisters and brothers.

B. Between Enthusiasm and Rejection
Is 50:4–7; Phil 2:6–11; Mk 11:1–10 and 14:1–15:47

We are approaching the celebration of the central mystery of the Christian message: the death and the resurrection of Jesus.

Jesus the Messiah

The Lord prepares every detail of his entry into Jerusalem where he is to confront death (Mk 14:1–6). His enemies have been on the lookout for years. The simplicity and the honesty of Jesus have rendered them powerless; his proclamation and his practice of love, especially for the most destitute, have confused them. The weakness of his adversaries' testimonies and arguments make them resort to force. Fear is a bad adviser. Aware of this, the Lord goes to his death riding a colt. The gospels show us the people who acknowledge him as the Messiah (Mk 11:7–10). This is just what the leaders of the people feared. In advance, the people point out the reason why Jesus will be executed: because "he comes in the name of the Lord" (v. 9), because the kingdom is approaching. The rest is irrelevant, mere attempts to conceal the truth. Jesus openly proclaims the truth in the temple (v. 11).

Something will be obtained by their deceitful arguments. Perhaps some of the people who acclaimed Jesus then would later shout in response to Pilate's question: "Crucify him, crucify him" (Mk 15:13–14). The powerful always have many recourses to confuse the people. But let us not just think of others; sometimes we are also examples of this inconsistency. At one moment, we acclaim and welcome the Lord; at another, we deny him. Holy Week is precisely a time for conversion, a time to hear the gospel calling us to be more consistent in our lives, a time to choose Jesus rather than Barabbas, a time to be in solidarity with Simon of Cyrene and the good thief (v. 21) and a time to be courageous and determined like the women of Jerusalem (vv. 40–41, 47).

The Servant of the Lord

Conversion means allowing the Lord to give us "the tongue of a disciple" (Is 50:4), that is to say, the ability to speak as followers of Jesus. The servant of the Lord is our model: he has a word of encouragement for those going through bad times, and with ears open and attentive to God's Word, not resisting the call, not turning back, he faces the difficulties with total trust in God who is at his side (vv. 4–7). To have a disciple's tongue, according to Isaiah's beautiful expression, is not only a matter of expressing ourselves in words but also in an attitude of humble service which includes the surrender of our lives (Phil 2:6–10). Without this, the message would be empty and without moral authority. This week is a suitable time to strengthen our commitment.

On the cross, Jesus utters his final words: "My God, my God, why have you forsaken me?" (Mk 15:34), words expressing the pain and the isolation of one feeling abandoned by God. Although he shouts his being abandoned in the opening words of Psalm 22, according to an ancient custom Jesus makes all the other verses his own. It is a painful complaint, but in the Bible lamentations do not exclude hope, which is clearly expressed in the following lines (see Ps 22:5–6). Pain and hope. On the cross, there is a profound communion with human suffering but also with the hope in the God of life. Jesus, "the forsaken," abandons himself into the Father's hands. From the cross, the Lord is calling us to follow in his footsteps.

C. Words of Encouragement
Is 50:4–7; Phil 2:6–11; Lk 22:14–23:56

Palm Sunday: the crowds are welcoming the Lord with leafy branches in their hands, but shortly after that he will be condemned to death.

No Turning Back

The accounts of the passion and the death of Jesus are the oldest in the gospels and they are to be read in the light of the resurrection. Today, we are listening to Luke's testimony in a clear language telling us about Christ's suffering: "His sweat became like great drops of blood falling down on the ground" (22:44). We cannot read these texts without feeling invited to share Jesus' suffering and also his complying with the will of the Father (23:46). Luke's account includes two scriptural passages which help us to clarify its scope.

The text from Isaiah is considered as the third song of Yahweh's servant, one of the figures of Christ in the Old (or First) Testament. In a style close to Jeremiah's, the prophet tells us about his vocation. It is God's initiative, and his mission is to encourage the weary (50:4). We are dealing with the theme of consolation that characterizes second Isaiah. For the prophet, consoling means liberating. It requires the ability to listen (v. 4); the Lord opens the ears of his messenger to enable him to hear the expressions of anguish and protest of those who are discouraged (v. 5). The abuse he receives in fulfilling his mission does not make him desist or turn back (v. 5). He knows that the Lord sustains him, and he says trustingly, "Therefore I have not been disgraced" (v. 7).

Today's liturgy attributes these feelings to Jesus. He has come to console and to liberate. His suffering and his death do not intimidate him or put an end to his mission. The Father is with him.

Emptying of Self

Paul's text brings us a beautiful and well-known christological hymn. Its basic theme is Jesus Christ's humility and his will to serve. The Son of God does not seek to cling to his privileges, but instead he empties himself to become one of us. And so from below, paying the price of the cross for fulfilling his mission, he gives us the fullness of life. Therefore, every tongue will proclaim that "Jesus Christ is Lord" (Phil 2:11).

Before the start of his hymn, Paul invites us to have "the same mind that was in Christ Jesus" (Phil 2:5) — in other words, to be able to let go of situations of privilege to carry out our task as witnesses of the Father's love. Many people live in inhuman conditions, in profound isolation and unspeakable deprivation; being in solidarity with them is imperative for all Christians and for the entire church. This solidarity does not imply giving from above but rather horizontal sharing; not palliatives in a situation that is deteriorating but words and gestures of encouragement and permanent commitment with a suffering people. This is the way we will make the name of Jesus known (Phil 2:10).

Holy Thursday

Do as I Have Done
Ex 12:1–8, 11–14; 1 Cor 11:23–26; Jn 13:1–15

Holy Thursday marks the start of what is called the paschal Triduum. Today's texts deal with the Passover.

The Washing of the Feet

Passover is the great celebration of the Jewish people. It commemorates their departure from Egypt and the end of their oppression. Before that date (according to John) Jesus eats with his disciples. He knows that his hour (an important theme in John's gospel) has come, the hour "to depart from this world and go to the Father" (v. 1). This is not an easy juncture as Jesus has close bonds with his milieu and he loves "his own." But this very love leads him to part with them (v. 1). This is the price he has to pay for having proclaimed the kingdom. One of the disciples had already decided to betray him (v. 2). At that undoubtedly painful point, Jesus has a growing awareness of his mission framed by his coming from God and his going back to God (v. 3).

Then, in a prophetic gesture not recorded in the synoptic gospels, Jesus rises from the table and starts to wash his disciples' feet (vv. 4–5). The abundance of verbs in these two verses stresses

Jesus' initiative and action. The washing of the feet was an expression of welcome and service, and it was practiced with people recognized as having some kind of superiority, social or otherwise. The Lord inverts the terms, and his love brings him to serve even the most humble. Peter's understandable protest does not stop him. On the contrary, Jesus' insistence points out the importance of what he is doing (vv. 7–10). The text does not say that Judas is not included in this gesture, but in a clear reference to him Jesus warns: "Not all of you are clean" (v. 11).

Have You Understood?

Unlike the other evangelists, John does not have a narrative of the Last Supper. Paul's text, on the other hand, presents it very faithfully in a version close to that of Luke (vv. 23–26). On Holy Thursday we celebrate the Last Supper and the institution of the Eucharist in a special way. The Exodus passage recalls the Passover feast, the celebration of God liberating his people on "a day of remembrance," the motive for thanksgiving "throughout the generations" (v. 14).

Everything indicates that by placing the washing of the feet in the place of the Last Supper narrative, John wants to underscore the meaning of the death and resurrection of the Lord. The surrender of his life is not an act of heroism or for personal consumption; it is an act of humble and loving service. Jesus asks affectionately, "Do you know what I have done to you?" (Jn 13:12). Then he explains to them precisely why he, the Master, has washed their feet. His message and his testimony are not seeking to secure privileges but to serve (v. 13). The meaning of his gesture must be an example of how to behave for his followers: "you also ought to wash one another's feet" (v. 14). In other words, they ought to serve one another and never take advantage of their condition and their mission to place themselves above others. Such a service may lead to the surrender of our lives. This is what the institution of the Eucharist is expressing.

Just as he has done at other times in John's gospel ("love one another as I have loved you," 15:12), the Lord proposes his own behavior as a model for his disciples telling them, you also should do "as I have done to you" (v. 15). The two accounts, the two gestures, the washing of the feet and the institution of the Eucharist, cast light upon each other. Both are remembered and repeated on Holy Thursday. Have we really understood?

Good Friday

My Kingdom Is Not Like Yours
Is 52:13–53:12; Heb 4:14–16, 5:7–9; Jn 18:1–19:42

On Good Friday, we always consider John's carefully written version of the passion and the death of Jesus.

Yes, I Am a King

John's account of the passion is a powerful affirmation of Jesus' identity. To those who are looking for Jesus of Nazareth, he says: "I am he" (vv. 5, 6, 8), a formula frequently used in John and repeated many times in these two chapters. The confrontation with Pilate is impeccably presented. To begin with, John points out that since it is the Passover feast, the Jews "themselves did not enter the praetorium, so as to avoid ritual defilement" (v. 28). This forces Pilate to come and go constantly (vv. 18:29, 33, 38; 19:4, 5, 8), during which time his stature weakens and decreases while that of Jesus increases.

Pilate comes on the scene sure of himself and of his power. At first, he does not even want to be in charge of the accused (18:28–32). Then, with indifference, he asks Jesus: "Are you the King of the Jews?" (v. 33). Jesus' answer is well-known: "My kingdom is not from this world" (v. 36). This affirmation does not mean, as is sometime alleged, that the kingdom has nothing or little to do with human history; that does not correspond to the gospel as a whole. When we pray for the coming of the kingdom, we are asking for it to come into our history, and at the same time we know that it transcends it.

With his "my kingdom is not from this world," Jesus is telling Pilate: my kingdom is not like the one you know, like the one of the world which you represent (v. 36). Yet, it is a kingdom that also impacts the present. Pilate seems to have understood: "So you are a king?" (v. 37). Jesus does not deny it: "you say that I am a king"; however, his kingdom is not one of domination like Caesar's but one of service. Theirs are two different ways of understanding the history and universality of human existence.

The Cross as a Throne

Jesus gives his life out of love, thereby showing the way of service to his disciples. As the text progresses, with Pilate's constant coming and going, an expression of his hesitation and irrelevance, Jesus' personality is growing stronger (19:8–10). The power of the representative of the most powerful king on earth does not intimidate him (v. 11). Jesus' adversaries make this Roman official choose between Jesus and Caesar and what they signify (v. 12). Earlier, Pilate had made them choose between Jesus and Barabbas (18:39–40); the same people demand a much more important decision involving risks for the procurator. As so many people do today, Pilate opts for temporal power and his sinecure (19:13). Subservient, Pilate orders the crucifixion of the Nazarene and the cross, a sign of his surrender and love, is transformed into the throne of the reign of service. When Jesus is led to his death, seemingly vanquished, John presents him as standing tall and victorious.

Beaten, his face disfigured, like the servant of the Lord portrayed by Isaiah, Jesus "shall startle many nations; kings shall shut their mouths because of him" (52:15). Likewise, in his surrender "he bore the sin of many and made intercession for the transgressors" (53:12). Jesus, the Son of God, is the "high priest" who sympathizes "with our weaknesses" (Heb 4:15). This is what we are celebrating today.

From the cross, the Lord is calling us to love fully. We welcome the kingdom of service which Jesus brought to us in solidarity with everyone and especially with the most marginalized, with those who need our friendship.

The Easter Vigil

A. The First Women Witnesses
Rom 6:3–11; Mt 28:1–10

The Easter Vigil is the feast of fire, light, and water or, more exactly, the feast of the risen Christ, energy, enlightenment, and life for all. We are incorporated into Christ through baptism, which has its most appropriate framework at the Easter Vigil.

Come and See

The death of the Lord had confused the disciples and made them withdraw, but the women were not intimidated. The four gospels tell us that the women were the first persons who went "to see the tomb" (v. 1). The verb "see" occurs several times in these verses: "come, see the place where he lay" (v. 6); "there you will see him" (v. 7 and 10). In fact, the point is to give testimony of what they have experienced in the most direct way: by seeing.

Several characteristics mark the event, making it very solemn and emphasizing the importance of what happened (vv. 2–4). But the women should have no fear of all that: "Do not be afraid" (v. 5). They are lovingly looking for "Jesus who was crucified," but the messenger (this is the meaning of the term "angel") tells them that they themselves have to verify that the tomb where they were to find him is empty. Matthew emphasizes this point. They leave the tomb "with fear and great joy" (v. 8). The expression is beautiful and nuanced; the inevitable fear they experience does not paralyze them as it did the guards who "became like dead men" (v. 4). They feel great joy, and joy is always contagious, which explains why "they ran to tell the disciples" (v. 8). On this Easter night, the overwhelming feeling is one of joy, a joy which has to mark our lives as believers.

Do Not Be Afraid

Jesus meets these faithful and courageous women, greeting them with a "Rejoice!" which our text translates less literally by "Greetings" (v. 9), but we are really dealing with rejoicing. Taking hold of Jesus' feet is another way of saying they are verifying that the risen one is real (v. 9), and this completes the event to which they are to bear witness. The "brothers" of Jesus, those who accompanied him during his preaching, also have to be his witnesses. They are to meet in Galilee, where Jesus had shared with them all the Father had entrusted to him (v. 10).

Through baptism, we are incorporated into Christ and his mission. We have been baptized into the death and the resurrection of the Lord. That is the passage we are celebrating on this night which begins at the Easter light (Rom 6:3–4). So we walk "in newness of life" (v. 4). Paul invites us to be aware of that newness. The resurrection of the Lord puts an end to the "dominion of death" (v. 9). Being witnesses to the resurrection means sharing our condition of "being alive to God in Christ Jesus" (v. 11). Evangelizing means communicating the joy of knowing that we are loved by God, the joy of knowing that life is the ultimate word in human existence.

B. A New Beginning
Rom 6:3–11; Mk 16:1–8

With the resurrection of the Lord, a new life is beginning. The gospel accounts present this perspective very clearly.

The First Day of the Week

Like Matthew, Mark indicates the day of the event twice: "when the sabbath was over," the day of rest, then comes "the first day of the week" (v. 1), which is now our Sunday, the day of the Lord. Mark insists on the timing: the women go to the tomb "very early," "when the sun had risen" (v. 2). The focus is on the idea of beginning, a new start. The women's intention is to anoint the body of the Lord (also found in Luke, differently from Matthew, who does not mention the subject). The names of the women vary slightly in the four gospels, yet one name is always mentioned, the name of Mary Magdalene.

The narrative is simple. There is no special event, other than the fact that in Mark the stone at the entrance of the tomb had already been rolled back (v. 4). The messenger is simply a young man "dressed in a white robe" (v. 5). He tells the women: "Do not be alarmed" (v. 6). They are amazed with a touch of fear, and he anticipates their eventual question: "Jesus of Nazareth, who was crucified, has been raised" (v. 6). This terse formula contains the essence; then he adds something which can be verified by the women: "He is not here. Look, there is the place where they laid him." The empty tomb is the sign of a new presence to which they are to bear witness. First, they are to communicate the news to the disciples, who may not have dared be the first to go and see Jesus' tomb. They must go to Galilee where "they will see him" (v. 7), just as Jesus had told them. They were all from Galilee, and there they had accompanied the Lord on his preaching journeys. The tomb will remain empty in Jerusalem, but from the marginalized region of Galilee the world will be filled with the presence of the risen Christ.

Mark immediately shows the women so seized with "terror and amazement" that they "said nothing to anyone" (v. 8). The text ends abruptly. The women's fear is understandable, but not their silence. In fact, Mark leaves open the possibility of their communicating their experience, while Luke shows the women carrying out the mandate to speak with the disciples. This has led some to think that Mark's gospel is not complete (hence the suspension points in the Jerusalem Bible). However, it may also be a new indication, a frequent occurrence in Mark, that believing is a long and difficult process, a process which is always beginning.

Baptized in Christ

Paul gives us the meaning of the baptismal liturgy so essential in the Easter vigil. Like every sacrament, baptism is a sign, an effective sign in the words of Christian tradition. Its significance is our bond with Christ. In the death of Christ, the power of sin, of self-sufficient egoism dies. We have been baptized into his death (v. 3). Paul reinforces the idea of the resurrection, adding that "we have been buried with him by baptism into death." Because of that, just as Christ was raised, we too have been called to walk "in newness of life" (v. 4).

Mark is also speaking of a new beginning. Paul specifies that "our old self," which "was crucified" with Christ (v. 6), has to die in us. In this way we will cease to be slaves of the power of death, expressed in sin, breaking up our friendship with God and one another. We are freed from this power by Jesus Christ (v. 7). As Jesus lives, we too must "live to God" (v. 10). Being witnesses to the resurrection means accepting the power of the Spirit of freedom and life in ourselves, getting rid of our own selfishness and liberating others from whatever prevents them from fulfilling themselves as human beings and as daughters and sons of God. A solidarity that is welcoming and committed to everyone and especially to the neediest is our bond with the risen Christ, the giver of life.

C. Look for Jesus among the Living
Rom 6:3–11; Lk 24:1–12

The resurrection of Christ calls us into the community of Jesus' disciples, witnesses to his life. Without the resurrection, Paul tells us, our preaching and our faith would be in vain (1 Cor 15:14).

The Empty Tomb

The testimony of the resurrection begins with a crisis. Many women, disciples of Jesus, go to the tomb, and to the names we already know Luke adds "and the other women with them" (v. 10). They find the tomb empty. The body of the Lord is not there (Lk 24:3) and their first reaction is confusion: "they were perplexed" (v. 4). Informed by the women, the disciples do not believe them. People considered as "inferior" are never believed. Peter goes to the tomb, but "he saw the linen clothes by themselves; then he went home, amazed at what had happened" (v. 12). Yet, this emptiness, this absence refers to the fullness of a presence. The body of Jesus is not in the tomb because he is alive. The messengers of the Lord ask Mary Magdalene, Joanna, and Mary the mother of James: "Why do you look for the living among the dead?" (v. 5). They are still asking us the same question today.

The God in whom we believe is the God of life. This is what we celebrate frequently in the midst of a situation which severely strikes the poor, marking them with the seal of premature and unjust death but also in the midst of generous expressions of solidarity on the part of the poor themselves. Believing in the resurrection implies defending the lives of the weakest members of society. In them, the poor and the oppressed, we have to encounter the Lord. In the living, though they are threatened by death, the risen Christ is present. Looking for him among the living leads us to make a preferential commitment for those whose right to life is constantly violated.

The Resurrection Is a Passover

Proclaiming the resurrection of the Lord is proclaiming life in the face of death. Thus, for Christians, the resurrection is a Passover, that is to say, a passage. In the Bible, Passover (regardless of the possible etymology of the Hebrew term translated this way) is the passage from oppression in Egypt to the promised land. Celebrating it signified remembering the gift of liberation. Jesus places his work in that context; it is a passage from oppression and death to freedom and life. We become incorporated into this passage through baptism, by which we are "dead to sin and alive to God in Christ Jesus" (Rom 6:11).

Life cannot be affirmed without passing through death, without confronting it. This is the witness that so many people in

Latin America have given us by their being faithful to the God of life and, as a result, have been confronted with unjust death. Their Passover, in communion with Jesus', illumines our reality. It makes us see the cruelty of poverty, injustice, and isolation, but it also spurs our hope in the One whom we must seek among the living because "he has risen" (Lk 24:6). And so we must also look for these people among the living, not among the dead.

The Easter Season

"Why do you look for the living among the dead?"

(Lk 24:5)

Easter Sunday

Between the Indicative and the Imperative
Acts 10:34, 37–43; Col 3:1–4; Jn 20:1–9

How are we to celebrate Easter joy with all the human suffering, especially of the poor and the have-nots, which seems to choke our shouts of joy in our throats?

Women, the First to Arrive

In the early days, Christians used to gather the entire night in vigil, in expectancy of the Lord's resurrection. They remembered the death of Jesus, and at daybreak they celebrated his victory over it. The Easter Vigil was everything. Later on, it was broken down, and with the addition of other elements it gradually became our Holy Week. Passover — the passage from death to life — was so important that in Spanish the term "Pascua" refers not only to Easter but also to Christmas, the feast of Epiphany and even to Pentecost.

At the paschal vigil, we read the accounts of Matthew, Mark, and Luke. Now the liturgy presents John's account. The women are the first to arrive at the tomb, but John mentions only Mary Magdalene (20:1). The disciples do not believe them, as Luke points out (Mark does too in a complementary text; see 16:9–11). John only infers it, and, along with Peter, he mentions the "other disciple" (v. 3). The Lord appears first to women, persons who were looked down upon at the time (as well as now). This may be the reason why the disciples do not believe them. The proclamation of life starts with the very persons who are marked by death, marginalization, and mistreatment.

Peter and the other disciple run to verify what Mary Magdalene has reported. The second, younger disciple (undoubtedly, John himself), arrives first, but he lets Peter go in first (4–6). Then John goes in: "he saw and believed" (v. 8). All they find is the empty tomb. In that absence, they perceive a new presence, the presence of the Lord who has overcome death and who gives us life.

Things from Above

If so many texts and discourses on the resurrection sound hollow to us, it is because their authors have not experienced unjust death. This may be why in Latin America the resurrection is charged with energy and it reaches a new depth. This enables us to have a better understanding of Paul's text. The indicative which recalls that we "have been raised with Christ" is followed by the imperative: "Seek the things that are above" (Col 3:1). The resurrection is the core of our faith and, therefore, the great model of our behavior. After Peter's first preaching (Acts 2) focused, like today's text (Acts 10:37–43), on the resurrection of Jesus, his listeners ask him: "What should we do?" (2:37). We should always ask ourselves the same question.

In biblical language, "the things that are above" are the things of God. We have to set our minds on them (Col 3:2). Life, all of it, is what characterizes God. No part of what we call material and spiritual, temporal and eternal escapes the gratuitous gift of life. Believing in the resurrection means bearing witness to him who is "judge of the living and the dead" (Acts 10:42). We will experience paschal joy only if, like the Christ of our faith, we are life-giving. In the midst of difficulties and problems, many people seek to express their solidarity with the neediest who, in turn, organize themselves to defend their rights and alleviate their suffering. Many of them do this prompted by their faith, and the joy of Easter gives vitality and meaning to their testimony.

Second Sunday of Easter

A. With Generous Hearts
Acts 2:42–47; 1 Pet 1:3–9; Jn 20:19–31

The center of Holy Week is the celebration of Jesus' resurrection. The texts for this Sunday echo this momentous event.

Peace and Mission

The author of the gospel plans to tell us about some of the many signs that Jesus performed. He writes "so that you may come to believe that Jesus is the Messiah, the Son of God and that through believing you may have life in his name" (Jn 20:31). Believing is having life. Having faith is believing in life. For John, everything begins with the experience, the encounter with Jesus (1:35–39). The evangelist presents himself as a witness to the deeds and words of the One who has overcome death and has risen from the dead. This testimony characterizes the disciples, those who, attentive and bewildered, followed Jesus on the roads of Galilee. For them, believing in the Master was a difficult and joyful process. When he died, they feared it was all over, but as today's passage from John tells us, the Lord appeared to them. His presence brought them peace (vv. 19–21 and 26), but at the same time it meant new demands for the disciples: "As the Father has sent me, so I send you" (v. 21). They are to continue his work.

We have received that testimony and with it peace and a mission. In some way, Thomas, who had not seen the risen Lord physically, represents us in the text. We have not seen him either. Jesus scolds Thomas for not accepting the other disciples' testimony. An affectionate reproach: "Do not doubt but believe" (v. 27). John, who insists so much on experience as the foundation of faith, wants to remind us of the experience of Jesus we can have now: the testimony of others. The gospel of the Lord comes to us through the testimony transmitted from one generation to another and through the present generation.

A Living Hope

The testimony of the Lord's resurrection builds up the community whose members are those who believe in life. Having faith implies sharing what we have according to everyone's need (Acts 2:45). Christian faith does not consist in proclaiming abstract truths; instead it means having life, and life presupposes communication. Only a church in solidarity with the poor of this world, a church formed by people who share what they have, not feeling superior to anyone because they are Christians or because of the position they might have in the ecclesial community, can celebrate the Eucharist "with generous hearts" (Acts 2:46).

The peace which the risen Lord brings us also entails a task, a mission inspirited by "a living hope" (1 Pet 1:3), the responsibility to communicate and to share that hope. When hope dies in a person or a people, only darkness and sadness are left. The resurrection can only be proclaimed in joy, a joy which forgets neither the presence of afflictions and trials (1 Pet 1:6) nor the signs of life which many followers of Jesus are giving. We have to live all this with generous hearts.

B. A Sending Forth
Acts 4:32–35; 1 Jn 5:1–6; Jn 20:19–31

The Easter season is a time of joy and also a time of sending forth, of responsibility for Christians.

Belief and Unbelief

The disciples of Jesus go through a moment of fear after the death of Jesus on the cross (Jn 20:19). In those circumstances, the risen Lord bursts in and gives them the necessary strength to carry out their mission (v. 21). Jesus opens the doors which fear had closed. He brings them peace, but that does not mean rest. On the contrary, peace is the prerequisite to go out to proclaim the gospel. The mission of the disciples is the same as the one the Father had given Jesus: "As the Father has sent me, so I send you" (v. 21). They will carry out their mission thanks to the impulse of the Holy Spirit (v. 22).

Thomas has passed into history as a skeptical, even incredulous disciple; he does not believe if he does not see. By resisting faith, Thomas earns a promise for us in the form of a beatitude proclaimed by the Lord: "Blessed are those who have not seen and yet have come to believe" (v. 29). Like Thomas, it is our turn to say: "My Lord and my God!" (v. 28). We are among those who have not seen Jesus with our own eyes and yet we believe.

Being Born of God

Jesus does not leave anyone indifferent; he transforms our lives in every aspect. Jesus' followers place everything at the service of others. They enter into a communion which affects every dimension of human existence. Luke tells us: "everything they owned was held in common" (Acts 4:32). In this way, they give their testimony to "the resurrection of the Lord Jesus" (v. 33). Such a love eliminates needs within the community (v. 34). As witnesses to the resurrection, they communicate life and take everyone's need into account (v. 35). This image of the first community has been the inspiration for many experiences in the course of history. This type of utopia is what makes history move forward.

Faith in Jesus means that we have been born of God (1 Jn 5:1), and it transforms us into conquerors of death because we believe in the risen Lord. Now we have to make the resurrection of the Lord believable through our own signs of life toward others. The love of God and the love of God's children are inseparable. This is what the first community did by putting everything they owned in common so that no one would be in need. In our own situation, we must decide what it means to give signs of life.

C. The Keys of Death
Acts 5:12–16; Rv 1:9–13, 17–19; Jn 20:19–31

On this Sunday, we are proclaiming a beatitude which affects us deeply: "Blessed are those who have not seen and yet have come to believe" (Jn 20:29), because by faith we share in life: "so that through believing you may have life" (v. 31). Our faith in the Lord is translated into works which generate life.

As the Father Has Sent Me

The resurrection does not impose itself as evidence, and the risen Jesus' appearances slowly impact his disciples' hearts. Faith opens us up to the risen presence of the Lord among his own: "the disciples rejoiced when they saw the Lord" (v. 20). Yet this presence and its fruit, joy, are not for the sake of intimate contemplation; instead they are power for the mission. Jesus appears among his disciples and he tells them: "As the Father has sent me, so I send you" (v. 21). A mission which comes from the Father and his love, from God's desire to forgive and give life (because "forgiving is giving life") and from his concern to "gather the dispersed children" (Jn 11:52). For that purpose, God sends his Son and his church, empowering them with the Holy Spirit, the "Lord and giver of life."

The Lord is present in his church to open it up to the world, but many times the church is afraid to risk its life and it tends to withdraw into sterile isolation, especially when hostility and death are ruling outside. As today's text says, the Lord's presence is found in the midst of a community "with the doors locked for fear of the Jews" (v. 19).

He Was Dead and He Lives Forever

The Father sent his Son into the world and the world killed him, but he did accomplish his mission: "by finishing the work you gave me to do" (Jn 17:4). To encourage his church, today the Lord says: "I was dead, and see, I am alive forever and ever" (Rv 1:18). He has been made the Lord of life. The church, like John the Evangelist, is called to be a witness to the life the Father seeks to transmit through our mission, but that also implies we are participants and companions in "the persecutions, the kingdom, and the patient endurance" (v. 9). This church, with a mission, which must risk its life, is told: "I have the keys of death" (Rv 1:18), "Do not be afraid, I am the first and the last" (v. 17).

We come to life through faith, but our faith and devotion to the Lord are translated into signs of life as attested by the early community. "Many signs and wonders were done among the people through the apostles" (Acts 5:12). To give testimony of the power of the resurrection means to serve the destitute and the poor who are subsisting at the limit of nonlife. In the first community, "a great number of people also gathered from the towns around Jerusalem bringing the sick and those tormented by unclean spirits and they were all cured" (v. 16). The power of Jesus' presence is experienced in life. At Easter, we celebrate the presence and the life of the risen Christ, the hope of mistreated and suffering men and women.

Third Sunday of Easter

A. In the Breaking of the Bread
Acts 2:14, 22–28; 1 Pet 1:17–21; Lk 24:13–35

Being Christian is to believe in the resurrection, which is, therefore, the nucleus of the preaching and testimony of the church.

A Rereading

This Lukan text has profoundly impacted the memory of Christians. Discreetly and in keeping with the customs of the time, Jesus joins the two disciples who are walking to Emmaus and talking with concern about what has just happened in Jerusalem (24:13–15). They are sad (that is to say, the opposite of what the resurrection should produce in believers) and, perhaps, disappointed. They are astounded that the stranger does not know what had happened in Jerusalem to Jesus of Nazareth, the prophet of God condemned to death by the leaders of his people (vv. 18–21). Moreover, the women of their group and a few others have told them about the empty tomb, but their faith is not mature enough to enable them to see in that absence the presence of the risen Jesus (vv. 22–24).

Believing in the resurrection and perceiving all its repercussions are a process that demands time. It also requires our being able to know how to read scripture. This is what the stranger who joins them does with patience and devotion: "he interpreted to them the things about himself in all the scriptures" (v. 27). As Saint Augustine said, Jesus is in fact the key to scripture. We never complete our reading of the Bible; we go to it with our questions, but in turn it questions us. We read it, but we are also read by it. It reveals God to us but it also reveals us to ourselves. The Bible reminds us that we encounter Jesus in those who are excluded and in those who suffer in the world. Following in the footsteps of the bishops at Puebla, the Santo Domingo conference has underlined this once again, and at the same time it invites us to lengthen the list of the poor in whom we are to recognize Jesus — a task that is not difficult, albeit painful, in our continent with increasingly more poor.

Witnesses to the Resurrection

The so-called Emmaus disciples still do not recognize Jesus, but they put into practice the welcome they have learned from their master: "Stay with us" (v. 29). The stranger takes bread, blesses and shares it, and then the disciples remember that Jesus had done just that (Lk 9:12–17), which makes them recognize him as the Messiah (24:18–21). In the gift of bread, he expresses his own surrender, which opens the eyes of the two friends. Then they see what their inertia and sadness did not allow them to perceive; the gesture of the Lord gives renewed strength to their reading of the scriptures (v. 32). Once they are back in Jerusalem, the disciples rejoice and comfort one another by sharing the news that Jesus has risen (vv. 33–35).

Bearing witness to this is a disciple's mission. When they have to select someone to join the twelve, they choose him from those who were witnesses "with us to his resurrection" (Acts 1:22). Our major question is the following: how are we to be witnesses to the resurrection and life in a world in which, as Peruvian poet César Vallejo said, pain and death increase sixty minutes per second? Let us look for the answer with our faith and hope set on God (1 Pet 1:21).

B. The Author of Life
Acts 3:13–15, 17–19; 1 Jn 2:1–5; Lk 24:35–48

The appearances of the risen Christ to his disciples seek to confirm them in their faith and to awaken them to their new responsibilities.

Sharing the Bread

Two disciples have just recognized Jesus in "the breaking of the bread" (Lk 24:25). Then, he appears to his followers and wishes them peace (v. 36). We understand the richness of this concept which implies fullness of life. Jesus had announced it to them while he was walking with them on the roads of Galilee, and now he is reaffirming the message. He shows them his hands and feet saying: "It is I myself" (v. 39). He is not a spirit or a ghost. The risen Jesus has flesh and bones (v. 39); he is hungry and asks them for something to eat as he had always done with them. He eats "in their presence" (v. 42). Meals are always a sign of life and of communion.

The text reiterates the unity between the historical Jesus and the risen Christ. The Lord repeats what he had told them before (v. 44). Now they understand him better, and their minds are opened to the scriptures. They clearly see that their task is to be witnesses to the message and the resurrection of the Lord "beginning from Jerusalem" (v. 48), the city where he was executed. For Luke, it is from there that the victory over death is to be proclaimed.

Witnesses of the Truth

Strengthened by the Spirit, Peter gives witness of "these things" (Lk 24:48). Jesus' adversaries had to choose between "a murderer" and the "author of life" (Acts 3:15). On various occasions, the

Bible tells us that we have to choose between life and death. This is what the leaders of the Jewish people had done. Jesus' proclamation had questioned their privileges, and their response was to decide against the one who was bringing the fullness of life — a futile deed, since God raised up the one they killed. Peter is a witness to this (v. 15). Defending a privilege always leads to choosing death.

Duplicity, disloyalty in terms of what we claim to believe, is a subtle way of choosing death. The person who does not practice what he or she professes is "a liar and in such a person the truth does not exist" (1 Jn 2:4). Believing in the risen One involves affirming and communicating life. If we do not share life, our love of God has not reached perfection (v. 5). Giving life means many things, including something seemingly simple which the risen Jesus himself asks for, namely, feeding others. Let us hope we always have a "piece of broiled fish" to share.

C. Obeying God Rather Than Human Authorities
Acts 5:27–32, 40–41; Rv 5:11–14; Jn 21:1–19

Christians are witnesses to the resurrection. This testimony of life may lead to difficult confrontations.

Come and Eat

The gospel of John had already presented two manifestations of the risen Jesus: the first one to Mary Magdalene and the second to the disciples behind locked doors for fear of the Jews. This time, Jesus appears to the disciples who had resumed their daily work of fishing. In each case, John points out that the Lord is not recognized at the first moment; his resurrection does not appear obvious to his disciples. Yet Jesus is there; his body bears the marks of the death which he had endured, and he becomes present in order to reveal that life overcomes death. This is why Jesus invites them to eat (v. 12): sharing a meal expresses life and friendship. To remember his death and his resurrection, shortly before he was arrested and crucified, Jesus had also asked his followers to gather for a meal, the Eucharist. The absence of the food to which every person is entitled goes against the message of abundant life brought by the resurrection of the Lord.

The dialogue with Peter places the responsibility to tend the sheep (vv. 15–19) in a context of love. The three questions seek to erase Peter's three denials (18:15–18). This time, the repentant disciple proclaims his loyalty and love. Loving the Lord is the prerequisite to carry out pastoral work, which must also be done with love for "the sheep," in other words, with respect for them and concern about their preoccupations and needs. Pastoral work is a dialogue, not something imposed by someone who knows and can do everything. Otherwise, it will not reveal the God who loves us and wishes to be loved.

Beatings and Insults

The resurrection of the Lord is the heart of the first apostolic preaching (Acts 2–3). For the people in power at the time, that proclamation of life is subversive. Thus, they try to prohibit teaching in Jesus' name and their being accused of shedding his blood. Nothing is more subversive than the truth which unmasks the will to kill hidden behind social and religious justifications.

Peter and the apostles respond firmly: "We must obey God rather than any human authorities" (Acts 5:29). Being witnesses to the gift of life and the love of God is not something optional for Christians, but instead it is what makes us Christians (v. 32). This testimony must be given even when it means facing insults, jail, and death (see also Jn 21:18–21). Not long ago, one more anniversary of Archbishop Romero's assassination occurred. What led to his death was precisely his repeating with Peter that one should obey God rather than human authorities, which is what he said to Salvadoran soldiers in his last homily. We should follow God and our consciences rather than the orders of military superiors and leaders who order the murders of their country's poor. Those who were defending their privileges at the price of the marginalization and death of many did not forgive him for saying that. Yet Romero's example as a witness to the resurrection continues to be present among us.

We must all decide how to obey God rather than our own fears, our desire to avoid problems, the whims and privileges of those who feel they own the country, or the application of harsh programs which do not take into account the life of the risen Lord.

Fourth Sunday of Easter

A. The Good Shepherd
Acts 2:14, 36–41; 1 Pet 2:20–25; Jn 10:1–10

In the midst of all the uncertainties in which we live, today's liturgy invites us to recognize Jesus as the good shepherd.

Life in Abundance

By calling Jesus the good shepherd, John found an image which has impacted the Christian conscience and memory. As it happens so often in the gospels, this image refers to a rural experience. In the Johannine text, Jesus presents himself as the pastor who loves and is concerned for his sheep. He knows them, calls them by name (Jn 10:3); he is close to them. The sheep also know him, "they know his voice" (v. 4). This two-way knowledge binds them indissolubly, especially if we keep in mind that in a biblical context to know means to love. We are dealing with an intimate knowledge which somehow creates a mutual affectionate dependence, whereby at the beginning of the text the good shepherd is the antithesis of the thief and the bandit (v. 1). The sheep "do not know the voice of strangers" (v. 5). The thief comes "to steal, kill and destroy," while Jesus has come so we may have life abundantly (v. 10).

What Should We Do?

Once again we are in the presence of the central alternative: life or death. Jesus makes us see what is really at stake within the church, namely, how responsibilities are to be carried out in the Christian community. Those who have the task to guide must be close to the Christian people, know their needs and their hopes, and, moreover, they must share their lives. Like the good shepherd, we must be the gate through which people enter into the justice and joy of the kingdom (vv. 7–9). Pastoral responsibility is a service, not a privilege. The shepherd who neglects the daily suffering of the poor and the abuses they endure becomes a stranger and, in the final analysis, a "thief and a bandit," even though these terms sound harsh. This is always a risk. The Lord's warning is severe and demanding for everyone.

Recently, the media reported a brutal eviction which occurred on some lots in the city of Lima. The judge, that is to say the person in charge of doing justice, was present. And so were hundreds of bullies in and out of uniform, on horses or on foot. They were all upholding the law, but not justice or human dignity: burned shacks, loss of scanty goods, dozens of people wounded, perhaps some dead, mistreated children. After hearing Peter's homily announcing the risen Jesus, his listeners asked: "What should we do?" (Acts 2:37). This is the appropriate question to the message of the one whom God chose but who was rejected (1 Pet 2:4). How should we proclaim the good shepherd who came to bring us abundant life? When we face situations like the ones we just mentioned, what should we do to be shepherds rather than bandits in Peru today?

B. Jesus, a Free Man
Acts 4:8–12; 1 Jn 3:1–2; Jn 10:11–18

Today's gospel has left an indelible impression in the imagination of the Christian community. One of the earliest representations of Jesus in Christian art was that of the good shepherd.

Mutual Knowledge

As usual, Jesus bases his parable on daily life. His listeners are familiar with rural life and they know the close bond uniting the shepherd with the sheep by experience. The shepherd knows his sheep and even calls them by name. In the Bible, to know is to love. The shepherd loves his sheep and they love him. The expression used in Jn 10:14 is almost that of the covenant: "I will be your God and you will be my people." Mutual love unites the Lord and his people, love not fear. The model of this union is the relationship of Jesus as Son with the Father. The depth of this bond enables the Lord to surrender his life for the people he loves.

Hired hands behave quite differently. They are with the sheep out of self-interest; love is not their motivation. Thus, they run away in the presence of danger, "they do not care for the sheep" (v. 13). The salary may be money, honors, feeling like the center of a small world. Only by pretending to be shepherds can some people attain social consideration effortlessly, something they would have a hard time attaining by any other means. However, such motives do not create strong bonds; they are shepherding themselves, not the sheep. They look after their own interests and prestige, not after the people they claim to serve. The Lord is very harsh with them ("they do not care for the sheep," v. 13) and with whatever denotes complicity on our part with this attitude. This is why Jesus invites us to imitate him in boundless solidarity with his brothers and sisters, especially with the most exploited and the weakest. Only then will we be able to call ourselves "children of God" (1 Jn 3:1), persons who know and love Jesus.

Giving One's Life

That solidarity can go to the point of laying down our lives (v. 15), a gift willingly offered, in full freedom, a commitment out of gratuitous love, not out of a formal obligation. No one takes away the life of Jesus; he lays it down. His death, his execution on the cross is not the outcome of some fate but rather his free decision (v. 18). Day after day, he chose to proclaim the kingdom of love, peace, and justice and he did so by favoring the least ones, the oppressed and the despised. This is why he was killed. He came to comply with the Father's will (v. 18), but those who did not want to lose their privileges rejected him.

This is the core of the imitation of Jesus. Being a shepherd is an option for life, not a profession. We are all shepherds of our brothers and sisters; we have a responsibility to them which we must freely assume. Commitment to the poor of the country, with their pains and their hopes, their limitations and their struggles, implies a daily option and a constant risk of misunderstanding and hostility. Yet, if we are not hired hands, we cannot "keep from speaking about what we have seen and heard" (Acts 4:20).

C. Giving One's Life
Acts 13:14, 43–52; Rv 7:9, 14–17; Jn 10:27–30

The Easter cycle brings us texts in which the Lord strengthens our faith and reinforces our commitment.

The Shepherd's Voice

John's gospel has just presented Jesus as the Good Shepherd who lays down his life for his sheep. The framework of the text, as well as today's passage, is one of conflict with the leaders of the Jewish people. Just before that, Jesus had said: "I know my own and my own know me" (10:14). Now he says that his sheep listen to his voice, that he knows them and they follow him (v. 27). Between Jesus and his disciples there is a dialogue based on mutual knowledge. Here, the relationship between the Lord and those who listen to his word is expressed in rural terms understandable for Jesus' contemporaries: the relationship between the shepherd and his sheep.

Jesus' gift is eternal life which overcomes death (v. 28). This is the mission the Father had given to him (v. 29) and Jesus gives his own life to carry it out. John likes to underline the union between Jesus and the Father: "the Father and I are one" (v. 30). In his gospel, this is a central element of Jesus' messianic awareness and the foundation of our union with Jesus.

With Courage and Boldness

The theme of the Good Shepherd unfolds over a backdrop of conflict and the threat of death (see the verses following our text in John's gospel). This was also the backdrop surrounding the first steps of the Christian community (Acts 13:45). The message cannot be announced without courage and boldness (v. 46). When we truly proclaim this message, we will find problems, not applause. The word of the Lord is demanding and it questions every undue privilege, every religious exclusiveness. The universalism of the Christian faith upsets those who seek to benefit from their religious position, those who use it to dominate rather than to serve: "the women of high standing" and "the leading men of the city" (v. 50). But the Lord is a light for everyone (v. 47). Because Paul and Barnabas understand that, they are persecuted and driven out of the area (v. 50).

In the face of the persecution to which the Christian community is submitted by the Jews and the Romans, the book of Revelation also reminds us of the universal character of Christianity calling peoples from every nation (vv. 7 and 9). The originality of the Christian faith is the cause of the difficulties suffered by those who embrace it. Today, going back to the sources of Jesus' message also places us at odds with a petty and unjust order. This implies closeness to those who suffer, the ability to wipe away their tears (v. 17). We will be sorry if on judgment day (Is 25:8) the Lord finds us dry-eyed because we have not been able to weep with those who weep.

Fifth Sunday of Easter

A. I Am the Life
Acts 6:1–7; 1 Pet 2:4–9; Jn 14:1–12

Giving one's life is a service, a diaconate. This has always been the understanding of the Christian community.

The Way to the Father

The last verses of John's eleventh chapter mark the beginning of Jesus going up to Jerusalem. There the Lord knows he will find death, and that awareness is troubling his disciples. Jesus asks them to deepen their faith in the hour of trial; believing in him is believing in God (14:1). Jesus' followers form a family, and they will dwell in the Father's house (v. 2). The Lord assures them of that (v. 3) and he has shown them the way but it is not easy to comprehend his teaching (v. 4). Thomas has his doubts and his question prompts Jesus to give a brief answer which is a profound revelation of himself: "I am the way and the truth and the life" (v. 6). We go to the Father through Jesus, whose life and message tell us that the way is the practice of loving God and others. Such a path represents a daily exigency. Being with Jesus is being with the Father.

We have to accept the truth and the content of Jesus' message, and as John himself says, we must put it into practice in order to come to the light, another major Johannine theme (3:21). Those who reject the testimony of Jesus, the "living stone" (1 Pet 2:4) upon which we must build our Christian existence, are living a lie. The ultimate meaning of Jesus' witness is life which comes from the Father and makes us God's children (John 1). In a situation of hunger, pain, and isolation, giving life is putting into

practice the truth that Jesus reveals to us and starting on our way
to the Father.

A God Close to Us

Jesus proclaims a God who is close to us. We know him by knowing Jesus, and seeing him we see the Father who sent him (v. 7).
Philip (to what degree are we like him?) has not understood that.
Jesus responds by reaffirming his deep oneness with the Father;
his works reveal him (v. 11). Works should also be the expression
of our faith. Believing in Jesus is doing the works that he does
(v. 12). Thus we will form part of God's own people (1 Pet 4:9).

This was the understanding of the first Christian community.
Witnesses of Jesus' gestures of love for everyone, especially the
most forgotten, they select collaborators of the disciples, deacons
who are to look after the needy (Acts 6:1–6). The diaconate, or
service, is a fundamental dimension of the church. Today it is
solidarity with the people excluded by the present economic system and driven into worse poverty, solidarity with those who
encounter closed doors and hearts because of their social insignificance (the sick and the elderly). But the diaconate also entails
raising our voices and denouncing that situation, even when this
upsets some people.

B. Only the Clean Bear Fruit
Acts 9:26–31; 1 Jn 3:18–24; Jn 15:1–8

The Easter season reminds us that being a witness to the resurrection signifies giving life.

Solidarity and Fruit

In the Bible, the vineyard is an image referring to the people of
Israel. It coincides with their daily experience; thus the vineyard
and the wine are an immediate and clear reference for Jesus' compatriots. It deals with the true people of God (Jn 15:1). Solidarity
with Jesus is the condition for bearing fruit (v. 2) and this bond
defines God's people. Without the vine, the branches dry up (vv. 4
and 6). Life can circulate only in a body in which each member
fulfills its function. We are all familiar with this Pauline theme.

Two chapters before, in chapter thirteen, John gave an account of the washing of the feet, which we remembered on Holy

Thursday. Its in-depth meaning is not an external purification, removing the dust from the disciples' feet. Jesus' attitude also entails humility, service, and love. It is an in-depth cleansing. Through the sign of water, this gesture makes the disciples enter the sphere of light and love, which means leaving darkness and the absence of fellowship. Those who find their identity in their bond with the Lord and in serving others are clean. Thus the Word cleanses us (v. 3), transforming us from within, making us different. Believing in the Word is bearing fruit, and if we separate those two aspects, we will fall into what James's epistle calls being "double-minded" (1:8; 4:8). The disciples are clean to the degree that they have welcomed Jesus' message and witness.

In Actions and Words

Becoming clean is a process, and this is why the Father prunes us: so that we may bear more fruit (v. 2). The Father is glorified by this (v. 8); his will is that we bear the fruit of love, that is, love in actions and not just in words. Such is the truth of Jesus' instructions (1 Jn 3:18). We are clean if we speak as we act and act as we speak. If we love in our actions (v. 18), we will know "that we are from the truth" (v. 19) and we will abide in God (v. 24).

The text from Acts tells us about the older disciples being afraid of Paul, the recent convert (9:26). This is undoubtedly due to their remembering him as the former persecutor of Christians. But there may have been more to it. Paul was showing a strength and a broad-mindedness which surprised and frightened Christians who had already settled in their lives without the missionary thrust which energized the new convert. He was preaching courageously, and he was not afraid of getting involved in arguments with Jews (and perhaps Christians too) of Greek descent. His message and his passion got him into trouble (vv. 28–29).

Paul took seriously what is so hard for us: loving our neighbors in their specific situation. He did not seek refuge in an alleged love of God, whereby, placing ourselves above history, we break our link with the vine with its deep roots in the ground. Loving God means entering fearlessly into the lives of our neighbors regardless of the difficulties which this may bring about.

C. The Door of Faith

Acts 14:21–26; Rv 21:1–5; Jn 13:31–35

During the Easter season we celebrate life. Life is expressed in love. The gospel of John which we are reading on these Sundays closely links these two themes: life and love. We come into this relationship through "the door of faith" (Acts 14:27).

Making the Lord Present

John presents Jesus saying goodbye to his disciples and leaving them a summary of his teachings. The Lord will depart soon, and he will not be on hand to be consulted about the challenges his followers will face. Yet, he will continue to be among them if they live according to the "new commandment" which he entrusts to them: "As I have loved you, you also should love one another" (13:34). This is new, not because it is the first time that Jesus mentions it but rather because love is a permanent creation, a daily innovation, the ongoing search of ways to get out of ourselves and make the other the center of our lives.

That is the way to make Jesus present at all times. "By this everyone will know that you are my disciples, if you have love for one another" (v. 35). Jesus will be recognized if we love as he did. That is, total love which excludes no one, by way of a special solidarity with the insignificant and the oppressed, keeping the reign of God always present and clearly denouncing those who are responsible for the injustice and mistreatment of the poor. "As I have loved you": without double-talk, without fearing the anger of the powerful, without seeking honors or convenience and without conniving silence. We should remember all of that to make Jesus' concrete love the model of our speech and our commitment before the challenges presented by the harsh reality of our country and our continent.

A New Earth

Only the testimony of genuine and committed love can change what now exists, the old earth (Rv. 21:4). To accomplish that, we need to act as Jesus did, to be close to those who are suffering, to be sensitive to their situation, to be concerned about concrete people, and to wipe the tears from the faces of those who are beaten down by hunger and discrimination. And so we will announce the day — for the second time, the book of Revelation alludes to the beautiful text of Isaiah 25:8 — when the Lord will dwell with us and "wipe every tear" (v. 4). Then, he will reject those who were unable to sympathize with others and as a result who did not make the Lord present among us.

Each one of us, the entire church must find ways to encourage people "to continue in the faith" (Acts 14:22) and to love others as Jesus loved us. To do that, we will have to let go of ourselves, our pettiness, our desire to be respected in the world because we are Christians or authorities in the church. The Son of God came to serve, not to flaunt his prerogatives. People will not recognize the Lord if we do not love as he did, if we do not place all that we have and all that we are as Christians and as church at the service of others, especially of those whose most basic rights are mocked and trampled upon. In this way, we will open "the door of faith" for them and for ourselves.

Sixth Sunday of Easter

A. Being With...
Acts 8:5–8, 14–17; 1 Pet 3:15–18; Jn 14:15–21

As we have done every Sunday after Easter, we continue to read John's gospel. Today, the texts are preparing us to celebrate the forthcoming feast of Pentecost.

Another Advocate

John relates Jesus' lengthy farewell discourses preceding his passion and death. In today's passage, we are told of the coming of the Holy Spirit, the one who is to continue the mission. The Lord calls the Spirit "another Advocate" (Jn 14:16) and by so doing he implicitly refers to himself. The term "Paraclete" (that is, "Advocate") means "being with," being the defender (the one who intercedes for). This is who Jesus is, someone who is at his friends' side, representing and defending them. John also calls Jesus Christ Advocate in one of his letters (1 Jn 2:1).

Continuing the Son's mission, the Spirit comes "to be with you forever" (v. 16), and we know him because he abides in us (v. 17). To the theme of the Spirit's closeness and "being with" is added another aspect: "the Spirit of truth" (v. 17). Thanks to the Spirit, we acknowledge that God is Father and Life. The Spirit is the opposite of "the father of lies," who prevents us from behaving with the freedom of God's children and who is "a murderer from the beginning" (Jn 8:44). Jesus and the Spirit are with the Christian community. They lead it to communion with the Father (Jn 14:21) and to "all the truth" (Jn 16:13). We must do what is true and put truth into practice, as John himself reminds us (Jn 3:21).

Giving an Accounting for Our Hope

The Lord is asking us to be with our sisters and brothers. Receiving the Spirit (Acts 8:15–17) must make us become "advocates," defenders, people who are with those who need us. We are called to serve, not to impose our ideas. This presupposes our living with others and sharing with them. If Jesus does not leave us orphans (Jn 14:18), neither should we leave those who need us orphans. This is true worship, sanctifying the Lord in our hearts (1 Pet 3:15).

In his surrender, Jesus gave us life. This gift from the Lord should make us respect and welcome our neighbors with their needs, their suffering, and their life projects. All of this makes up the "good conduct in Christ" to which Peter is calling us (3:16). We cannot, therefore, allow people to set themselves up as masters of the lives of others. The right to life is the primary right of the human person.

Being with our neighbor, whoever he or she may be, will enable us to give an accounting for our hope (v. 15) in the presence of the Spirit among us.

B. Friends, Not Servants
Acts 10:25–26, 34–35, 44–48; 1 Jn 4:7–10; Jn 15:9–17

Throughout this season, the liturgy of the church has presented us with all the accounts of the risen Jesus' appearances. Then it has reminded us of the gospel passages celebrating the meaning of the victory over death: love.

As I Have Loved You

The fifteenth chapter of John is marked by the tenderness of the Lord with his disciples. His message is: abide in my love;

it is the same as the love of the Father for me (15:10 and 12). This must be the source of our joy (15:11). Jesus expresses this world of relationships with one word: friendship. Being Christian means being the Lord's friend. Friend, not servant. Servants do things because they receive an order, not because they know and share their master's thoughts (15:15). The servant's relationship is cold and formal. A friend's conduct comes from within. Friendship presupposes communication, our having made our own the objectives and feelings of the person we appreciate and love.

The warmth of friendship implies a sharing which creates equality and breaks the categories of domination and servitude. Love can exist only among equals. Our Christian life lies in our ability to make others our friends. If we cling to an alleged or apparent superiority, considering others inferior to ourselves, we will not be able to share the gospel with them (Acts 10:26). Christian solidarity is never impersonal. There will be no commitment to the poor and the oppressed if there is no friendship with them. It is only in friendship that we will abide in love.

Knowing God

The Lord tells us that he calls us friends "because I have made known to you everything I have heard from my Father" (15:15). He has shared with us the profound motivations of his testimony. He has made us his "equals." In other words, he has shared what he knows with us, that "God is love" (1 Jn 4:8). This is to know him. In the Bible, knowing God means loving God. The primary reason for that is that God is love. He chose us and love is our response to his free and gratuitous initiative (15:16).

Whoever does not love does not know God (1 Jn 4:8). That love has to bear fruit (15:16). The Father manifests his love by sending us his Son (1 Jn 4:9). Now we understand his commandment better: "love one another" (15:17). This is the way to respond to God's love for us. Those who involve themselves with the needs and aspirations of others are close to God. "God shows no partiality but in every nation anyone who fears him and does what is right is acceptable to him" (Acts 10:35). The work of God's friends is to live equality and to practice what is right. "In this is love" (1 Jn 4:10).

C. Peace and Love
Acts 15:1–2, 22–29; Rv 21:10–14, 22–23; Jn 14:23–29

We are approaching the conclusion of the Easter cycle and the feasts of the Ascension and Pentecost. Thus, this Sunday's readings direct us to the celebration of the new presence of Jesus through the Spirit.

Jesus Is the Way

Following Jesus, keeping his word as the text of Saint John says (v. 23), is the proof of love, of true discipleship. At the same time, it is the only way to the Father. It is possible to come to God only through Jesus. This is one of the major themes of the gospel of John: Jesus is the Word, the Son, the revelation of God (v. 24) in our human history. This is why there is no other way to God except by "keeping his word."

To come to the Father is a matter of life and of practice. It entails believing in Jesus and loving him, a love which is expressed by paying attention to his word and by striving to put Jesus' way of life into practice. This is the first major statement of today's gospel. The reading from Acts offers us a precise example of putting into practice the way of Jesus. At a time of profound tensions between Paul's communities and the Jerusalem community concerning the Jewish practice of the circumcision, Christians sought to resolve their differences in an atmosphere of friendship and respect (vv. 22–29). Today this can serve as an example for dealing with conflicts inside and outside of the Christian community.

The Spirit of Jesus

Jesus' presence in human history is taking on a new form: the Holy Spirit. Sent by the Father, the Spirit will teach and enable us to remember Jesus, his words and deeds (Jn 14:26). This trust in the presence of the Spirit of God in our midst gives meaning to Jesus' "testament": the gift of peace. "Peace I leave with you, my peace I give to you" (v. 27). As we know, it is the Hebrew word *shalom* which we translate by "peace." Jesus' testament must be understood in terms of *shalom*, which means well-being, life, harmony, and therefore peace. Here on Jesus' lips, "peace" expresses his desire for his disciples to attain the fullness of life.

May Jesus' followers experience life in abundance; this is the concept expressed by the gospel, and it is possible only if they are filled with the Spirit of Jesus, the Spirit of the fullness of life and, therefore, the Spirit of peace.

The Spirit of Jesus enables us not to be troubled and afraid (v. 27), experiences and feelings all too common in the context in which we live. It is not a matter of denying our feelings but rather of living in the "peace-shalom-life" of the Spirit of Jesus. In this way, we will build up a city illumined by "the glory of God" (Rv 21:23).

The Ascension of the Lord

A. All Nations
Acts 1:1–11; Eph 1:17–23; Mt 28:16–20

The physical absence of the Lord brings specific responsibilities to his followers. From that moment on, they will continue his work.

Go to the Whole World

The last five verses of Matthew constitute a sober and at the same time an encompassing conclusion of the message presented to us in this gospel. The scene takes place in Galilee, just as we have been told (28:10). Galilee was the main setting of Jesus' preaching, a subtle touch seeking to underscore the identity between the historical Jesus and the risen Christ. The encounter is very simple. There are no marvelous elements to make this moment spectacular. In biblical tradition, the mountain is the place of God's revelation, and this is what we have here (vv. 16–17).

The presence of the Lord gives rise to worship and doubts (v. 17). In the chiaroscuro of faith, doubt forms part of the process of believing. Jesus addresses his final words to the eleven disciples, and in them he invokes his authority. "Heaven and earth" is a classical expression referring to all that exists. Jesus' authority is universal (v. 18). Then comes the sending, the mission which consists in "making disciples." It is a very concrete way of saying "proclaim the good news," an expression which we find in Mark

(16:15). Being disciples means accepting the gospel, entering into a personal relationship with Jesus and following him, and faith is lived as a community, as *ecclesia* (v. 19).

All "peoples" must be made disciples; there are no national or ethnic boundaries. Just as Jesus' authority is universal, the task of making disciples must also be universal. "Peoples" can also be translated by "nations." This probably refers to the pagan world. The problematic Israel-Gentiles issue may seem distant and irrelevant to us. Yet it reminds us of the permanent risk of appropriating the gospel to serve a society or a culture instead of using it to live it in small and private circles without a missionary spirit. The Lord's mandate applies to all of us.

Keeping the Mandate

Baptism is the effective sign, the sacrament of entering into the Christian community (v. 19), the Body of Christ, as Saint Paul will say. It involves the mandate to teach to obey all that the Lord has commanded (v. 20). Baptism in the name of the Trinity is inseparable from putting Christ's teaching into practice. Thanks to the work of the Spirit, that message enlightens the eyes of the heart to know the hope to which we have been called (Eph 1:18). The feast of the Ascension reminds us that this hope has to sustain us in our mission as witnesses (Acts 1:8).

The disciples receive their mission in Galilee, a marginalized region, close to the pagan world and, as a result, an area viewed with contempt by the practicing Jews of Judea where Jerusalem is located. The proclamation of the gospel starts from an insignificant and despised land. This is not just a matter of geography; it is highly significant. It serves as an example. For us today, Galilee is the world of the poor, our starting place to proclaim the gospel to everyone without exception. We will do that with the conviction that the Lord will always be with us (Mt 28:20).

B. The Challenge of Adulthood
Acts 1:1–11; Eph 1:17–23; Mk 16:15–20

The historical mission of Jesus is over. Now it is the disciples' turn to give witness to his resurrection.

Making Their Decisions

The precise authorship of Mark's conclusion is subject to discussion. Be that as it may, it is an ancient text and tradition acknowledges it as an integral part of the gospel. The similarity with Matthew's text is obvious. It deals with the mission which the community of the disciples has to undertake. Mark establishes an immediate connection between the mission and the Lord's ascension (16:19–20), something not found in Matthew, who says nothing about the ascension. The connection is not fortuitous; it is very significant.

Mark's account of the ascension is very concise. After speaking with his friends, Jesus "was taken up into heaven and sat at the right hand of God" (v. 19). The formula in the passive voice ("he was taken up") indicates that the Father is the one at work. The physical absence of the Lord opens up a new time: the time of the community of the disciples. This is why the book relating their Acts starts with the ascension. After that, Jesus' followers will not have him on hand, and neither do we, to ask him what to do at every moment. They will have to make their own decisions. The Lord says to them, you "will be my witnesses" (Acts 1:8). It is not enough to report what they saw and heard; they also have to know how, to whom, and when to do it. In addition to the experience of the Lord, this implies historical insight and wisdom. Before ascending into heaven, the Lord entrusts the continuation of his mission to his disciples. This trust represents a challenge, a call to apostolic adulthood.

Looking toward the Earth

After the brief presentation of the ascension, Mark's text reads: "They went out and proclaimed the good news everywhere" (v. 20). The trust which the Lord has placed in them spurs them on to the mission. The church dies when it falls back upon itself, upon what it has acquired and perhaps upon the defense of the privileges of a few. The Lord's ascension presupposes the disciples' onset of their mission, a task that will lead them to face new historical realities, to test their faith in the presence of the resistance, the indifference and even the criticism of others. As Paul says in quoting Psalm 68:19, when ascending on high, the Lord gives his followers gifts that must bear fruit (Eph 4:8). Comforted by the Lord (Mk 16:20), their responsibility is to bear fruit.

The task will not be easy. Proclaiming the gospel also means listening to the problems and the demands of the people we address. They question us and cause doubts in the gospel bearers. The Lord assures us of the "power of the Spirit" (Acts 1:8), insight and discernment in the mission entrusted to us, as Paul says elsewhere. Despite the promise, the disciples remained there standing still, perhaps struck by the absence of Jesus and afraid to begin to proclaim the gospel. They stand there "looking up toward heaven" (Acts 1:11). The messenger of God reproaches them for that attitude. They still have not understood — even today — that they have to look toward the earth, history, the place where they must be witnesses of the risen Christ.

We have to proclaim life in the midst of situations of long-standing and increasing injustice, of different types of violence trampling upon basic human rights. This proclamation has to be done with "humility" (Eph 4:2), without fear of the powerful of this world, rather than with generic words or with the attitude of possessing the truth in every field. This is the basic message of the ascension.

C. The Absence of Someone Who Is Alive
Acts 1:1–11; Eph 1:17–23; Lk 24:46–53

The Easter season is coming to an end. During this time, we have heard again and again the core of the gospel message: the Lord is alive. He has conquered death and what it produces. This is the source of our hope (Eph 1:18).

Witnesses of These Things

The gospels of Matthew and Mark conclude with the sending on a mission. What characterizes disciples is their preaching the good news. It consists in giving testimony of their encounters with the risen Christ. From that perspective, they see Christ's teachings in a new light. These are the gospels: an understanding of the deeds and words of Jesus from the perspective of Easter, the passage from death to life (Lk 24:46). The witnesses have come to that understanding (Lk 24:48 and Acts 1:8). In fact, witnesses do not limit themselves to reporting an event; they become involved with it, making it their own. Jesus "opened their minds to understand the scriptures" (Lk 24:45). This is why "after his suffering he presented himself alive to them by many convincing proofs, appearing to them during forty days and speaking about the kingdom of God" (Acts 1:3). Thus they are witnesses of the kingdom of life.

Perceiving the significance of events is not enough; it is also necessary to assume the responsibilities that witnessing involves. While Matthew and Mark emphasize the sending on a mission, Luke insists on the absence of Jesus while the disciples bear witness to him. Jesus has left them in charge of his mission, which they have to pursue on earth. The Son ascends into heaven at the right hand of the Father. But according to the lesson of these past Sundays, it is the absence of someone who is alive, not that of a dead man. This is why Jesus sends "what the Father promised": the Spirit (Lk 24:49 and Acts 1:4). The Spirit will help us make Jesus, the living one, present in the midst of a reality made of selfishness, of undue privileges, of the arrogance of political and religious power, of indifference toward the poor, and of hunger. In other words, death.

Why Do You Stand Looking up toward Heaven?

Ascension and Pentecost are feasts of Christian maturity. They are a call to continue Jesus' mission with our insight into reality, our criteria and decisions. The "power of the Spirit" (Acts 1:7) is with us. We must not stand still looking up and lamenting the absence of the Lord; instead we must set on our way to take his gospel "to the ends of the earth" (Acts 1:8). This is why every attempt to keep Christians in an attitude of dependency and immaturity without real responsibilities and voice in the church is contrary to the meaning of the feast we are celebrating today. The Second Vatican Council strongly emphasized this. Being mature in the faith is a requirement of the gospel, and adults have — ought to have — their opinions about the common task.

We are encouraged in this by the assurance that the Lord will return (Acts 1:11) because he is alive (Eph 1:20). But we are also concerned because at that time he will ask us to give an account of the talents he has entrusted to us.

Pentecost

The Power of the Spirit
Acts 2:1–11; 1 Cor 12:3–7, 12–13; Jn 20:19–23

Pentecost is one of the great Christian feasts. This is when we celebrate the power of the Spirit present in the church of Christ.

The Spirit and Fear

Jesus' death has been a tremendous blow to the disciples. The confrontation with the leaders of the people in collusion with the Roman authorities has terrified them. "For fear of the Jews" (Jn 20:19) they have gathered behind locked doors. The Master gives them his final instructions: he wishes them peace, *shalom*, that is to say, integrity of life, search for justice and harmony. In addition, he tells them to continue the mission that had led him to an ignominious death, which frightens his followers (v. 21).

The Lord asks them to have the courage to announce the gospel without worrying about the resistance and hostility they are to encounter. They will be able to do that only by receiving the power of the Spirit (v. 22), the Spirit of love, the antithesis of fear, as John himself says in his first letter (1 Jn 4:18). In fact, the fear of speaking clearly and of proclaiming the word of God precisely and opportunely reveals a lack of love. The presence of the Spirit in the church, in each one of us, must lead us to defend the dignity of God's children whose rights to life and truth are being violated. Becoming paralyzed with fear of the powerful or of losing our comfort and privileges in society means that we refuse to receive the Spirit of love.

In the Native Language of Each

In Israel, Pentecost was the festival of harvest (Ex 23:16, 34:22). Later on, it was transformed from an agrarian feast to a historical one to commemorate the promulgation of the law on Sinai. On that day, the city of Jerusalem filled up with believers from various places coming to the festival. As we already know, the disciples are fearful and they are gathered without knowing exactly what to do. The gift of the Spirit will empower them to proclaim the good news to all the peoples who have come to the city (Acts 2:1–11).

Inspired by the Holy Spirit, the disciples find the suitable language for the proclamation. The text provides us with an important detail which contradicts a superficial, though frequent, interpretation. It is not a matter of using only one language but rather of being able to understand one another. The text is clear: the people hear the disciples "speaking in the native language of each. Amazed and astonished, they ask, 'Are not all these who are speaking Galileans?'" (Acts 2:6–7). They all understand in their language, from their own cultural world.

Thus, evangelization does not mean a superimposed uniformity but rather fidelity to the message and to understanding in diversity. That is the church, a communion in which every member has a function (1 Cor 12). All members count and must, therefore, be respected in their own charisms. The feast of Pentecost calls us to have the courage to proclaim the gospel and the true meaning of ecclesial communion.

In the Native Language of Each
Acts 2:1–11; 1 Cor 12:3–7, 12–13; Jn 20:19–23

On Pentecost, we celebrate the presence of the Holy Spirit in the Christian community, the church.

Peace and Forgiveness

The death of Jesus, his execution on the cross, produced terror in those who had followed him. All the gospels speak of the fear these events had caused. The same gospels, John in particular, tell us that fear is the antithesis of faith. Having faith means trusting. John tells us that instead of announcing the message, the disciples had gone in a house and locked the doors (20:19). The Lord appears and wishes them peace, namely, life, health, and integrity. In this new encounter with Jesus, they experience a feeling of joy. The Lord associates them to his work. They are to pursue his mission. The sending which Jesus had received from the Father is the foundation of the responsibility they are to assume as disciples. Its source is found in the mission entrusted by the Father, and we must always return to it because we always find new waters in this source.

Jesus' commissioning his followers is reinforced by the gift of the Spirit. The term "spirit" means gust, vital breath, power. We have to relate it to peace, *shalom*, according to the Hebrew expression. Peace and life are shattered by sin, which expresses our refusal to love. This is why forgiving is giving life. Forgiving someone means trusting that such a person can recover the ability to love, to reestablish the friendship with God and others which had been cut off by sin (v. 23). Forgiving requires courage and risk taking, the opposite of the attitude of the disciples before they receive the gift of peace and of the Holy Spirit. Without courage and risk taking, it is impossible to make the gospel present in the midst of the conflictive situations we are encountering now. Today we often see that human life has little value. As church, we have to denounce such an attitude instead of staying home behind locked doors (v. 19).

Unity and Diversity

The presence of the Spirit within the Christian community gives it its profound unity (1 Cor 12:3–4). But each member has his or her own function (vv. 12–13). The text from Acts also confirms this in a special way. The power of the Spirit leads the disciples to announce the kingdom of God, the core of Jesus' message (2:1–4). Contrary to what is often said, Pentecost is not the day when people understand one another by speaking the same language. Its significance is much deeper. Those who were in Jerusalem then heard the disciples of Jesus "speaking the native language of each" (v. 6). The text repeats that they are amazed because they hear "their own native language" (v. 8). Each one is speaking his or her own language, but they understand one another. Pentecost does not erase differences but it does shorten them.

The language about God comes from the Christian message. But it also comes from the way we put it into practice. This depends on precise historical circumstances. We have to respect the different ways of expressing the gospel if we do not want to sin against the Spirit: no coercive uniformity but instead understanding in diversity. It is important to keep that in mind today vis-à-vis the attempts to impose a single lifestyle at the personal and societal level.

Ordinary Time

"Just as you did it to one of the least of these who are members of my family, you did it to me."
(Mt 25:40)

The Holy Trinity

A. God So Loved the World
Ex 34:4, 6, 8–10; 2 Cor 13:11–13; Jn 3:16–18

Major feasts follow one another. After the Ascension came Pentecost and now the feast of the Trinity. In some way this feast is like the "anniversary" of the one triune God.

Sending Forth and Salvation

The third chapter of John's gospel presents the essence of the message of Jesus. At the beginning, we are reminded of the necessity to convert to be a disciple of the Lord. John uses the image of being born anew (v. 7). Jesus has come to testify to this new life (v. 11), the definitive life, eternal life (v. 15). This is why he has descended from heaven (v. 13) as the Holy Spirit has done (Jn 1:32). He will return to heaven after having completed his salvation mission (v. 13).

The verses of today's text specify the origin of that mission: the love of God the Father. He so loved the world "that he sent his own Son" (v. 16). In this text, the term "world" does not have the meaning of rejecting God but the neutral sense of human reality or history. God's greatest gift is the sending of his own Son whose work is to save (v. 17), namely, to establish God's friendship with human beings. This is salvation in the biblical message; it means welcoming the life which Jesus brings.

We enter into this life through the door of faith as we freely accept or reject this life. Believing in the "name of the only Son of God" (v. 18) is accepting his testimony and his message. It means trusting in "a God merciful and gracious, slow to anger and abounding in steadfast love and faithfulness" (Ex 34:6), according to one of the most beautiful descriptions of God we find in the Bible.

Agreeing with One Another

Faith should make us compassionate, merciful, and faithful like the God in whom we believe. A few verses later, we read in John's text for today that "those who do what is true come to the light"

117

(3:21). The truth which Jesus passes on to us is not just a matter of accepting and agreeing; it is a question of praxis, a daily task.

Empathizing (suffering with others) means that we make ours the sufferings of people who struggle for survival in the midst of so many violations of their most basic rights. Being compassionate (with our hearts focused on those who endure misery) implies that no situation of injustice (like what so many people in Latin America are enduring) is foreign to us. Being faithful (having faith, trusting) requires being steadfast in our commitments, courageous in the face of the difficulties encountered today when we are witnesses to the God of life.

If we proceed in this fashion, we will assume Paul's final recommendations to the Corinthians: we will experience the Easter joy and we will "agree with one another." The vital hope that the "God of love and peace will be with us" (2 Cor 13:11) will sustain us.

B. The Voice of the Living God
Dt 4:32–34, 39–40; Rom 8:14–17; Mt 28:16–20

Today's feast reminds us of a central point of our faith.

Making Disciples

From Galilee, where Jesus chooses to carry out his ministry, the disciples are sent to proclaim the gospel and to baptize "in the name of the Father and of the Son and of the Holy Spirit" (Mt 28:19). The living God is proclaimed (Dt 4:33) from the province, the land that is despised by the proud inhabitants of Jerusalem. The sending occurs on a mountain, the traditional place of an important revelation in the Bible. It is a sober scene; there are no extraordinary elements, simply "when they saw him, they worshiped him" (Mt 28:17). Jesus evokes his power to serve, not to dominate (v. 18).

The mission consists in "making disciples" (v. 19), a concrete formula to signify "proclaim the gospel." The expression coincides with Matthew's approach, the central theme of which is discipleship. The proclamation of the gospel should lead to transforming listeners into followers of Jesus, into people taking his teaching as the guideline of their lives. The gospel is not transmitted only by words; these have to be accompanied by deeds.

Giving witness to the gospel implies being attentive to these two aspects. Words without commitment are empty and deeds without words lack clarity. We have to follow the way of Jesus, who gives life and explains its meaning by his message.

Under the Guidance of the Holy Spirit

The mission is to make disciples "of all nations" (Mt 28:19), all people. Disciples are not isolated persons. Faith is lived in community and faith also proclaims a God-community. This community (Trinity) within God is the expression of the divine life in which we have to be baptized (Mt 28:19). The text from Deuteronomy recalls the faith of a people in the living God: creation (v. 32), the covenant (v. 33), the Exodus (v. 34). A God who is present in history out of love, this is what we have to meditate in our hearts (v. 39).

Faith in the living God frees us from fear. Being disciples is being free, not slaves (Rom 8:15). Children are heirs, not servants (v. 16). This spirit of freedom liberates us from any "magical" way of living our Christian faith. Disciples of the Lord do not live expecting what is extraordinary and exceptional. On the contrary, through their actions and words, disciples are to incarnate the gospel of love and justice in history. That means in daily life with the lack of the most basic things, with unemployment, mistreatment of the poor, social conflicts, struggle for justice. If we accept being "according to the Spirit" (Rom 8:14) and to offer friendship, Jesus will always be with us (Mt. 18:20).

C. Hope Does Not Disappoint
Prv 8:22–31; Rom 5:1–5; Jn 16:12–15

We have just celebrated Pentecost, one of the greatest Christian feasts. The power of the Spirit is in the midst of the Christian community. Today's texts invite us to ponder the significance of this presence.

Into All the Truth

John's text comes from the farewell discourses of Jesus. One of their themes is the promise of the coming of the Spirit, the breath of God guiding Christian life and continuing the Lord's mission. Jesus has announced the kingdom and the love of the Father.

Jesus' message is life, and it goes beyond any formulation. Its demands, which the Spirit will make known to us, are always new and surprising. The Spirit will guide us "into all the truth" (v. 13) which comes from the Father (v. 15).

Jesus shows us the way to the Father, and the Spirit will be with us on our journey. If the feast of the Ascension reminds us that we must take the Lord's work into our hands, Pentecost assures us that such a mission is possible because the Spirit is with us. The Spirit may lead us on paths we have not foreseen and which, therefore, make us somewhat afraid and perhaps distrustful. We prefer our being settled to having to change. But how are we to be faithful to the one "who makes all things new" (Rv 21:5) if we cling to our paltry security? How are we to be in solidarity with human suffering if we are not imaginative in our ways of expressing our commitments? Fear is a denial of faith.

Delighting in the Human Race

The passage from the book of Proverbs we are reading this Sunday is very poetic, or, to put it literally, it is creative. To whom does the poem to wisdom really refer? It is a subject of discussion among specialists. But it is clearly an expression of God, the triune God as we are told today. The text invites us to hope because everything is in God's hands from the beginning (v. 23). And everything was created out of love, gratuitous love, as if rejoicing, and delighting in the human race (v. 31). Delighting is not to be understood as something superficial and whimsical. It is creative; it requires inventiveness as we can easily see with children. There is a certain type of "education" which destroys children's creative ability. As a renowned educator used to say: "My education was interrupted when I was six years old and I started school...."

Faced with the enormous problems we are experiencing today in our country, it takes humility to acknowledge that our predictions have been cast aside and courage to face new situations. In various areas, we live a difficult and seemingly hopeless situation, at least for the near future. We need to return to the sources, and for Christians one of them is hope. Paul tells us that "hope does not disappoint" because it comes from the Spirit (Rom 5:5). We have to be witnesses to hope.

Corpus Christi

A. Bread and Life
Dt 8:2–3, 14–16; 1 Cor 10:16–17; Jn 6:51–59

The feast of the body and blood of Christ is the celebration of his total surrender. We have to embrace that surrender.

Abiding in Christ

John's lengthy sixth chapter is centered on the theme of bread. Today's passage takes on a sacramental perspective which was less clear in the previous verses. Some assume that the realism in speaking of the flesh and blood of Christ is addressed to people close to the Johannine community skeptical about the incarnation of the Son of God. Be that as it may, the message leaves no room for doubt: the gift of God becomes concrete through what is human. This is the gift of life, and therefore whoever "eats of this bread will live forever" (v. 51). This bread is the flesh which the Word assumed, as John has said at the beginning of his gospel (1:14). And the Word came into the world to bring life.

The objection of the listeners (v. 52) shows how difficult it is to accept that presence of God in history. The Lord gives his flesh through his total surrender, and thus he transmits the life thanks to which we abide in him (vv. 54–56). These verses provide the final interpretation of the text about sharing bread found at the beginning of chapter 6. Jesus has come to give himself and to share his life with us.

We Do Not Live by Bread Alone

Paul returns to the theme, opposing the risk of idolatry which is threatening the Corinthians. The significance of the supper in which we recall the death and the resurrection of Christ is our communion with the Lord. "The cup of blessing" and "the bread that we break" (v. 16) lead to this. Thus, we share in Jesus' message of love, in his commitment to the most destitute, in what led him to the cross and in his victory over death. In Christ, we are "one bread and one body" (v. 17). Communion with him is profound union.

Union implies closeness and mutual knowledge; this is the theme of our text from Deuteronomy. The book is a reflection on the events of the Exodus. A crucial question is raised in this chapter: the meaning of the long march to the promised land. The answer consists in saying that those forty years allowed God and his people to know one another. Through deprivation and afflictions, the Lord has tested his people to know what was in their hearts (v. 2). In turn, thanks to the living presence of the Lord who took care of nourishing them with the manna (v. 3), the people understood God better. In this process, they learned that "one does not live by bread alone but by every word that comes from the mouth of God" (v. 3). This word and this bread are life-giving.

After that experience, God and his people know one another more in depth, and this is the foundation of the covenant. The Last Supper is the celebration of the new covenant, of the friendship with Jesus who died and rose and who is present with us. Friendship is one of the central themes of John's gospel.

B. Worship and Justice
Ex 24:3–8; Heb 9:11–15; Mk 14:12–16, 22–26

The celebration of the feast of Corpus Christi presents us with texts dealing with the significance of the worship of the old and the new covenant.

The Paschal Context

The Last Supper of the Lord with his disciples, during which the Eucharist is established, takes place at the Passover feast (Mk 14:12, and 16). Passover is the passage from Egypt, a land of oppression and injustice, to the promised land, a place of freedom and justice. This passage of the Jewish people takes place thanks to God's liberating intervention. This historical event is the foundation of the faith of Israel and its significance has to be permanently pondered by believers. This reflection leads them to see that sin is the root of injustice and that the response to the Lord's gratuitous love is expressed in the creation of just and loving relations between people. Therefore, in its deepest sense, Passover is the passage from sin to grace.

We cannot separate the Eucharist from the Jewish Passover which forms its historical and theological context. Both in continuity and rupture, the giving of the body of the Lord and the pouring of his blood seals the new covenant (Mk 12:22–24). The Last Supper of Jesus is the anticipated celebration of what was soon to happen to him: the giving of his life. With his life, the Lord gives us new life and commits us to being faithful to his will to love, to the kingdom of God (Mk 14:25).

Repenting Means Changing

The covenant entails a twofold obligation: it indicates reciprocal belonging and possession. God is committed to the people who also acquire responsibilities toward God. The Exodus text we are reading today shows the close link between worship and accepting God's will. The major thrust of this passage is what "the people answered with one voice, all the words that the Lord has spoken we will do" (Ex 24:3, see v. 7). In fact, it is useless to offer sacrifices to God without putting into practice God's plan for life, love, and justice.

If this is true of worship in the old covenant, it will be even more so of the sacrifice of Jesus. Thanks to him, we will rid ourselves of the sin that is expressed in deeds of death and injustice and we will be ready to "worship the living God" (Heb 9:14). Such a worship demands deeds of life, love and respect for the rights of everyone.

This Sunday's texts remind us that if we do not do "what the Lord has spoken" (Ex 24:3), we are turning our backs on the Lord's surrender of his body and blood. If we do not practice his will of life and justice, our participation in Christian worship, in the Sunday Eucharist, is devoid of all content. Beyond sincerity and personal itineraries, the situation of injustice and marginalization of the poor appears as a clamorous departure from the demands of the new covenant sealed in Christ's blood. Every Eucharistic celebration ought to remind us of "the structures of sin" (cited by Medellín and John Paul II) existing in today's world. Our repenting for having contributed to these structures not only involves saying so in solemn moments, but above all it involves beginning to build this society on the basis of the needs of the oppressed and of those who are excluded from it.

C. In Remembrance of Me
Gn 14:8–20; 1 Cor 11:23–26; Lk 9:11–17

The body and the blood of Christ express, at the same time, the death and the life of the Lord.

Until They Were Filled

When the disciples return from the mission, Jesus wishes to speak privately with them in Bethsaida (Lk 9:10). Perhaps this can occur later (9:18–22) but for the time "the crowds" do not allow it as they are following him (v. 11). Even though his plans are upset, the Lord welcomes the people. In addition, he announces the heart of his message to them: the kingdom of God. He represents something very different from what the crowds are experiencing at the time. They are poor and marginalized. Jesus also attends to their health needs, healing them (v. 11). It is a sign of the kingdom which is a kingdom of life. The account which follows is another expression of that life.

Perhaps because they are tired, the disciples want to end their day and ask that the people be sent away to look for lodging and food (v. 12). But Jesus has other plans. The disciples are to give them something to eat; that is part of their mission of announcing the kingdom. Their refusal makes sense; they are sorry but they have neither food nor money (v. 13). Theirs are the categories of the unjust society that the kingdom challenges. For Jesus, the exigency goes much further, and it belongs to another level: it is a matter of sharing. This gesture knows no limits; love is always abundant and orderly: the people are to sit down in "groups of about fifty each" (vv. 14–15), groups of fifty like the groups of prophets mentioned in the book of Kings (1 Kgs 18:4; 2 Kgs 2:7).

Then Jesus shares what they have, and the disciples serve as intermediaries (v. 16). The crowds eat and the hungry are filled. Food is another sign of the kingdom because life depends on it. Despite the lack of food alleged by the disciples, there are twelve baskets left over. Twelve is a symbolic number: there is enough food for all (the twelve tribes). Let us not respond to the hunger that exists in the world by saying we do not have anything to give. Sharing increases our possibilities: in this way, we proclaim the kingdom.

Bread and Wine

In remembrance of the Lord's Last Supper, bread and wine are transformed into his body and blood because bread and wine are the basic nourishment of Jesus' people. When Abraham met Melchizedek, they shared bread and wine, a sign of friendship and blessing (Gn 14:18–19). This was the sign, the sign of food, that Jesus chose to be present in our midst. He ate with his disciples and in the Christian community, the remembrance (and the renewal) of that supper preserves alive the life which the Lord gave for us and which the resurrection made definitive (1 Cor 11:23–26). That is the life which we proclaim with the kingdom, the life which Jesus is sharing with us.

Second Sunday

A. Recognizing Jesus
Is 49:3, 5–6; 1 Cor 1:1–3; Jn 1:29–34

John's gospel has just presented John the Baptist in his mission, attesting that he is only the one who makes straight the way of the Lord. Now the time has come for John to recognize gradually who really is this Jesus whom he precedes.

The Lamb

John the evangelist does not relate the baptism of Jesus, except through the Baptist's indirect testimony, a testimony which is succinctly presented in a few verses.

"Here is the Lamb of God" (v. 29). This is the first time the Baptist points out Jesus. As is often the case with John, there is a reference to the book of Exodus, an immediate remembrance of the Passover lamb (Ex 12): the rite celebrating the original liberation of the Israelites. The lamb will be sacrificed as Jesus will be on the cross; it will be consumed as the body that Jesus will offer in the supper. The image of the lamb also refers to the servant of the Lord (Is 49:3) sacrificed as a lamb (Is 53:7) who will bear the sins of others and justify them. From the first pages of his gospel, the evangelist insists on Christ's redemptive mission (see also the victorious lamb, Rv 5– 6). Paul also dares to say that "our paschal lamb, Christ, has been sacrificed" (1 Cor 5:7).

The Spirit

Yet the Baptist states twice: "I myself did not know him" (vv. 31 and 33), and he senses that his own baptism ("in water," v. 33) is not important; it serves only as a preparation, a sign. But John continues to advance in his experience and he is able to testify that he has seen the Spirit descend and remain on Jesus (v. 32). It is the Spirit of the power of God sweeping over the primeval waters (Gn 1:1) (hence the image of the dove), the same Spirit given to the servant of Yahweh, making him "a light to the nations" so that his salvation "may reach to the end of the earth" (Is 49:6). This Jesus belongs to the category of prophets, permeated by the Spirit of the Lord.

However, the Baptist's knowledge is still insufficient until the Lord inspires him to understand that this Jesus, this servant who receives the Spirit, is the one who "baptizes with the Holy Spirit" (v. 33). In other words, he is the one who will give abundant life to humankind once he is invested with power through the resurrection.

It is neither easy nor instantaneous to recognize Jesus; it is something which occurs gradually. The forerunner who has seen can, in a more conscious way, give a new testimony: this is the Son of God, recognized in advance. John's entire gospel details his mission and his work. Thus he indicates the path we are to follow. In some way we are all precursors of Jesus. We present him to other people as John presented him to his disciples and Paul to the Corinthians (1 Cor 1:1–3).

B. It Was the Tenth Hour

1 Sm 3:3–10, 19; 1 Cor 6:13–15, 17–20; Jn 1:35–42

Christian life always begins with a call from God. The Bible gives us countless accounts of vocations.

An Experience

John the Baptist makes way for Jesus, and he invites his disciples to follow the one whose path he has prepared. The first disciples come from the Baptist's group (Jn 1:35–37). John recognizes

Jesus as the "Lamb of God" (v. 36). The framework of Exodus, so present in this gospel, suggests the theme of liberation through death. The image of the lamb is an expression of this, but it also deals with a victorious lamb as he is presented in the book of Revelation. Therefore, the two disciples who follow Jesus are warned of the difficulties and the risks of their option (v. 37).

Jesus asks them: "What are you looking for?" (v. 38). This question seeks to specify the quality of the faith of the disciples who just arrived. They respond by calling him "Rabbi" (which translated means Teacher), and asking, "Where are you staying?" (v. 38). Their question seems to express a desire to share the life of Jesus. Jesus' answer is also very concrete: "Come and see" (v. 39). Everything is taking place at the level of direct experience.

The one who inspires this account, John the evangelist, never forgot the hour of his encounter with Jesus: "It was about the tenth hour" (v. 39), or about four in the afternoon. Like every event which marks our lives, the remembrance of that encounter stays on with all its circumstantial details, leaving indelible imprints on our memories. The indication of a precise hour does not seem to have much significance for us. It would not matter if the text had said ten in the morning or two in the afternoon. But it is not the case for those who have experienced the event. The text is the testimony of that event with a personal imprint. The apparent insignificance of this detail contains a strong message. We all have our similar "four in the afternoon," our peak moments of encounter with the Lord. They sustain us in difficult moments.

Speak, Lord

The encounter with the Lord is not limited to these first disciples. The very nature of the event leads to communication. This kind of experience must be shared. Following Jesus is not an individual matter; it is something that is done in community. The itinerary of the messianic people begins with a direct encounter with the Lord. This encounter takes place in community: "We have found the Messiah" (v. 41).

The book of Samuel offers a beautiful vocation account. Not understanding the call at the beginning, young Samuel is confused, and he thinks Eli is calling him. Finally, following the priest's advice, he recognizes the voice of the Lord and places himself at his service: "Speak, Lord, for your servant is listening" (3:10). We have to be totally available because everything in us is

part of the Lord's call (1 Cor 13–15). Our bodies are temples of
the Holy Spirit (v. 19).

C. The God of the Celebration
Is 62:1–5; 1 Cor 12:4–11; Jn 2:1–11

Between Epiphany, which means manifestation, and Lent, we are
following the mystery of the Lord's revelation to his people. The
context of today's texts is highly symbolic: a new God appears to
us in the middle of the wedding and the celebration.

A New Name

In a postexilic situation and with the people weary, abandoned,
or despairing, the prophet feels the urgency and impatience to
speak of the "new" things the Lord has in store for his people:
a new name (Is 62:2), a new covenant. Here Isaiah uses marriage
symbolism, rather frequent in the Bible, to speak of the tenderness, the intimacy, and the affection of God's new relationship
with his people. God is not a severe and despotic God but rather
the bridegroom and the friend who can love with tenderness and
passion and who can delight in the love of his people.

In taking up that theme, the gospel of John presents not only
Jesus' first miracle but also the first of his "signs," the central
theme of this evangelist. This event is very meaningful. "Jesus
and his disciples have also been invited to the wedding" (Jn 2:3).
Or perhaps Jesus is the one who is inviting. He is inviting us to
know him. The God of Jesus does not reveal himself in a church
or on a mountaintop surrounded by imposing majesty, but instead at a wedding and in the company of his friends. God is
preparing his people for a celebration, a new alliance. What is
presented as a symbol will be full reality when the hour comes
(v. 4). This is the new relationship of God with his people, as
different from the previous one as water is from wine.

The Good Wine

John tells us that Jesus asks the servants to fill six stone jars for
the "Jewish rites of purification" (v. 6). Water and the purification
rites are referring to certain religious customs of Jesus' day. From
that time on, religion will no longer be based on the law and con-

stant ablutions (a sign of their uselessness) or on the observance of precepts followed under the fear of punishment and guilt.

This is precisely what John is telling us: the presence of Jesus is the epiphany of this new and different God — not a God of fear and punishment, distant from us and delighting in sacrifices but instead a God who is close, in the setting of a feast, sharing our joys and our concerns. At the wedding when they run out of wine, the "good wine" is served, the best revelation of the face of God. Religion will be joyful and festive because we share in God's joy. "As the bridegroom rejoices over the bride, so shall your God rejoice over you" (Is 62:5). Through the Spirit we have entered into God's family by becoming God's children. God is building the church in unity and diversity because "to each is given the manifestation of the Spirit for the common good" (1 Cor 12:7). Like the God in whom it believes, the community will not rest "until her vindication shines out like the dawn" (Is 62:1).

Third Sunday

A. The Beginnings of the Proclamation
Is 8:23–9:3; 1 Cor 1:10, 13–17; Mt 4:12–23

Immediately after the episode of the temptations, Matthew relates the beginning of Jesus' public life. John the Baptist's mission has ended abruptly and brutally.

The Message

Jesus comes on the scene choosing Galilee (Mt 4:12), a marginal region despised by the Jews from the capital and by the system. The province is close to pagans, and its somewhat mixed religion is suspect in the eyes of those clinging to cultic purity. Matthew quotes Isaiah's words (see also the first reading) calling it Galilee of the nations or of the pagans: the true light will be for those who are closer to the darkness (Is 8:23–9:2–3). This is an early prelude of the final commissioning of the risen Jesus (Mt 28:19): make disciples of all nations, all peoples (a universal perspective in a gospel which expresses the Jewish mentality so clearly).

The great teaching will start soon in the sermon on the mount, but this text gives a summary of its essential elements to situate the framework and the personages in a kind of introduction. The kingdom is near; its contributions and treasures will be specified later. But at that point, people are invited to repent, to turn their lives around (Mt 4:17). In a summary (v. 23), the evangelist presents Jesus in his teaching mission (the first in Matthew) "proclaiming the good news of the kingdom," which for Matthew includes the entire content of his book on Jesus. At the same time, the works of Jesus show that the announced kingdom is already being fulfilled; it is already working: the healings confirm the validity and the power of the proclaimed message. They are a message of life.

The First Followers

Between the message and the multitudes who will receive it the initial framework of Jesus' public life is completed by a concise and essential call to the first disciples. Here the key words are: "they followed him" (vv. 20–22). They are two sets of brothers. Jesus finds them in their family and work environment, and he proposes another option to them: "to fish for people." Without really knowing what that task will entail and before entering into the content, they give an immediate response. They will be followers and intermediaries between Jesus and the people. Like them, all future "disciples" will be invited to follow the Lord proclaiming the good news and putting it into practice. We are called to that same mission: to proclaim the gospel beyond the sterile disputes about primacies which forget what is essential (1 Cor 1:13–17).

B. The Time Is Fulfilled
Jon 3:1–5, 10; 1 Cor 7:29–31; Mk 1:14–20

Jesus is baptized by John in the Jordan, where he receives the Father's investiture through the Spirit. Mark's gospel moves very rapidly. A few verses later, Mark gives us a summary of Jesus' preaching and the call to his first disciples.

From Galilee

For the people of Judea, the other Jewish province, Galilee is a despised and suspect region. With pagan peoples as its neighbors, Galilee is influenced by them in its customs, its religiosity, and its way of speaking. Good Jews think that nothing good can come from Galilee. As a result, Jesus the Galilean (Nazareth is in Galilee) is announcing his message from an insignificant and marginal place (v. 14). The word of the universal love of the God of Jesus Christ is coming from the poor and the despised. The powerful and the privileged resist hearing the call, as the evangelist underlines by pointing out that John had been arrested (v. 14) — a premonitory warning of what will happen to Jesus.

With Jesus' testimony affirming that "the time is fulfilled" (v. 15), the day of the Lord has come. The will of God concerning history, the kingdom, is revealed in him. It is not a purely interior reality which happens in the depth of our souls. It is the plan of God which takes place in the heart of history in which human beings live and die. The reign of love and justice is God's design for human history, and because of that it challenges everyone.

The Signs of the Times

Being Christians means being attentive to this *kairos*, this special moment of the manifestation of God in the here and now. This is where the authentically prophetic dimension of every Christian life is at stake: being attentive to the judgment of God concerning the life situation of most of the people of Latin America and of our country, being attentive also to reactions against a state of affairs contrary to the kingdom of life, to gestures of solidarity among the poor, to the testimony of Christian communities emerging from among the poor and marginalized people of this world, to expressions of respect for every dimension of the human person, to the joy and hope of the poor in the midst of their sufferings, and to the learning of in-depth prayer in the midst of the struggle for liberation. All of these are signs of the presence of the kingdom in our own history.

Welcoming the reign of God demands that we "repent" (v. 15). This is an urgent demand — "The appointed time has grown short" (1 Cor 7:29) — which comes with the gift of the kingdom and generates a new attitude toward God and others. Jonah is given the mission to call for the conversion of Nineveh, the capital of the empire, enemy of Israel (1:1–2). The prophet, a Jew who loves his country, does not want to carry out that task, but he finally accepts the Lord's will to forgive, which has no racial or religious limits (3:1–5). The kingdom is grace, but it also makes demands upon us. The first disciples hear "the good news" and they are called to be part of Jesus' mission (Mk 1:16–290). The gospel changes their lives, and it must also change ours.

C. The Messianic Program
Neh 8:1–4, 5–6, 8–10; 1 Cor 12:12–30; Lk 1:1–4; 4:14–21

This Sunday brings us very rich texts, each of which deserves a separate commentary. As usual, we will focus on the gospel.

Poverty and Freedom

The Lukan text shows us the scope of Jesus' ministry, which begins in Galilee (v. 14). Like Ezra (see Neh 8:3), Jesus is reading the scripture, and the text from Isaiah provides the content of the kingdom he has come to proclaim. The different human situations which are listed (poverty, captivity, blindness, oppression; see Lk 4:18) appear as expressions of death. The proclamation of Jesus, anointed as the Messiah by the power of the Spirit, will make death lose ground as Jesus introduces a principle of life to bring history to its fullness. Therefore, in this programmatic text we find the life-death alternative, central in biblical revelation. Faced with this alternative we are required to make a radical option.

All these situations are not on the same level. The fundamental affirmation is "to bring good news to the poor" (v. 18), who are the people who lack what is necessary for life. Liberation is communicated to the poor. The captives, the blind, and the oppressed involve deeper aspects of the conditions of the poor. In all these cases, we have a proclamation of freedom. This is also the meaning of the expression of recovery of sight to the blind. If we refer to Isaiah's original text (in Hebrew), we find that he spoke of "the condemned" whose "eyes were opened" when they were taken out of their dark dungeons. The Greek translation of this text cited by Luke uses the image of the blind. The lack of light in prison prevents them from seeing. On the other hand, when Isaiah's text speaks of "healing hearts that are broken," following another text from Isaiah (58:6), Luke replaces it by "letting the oppressed go free." The good news which Jesus proclaims to the poor is the nucleus of liberation.

This approach characterizes and it must characterize the proclamation of the gospel by the church, a body in which each person has a necessary function to carry out (1 Cor 12:13–25).

Prophecy Remains

Luke insists on the perspective of his text by speaking of the proclamation of the "year of the Lord's favor" (Lk 4:19). It is a jubilee year to be celebrated every fifty years when "everyone shall return to his property" (Lv 25:13) because, in the final analysis, the Lord alone is the owner of the land. Breaking with all unjust inequality, this year of favor was supposed to contribute to the permanent establishment of friendship among the members of the Jewish people and finally to communion with God.

The reign of God, the reign of life, is the ultimate meaning of human history, but its presence starts now on the basis of Jesus' concern for history's forgotten people. This is the testimony of the Lukan text, "today this scripture has been fulfilled" (v. 21). This is the time of integral liberation in Christ; in the person of Jesus, the kingdom becomes present. Now it is our turn as his followers to carry out fully our roles as prophets, teachers, authorities (1 Cor 12:27–30). The poverty of our people demands that we fulfill the prophecy of Isaiah and Luke.

Fourth Sunday

A. God Chooses What Is Weak
Zep 2:3; 3:12–13; 1 Cor 1:26–31; Mt 5:1–12

These are the Sundays following Epiphany, the great feast of the universality of Jesus' gospel.

Poor in Spirit

The predominant beatitude in Matthew's text is undoubtedly the first one. The addition of "in spirit" with regard to Luke has been the theme of many debates. What is its meaning? In the biblical mentality, this expression signifies dynamism; the spirit is breath, a vital force. It implies the dynamic aspect of human beings.

"Poor in spirit" designates something broader and more demanding than a mere attitude of detachment with regard to material goods. The addition of "in spirit" transforms the reference to an economic and social situation ("poor") into a disposition to accept the word of God. We are really in the presence of a central theme of the biblical message: *spiritual childlikeness*. It deals with living in total availability to the will of the Lord, making it our food, as Jesus says in John's gospel. This has to be the attitude of those who know they are God's sons and daughters, brothers and sisters of others. Being poor in spirit is being disciples of Christ. This is fundamental.

Assuming material poverty is an essential manifestation of being spiritually childlike, but being disciples is not limited to that. This condition implies, first and foremost, being open to God's gift of love and a preferential solidarity with the poor and the oppressed. Opting for a lifestyle of the poor makes sense only in this context. In and of itself, material poverty, or lacking the necessary goods to live with dignity, is not willed by God.

The remaining seven beatitudes refer to other attitudes of disciples, of the poor in spirit: meekness, affliction because of the Lord's absence, hunger and thirst for righteousness, compassion, purity of life, peacemaking, persecution on account of justice. These enhance and deepen the first beatitude.

Seeking the Lord

The notion of the poor in spirit comes from the prophet Zephaniah. The "humble" to whom he is referring are the *anawim,* according to the Hebrew term (2:3). They are those who seek God and justice. This text inspires Matthew 6:33: "Strive first for the kingdom of God and his righteousness," a verse which, in some way, summarizes the sermon on the mount. This characterizes the "remnant of Israel," that is to say, those who keep the covenant alive as they are expecting the Messiah.

The Christian community is linked with that "remnant of Israel." The church of Corinth is made up of people who are despised by the powerful because they are poor. To become aware of this, they only need to look at themselves (1 Cor 1:26). God has chosen the lowest members of society to make them disciples: "what is weak in the world to shame the strong" (v. 27) — people who are open to God's word and, as a result, are in solidarity with the poorest.

B. Revelation and Liberation
Dt 18:15–20; 1 Cor 7:32–35; Mk 1:21–28

Capernaum is the center of Jesus' activity in Galilee. Accompanied by his disciples, he proclaims the coming of the kingdom.

A New Teaching

Jesus challengingly chooses the time and place of his preaching on the sabbath and in the synagogue (Mk 1:21), a frequent occurrence in this gospel. The Lord is not afraid to face those who refuse to accept his message. The people see the difference between Jesus' proclamation and the teaching of the scribes, between the call to love and religious formalism (v. 22). Jesus' practice reveals the liberating aspect of his word which loosens the bonds of servitude, of false ideas, of false gods, and of deceitful practices (vv. 23–26). The Lord wants us to be free to be able to devote ourselves to what is asked of us, to take part in the coming of the kingdom — in Paul's words, free to love.

Those who are listening to Jesus are amazed. What they hear seems "a new teaching with authority" (v. 27). To a mentality closed to change, new is synonymous with false. But the message of love is always new because it calls us to abandon the way of selfishness and of formalism and to take the path of generosity and consistency. Jesus is at the beginning of his mission, as Mark presents it and he fulfills it along these lines. Known as Jesus "of Nazareth" (v. 24), he is opposed to the forces of evil. His life will force back the presence of death. His testimony became known and "spread throughout the surrounding region" (v. 28). We have to take the proclamation of the kingdom of peace and justice beyond Galilee, "to the ends of the earth" (Acts 1:8) and to our innermost selves.

Prophet and Friend

The prophet is one of us, a member of the people, a friend, chosen by the Lord to speak in the name of God (Dt 18:15). In this way, the people will remain faithful to the Lord. God speaks to us through those he sends, through their mouths. God provides the words. Prophets tell the people what is the will of God. Those who do not listen to the prophets will be accountable to God (v. 19) who will do the same with prophets who do communicate what God has commanded them to say (v. 20). In Latin America and in this country, God is also raising prophets to speak to us in his name. Through these prophets, many of us on this continent have learned what God wants from us today. But Jesus is the prophet par excellence, and his prophecy is the norm for our lives. His teaching is always new to us.

The Lord wants us to be free to know how to listen to what he entrusts to his prophets. This is what Paul is asking (1 Cor 7:32–35). However noble and important other responsibilities may be, they have to be subordinated to the primary task: proclaiming the kingdom in terms of concrete gestures of love for others.

C. The Way of Love
Jer 1:4–5, 17–19; 1 Cor 12:31–13:13; Lk 4:21–30

The text of Luke which we are reading today comes immediately after the one in which Jesus presents his "messianic program," an incisive foretaste of his proclamation of the kingdom.

The Day of Fulfillment

The promise of liberation to the oppressed and of evangelization of the poor is fulfilled in Jesus (Lk 4:21). His Nazareth neighbors, his people cannot believe him even though they claim to know who Jesus is, the carpenter "son of Joseph" (v. 22), and this is what prevents them from seeing beyond the appearances. This contrast marks the proclamation of the kingdom: the gift of God comes in humble and unexpected clothing. Those who pretend to know everything are not open to learning and even less if the teaching comes from someone whose value they refuse to admit out of pettiness and envy. In a lapidary phrase, Jesus says: "No prophet is accepted in the prophet's homeland" (v. 24).

This idea is illustrated in the following verses. The great prophet Elijah was not sent to someone belonging to the Jewish people but to a widow from a pagan country (vv. 25–26). And so the message of God comes from the fringes. The same happens with Elijah's disciple, Elisha, who cleanses a leper, also a pagan and, therefore, scorned by Jesus' listeners — a pagan, not a member of the chosen people (v. 27). Jesus' compatriots understand the message and they become furious. They drive him out of the city and try to hurl him off the cliff (vv. 28–29).

Believers frequently attempt to monopolize God and even to put God at their service. As Christians and as church, we fall prey to the same temptation. What we think we know prevents us from paying attention to what is new, especially if it comes from what is insignificant and marginalized. The Lord reminds us that he is challenging us through those we do not know how to appreciate.

The Primacy of Love

Jeremiah is a shy youth and he may have stuttered. Yet God chooses him as a prophet (Jer 1:4–5). Conscious of his limitations, Jeremiah protests, but the Lord makes him see that power comes from God rather than from the prophet's personal qualities (vv. 17–18). The prophet's role is to announce the love of God, a love which can be manifested in building up or in destroying, but it is a love which is always aimed at life.

This is why love lasts forever, as Saint Paul's extraordinary text reminds us. Love is what gives Christian existence its ultimate significance; it is "the more excellent way" (1 Cor 12:31). Without love, nothing has any value (13:1–3). Love presupposes understanding others, respecting and serving them. Love does not force itself; it is offered (vv. 4–7). At times, we make commitments more to unburden our consciences than to serve others. Service requires our being able to listen and to be interested in what others desire and seek.

Love abides because it has its origin in God (13:13). John tells us: "God is love." All of us have to find out how to follow the concrete way of love in our lives.

Fifth Sunday

A. Being for the World
Is 58:7–10; 1 Cor 2:1–5; Mt 5:13–16

In today's gospel, we read a passage which forms part of the group of the beatitudes and which continues the theme of disciples' attitudes.

Let Your Light Shine

"Salt of the earth," "light of the world" (5:13 and 14): earth and world designate all human beings and all creation. The message of the great sermon starting with the beatitudes has a universal and cosmic outreach. "You," the disciples, are called to hand down this message to everyone: a personal, powerful, and demanding call.

Salt is small and modest, but it is effective. Besides giving taste to food, salt is used by fishermen to keep fish fresh, and it contributes to our own nourishment. At the very least, it preserves the essence and taste of food. The insignificant and weak disciples, as Paul says of himself (1 Cor 2:3), are to communicate through very simple means something irreplaceable, namely, the love of the Lord. If they should fail in that mission, they would lose their raison d'être.

Jesus is the true light, a light for those who sit in darkness (Mt 4:16), a light that will break forth "like the dawn" (Is 58:8), light because it reveals the Lord in his word and deeds. The disciples are witnesses of the light insofar as through them we can see some of the Father's goodness revealed in the Son. Naturally, that light must be visible, accessible to everyone rather than hidden by veils and human fears (Mt 5:15). The grace of being a disciple is not for our private use; it has to be communicated. It must shine despite the weakness of its bearers. Truth should never be hidden because those to whom it is destined have an urgent and boundless need of it.

Not Hiding Ourselves from Our Own Kin

Matthew tells us that the light will be manifested in "good works" (5:16). Isaiah describes them in terms similar to those used by Jesus (in Mt 25), in precise deeds with very concrete neighbors: sharing bread, providing housing, clothing the naked. If we do that, we will not be hiding ourselves "from our own kin" (Is 58:7), as the prophet beautifully writes. If we do that, we will break the darkness, and "light will rise in the darkness" (Is 58:10).

These "good" works are a substantial part of the mission: they are the revelation of another's message. They do not refer back to those who carry them out as if they were seeking personal glory. Instead in these good works, we see and give glory to the Father of all goodness (Mt. 5:16). In the sermon on the mount we find constant references to the Father: the works, our works, provide a glimpse of the Father's goodness and love for humankind.

B. Solidarity with the Weak
Jb 7:1-4, 6-7; 1 Cor 9:16-19, 22-23; Mk 1:29-39

According to Mark, Jesus starts his ministry in Capernaum, a Galilean city. The evangelist had deliberately told us that Jesus went to a synagogue on the sabbath (1:21). His message is called a "new teaching" (1:27) which is appreciated by some but undoubtedly rejected by others.

Disciples Are Those Who Serve

On the same day, after leaving the synagogue, Jesus goes to a friend's house with his disciples (v. 29). There he performs the first healing mentioned by Mark. He restores Peter's mother-in-law to health as a sign of the kingdom of life which he has come to announce. He does this on the sabbath, a day of rest and prayer which the Pharisees' casuistry had transformed into a straight-jacket by forbidding any kind of work. As this gospel will point out on several occasions, Jesus considers it more important to give life to a person than to observe empty formalities under the pretense of religion.

This new disciple responds to the gift she receives by her service (v. 31). All followers of Jesus should imitate this woman's conduct: we truly welcome the kingdom when we place our lives at the service of others (Mk 9:33–35). The book of Job (7:1) tells us that "human beings have a hard service on earth." The sign of life through healings continues (Mk 1:34). This is the way Jesus seals his teaching. We have to keep in mind that in those days, the sick were often considered to be sinners. The multitude approaching the Lord is probably made up of weak and marginalized people.

Praying and Evangelizing

Jesus withdraws to pray in a deserted place (v. 35). On various occasions, the gospels indicate those moments of prayer which invite us to be in union with the Lord in contemplation. This is related to the evangelizing concern. "Let us go on to the neighboring towns" (v. 38), Jesus says to his disciples. Proclaiming the gospel is a powerful activity of the community. The Messiah leaves Capernaum and goes throughout Galilee as an itinerant preacher pointing the way to the Father.

Paul tells us about the intensity of evangelization. I have to proclaim the message, the Lord says in Mark's gospel (v. 38). Paul echoes: "Woe to me if I do not proclaim the gospel" (1 Cor 9:16). We must announce the message in the only way possible: freely and without expecting rewards. What is freely received must be freely and unselfishly given. This spiritual freedom will enable Paul to identify with those to whom he is proclaiming the gospel, embracing their condition and becoming one of them. Paul presents the golden rule for evangelizers: "to the weak I became weak" (v. 22) — in solidarity with those who are abandoned like Job, so that the hope of the kingdom of life may spring up in them.

C. The Grace of the Calling
Is 6:1–2, 3–8; 1 Cor 15:1–11; Lk 5:1–11

We find numerous accounts of prophetic vocations in the Bible. Today's first reading is one of these examples.

The Image of Fishing

In the gospels, many events take place beside the lake of Gennesaret, the Sea of Galilee. A large crowd is gathered in that place (Lk 5:1). Jesus asks some fishermen to collaborate with him, and from their boats he carries out his mission of announcing the gospel to the poor (v. 3). Luke mentions only one name, that of Simon, who will be the first one called (v. 10). After teaching the crowd, a more intense dialogue takes place with the fishermen who had allowed him to preach. The conversation deals with their work (vv. 4–5). Thus, they will have a better understanding of what Jesus is going to tell them. The failure of their fishing expedition the night before has made them skeptical. This often happens to us also when we do not obtain what we had planned. They are thinking that nothing can be done. But Simon shows his trust: "if you say so, I will let down the nets" (v. 5). The result amazes them, forcing them to work as a team, and they become partners (vv. 6–7).

Jesus' proclamation of the kingdom (vv. 1–3) and fishing, the daily work of these people (vv. 4–7), are interrelated. Jesus' gesture enlightens Simon, who humbly declares he is a sinful man (vv. 8–9). The same thing happens to James and John (v. 10). These three former fishermen constitute the nucleus of the disciples. They are called to collaborate with Jesus in proclaiming the kingdom, something totally new and radical for them ("they left everything and followed him," v. 11). Jesus makes himself understood by using the language they can comprehend: "you will be catching people" (v. 11). This simple and instructive dialogue provides an example for us: the gospel must be proclaimed on the basis of people's daily lives. Apart from that experience, the proclamation has no grasp on reality.

A Mission

The work of evangelizing is a mission. It starts with a calling from God. We hand down what we have been graced to receive (1 Cor 15:3). At the starting point of Paul's mission, there is his direct experience of the risen Lord (v. 8). Our mission consists in making God's gift bear fruit in us, an endeavor which is also presided over by grace (v. 10). We have to proclaim this primacy of grace, the principal content of the gospel, as we believe in God's gratuitous love (v. 11). Isaiah's prophetic vocation had its origin in his contemplation of God (6:5). In the presence of his call, like Peter, Isaiah acknowledges his unworthiness. The Lord gives him courage and finally Isaiah gives in: "Here I am; send me!" (v. 8).

After the prophet expressed that he is available, what is to follow will not be easy. But he will be able to face those difficulties with serenity because he knows that in serving others the Lord's grace is with him.

Sixth Sunday

A. No Noncommittal Answers
Sir 15:16–21; 1 Cor 2:6–10; Mt 5:17–37

The sermon on the mount is a demanding synthesis of Jesus' preaching.

Yes, Yes; No, No

Christ represents both a continuity and a break with the law of Moses. His reaction is more against the distortions which "the scribes and Pharisees" (Mt. 5:20) have introduced in the law. The kingdom proclaimed by Jesus presupposes the practice of justice, not legal and formal justice but profound and reasonable justice. It is always easier to follow rules than to be committed and to share out of love. The Lord also indicates some guidelines to follow: "you have heard . . . , but I say to you," and in each case the Lord's demand is much greater. The central idea is indicated in verses 23–24.

Our offering at the altar is worthless if we deprive or forget others. It is not a matter of personal scruples but something objective: if "your brother or sister has something against you" (v. 23). Others are our reference point. In spite of that, today we do not see Christians turn back on Sunday when they come to church to celebrate the Eucharist. . . . Reconciliation with others implies our respecting their rights and opening our hearts in concrete gestures. But we must not stop there either; we have to come back to present our offering (v. 24) to complete the circle. Prayer and commitment go hand in hand. The Eucharist demands that we create human solidarity. Only thus will our words be authentic rather than vague, a "Yes, Yes or No, No" (v. 37).

In the Face of Death and Life

The book of Sirach presents the option to us with the same clarity: "Before each person are life and death and whichever one chooses will be given" (15:7). This is our alternative, an idea already found in Deuteronomy 30:15. The decision is in the hands of human beings, whom the Lord has created free (15:14).

Believing in God is choosing life, the purpose of the practice of righteousness which is demanded in the sermon on the mount. Those who limit themselves to the formal observance of the commandments of the Lord betray God's will for life. Under religious appearances, they are living a lie, and "God will not let liars go unpunished." Believers always run the risk of falling into the hypocrisy of the Pharisees.

What will enable us to discern is wisdom, the gift of God, not the alleged and calculating knowledge of the rulers "of this age" (1 Cor 2:6). If we confine ourselves to a religion of formal and external precepts, if we do not unite prayer with the practice of justice, if we do not choose life, we are crucifying Jesus again (2:8).

B. Returning to Communion
Lv 13:1–2, 44–46; 1 Cor 10:31–11:1; Mk 1:40–45

Jesus' miracles are signs of life, the totality of life, physical, social, and spiritual.

The Lord's Compassion

Jesus continues to proclaim his message in the synagogues (Mk 1:39) where Galileans gather to listen to the reading of scripture and to pray. Synagogues are the symbol of the religious institution of that region (the temple is located in Jerusalem in Judea). The leper is a being marginalized by society. His disease inspires terror (like what is happening today with the leprosy of our time: AIDS), moreover lepers are considered as sinners. In addition to their physical suffering, they are social outcasts. The text from Leviticus is a harsh expression of such a situation. Those who are suffering from a skin disease have to be examined by a priest (vv. 1–2), and in the case of leprosy they are considered unclean. So lepers are forced to live alone, outside cities, and they themselves have to proclaim out loud that they are unclean (vv. 45–46).

The man who approaches Jesus with trust is a leper: "if you choose, you can make me clean" (Mk 1:40). The Lord is moved with pity; that is to say, he makes the man's suffering his own, he does not avoid him out of fear. Jesus stretches out his hand and touches the leper (v. 41) at the risk of his own health; he does not take any precautions. Here we have an important example for the Lord's followers. Experiencing the pain of others as our own, we make them our neighbors, people close to us. But getting close to people may entail difficulties and problems, and we prefer loving without costs, without risks for ourselves and our own people.

Imitating Christ

The Lord grants the leper's request, telling him: "I do choose. Be made clean!" (v. 41). Jesus does not want people to be outcasts.

By making him clean, he heals the physical body and reincorpo-
rates him into society. By touching the leper Jesus has violated
the law, but his gesture corresponds to something much more
profound, love for the despised. On the other hand, his compassion may have taken him further than what he had anticipated;
it is too early for Jesus' radical and questioning message to be
known. Jesus tells the former leper to show himself to the priest
(condition to be readmitted to society) and not to say how it happened (vv. 43–44). However, the man cannot keep quiet, and that
creates immediate difficulties for Jesus' mission. But the kingdom
has been opened for the pariahs of society.

Our refusal to open our hearts to others, to stretch out our
hands to them, including the disenfranchised, scandalizes those
who do not belong to the church: Jews and Greeks in Paul's day.
Only a testimony of love and generosity can reach out to those
who consider themselves far from Christ (1 Cor 10:32). We must
follow the example of Paul, who does not seek his own advantage
(v. 33) in what he does, because he is imitating Christ (11:1).

C. The Sermon on the Plain
Jer 17:5–8; 1 Cor 15:12, 16–20; Lk 6:17, 20–26

The connection between the readings in the Sunday liturgy often contains a clue for their interpretation. This is the case of
today's readings, which, at first glance, do not seem to have any
interconnection.

A Challenge

The gospel presents the beginning of the sermon on the plain (in
Matthew, the sermon on the mount). Jesus came down from the
mountain where he had spent the night in prayer, and he meets
"a great crowd of his disciples and a great multitude of people"
(v. 17). Luke likes to emphasize the frequent presence of multitudes around Jesus. What Jesus is about to tell them does not
apply to a select few but to all "who had come to hear him and
to be healed" (v. 18).

"He looked up at his disciples" (v. 20) directly, addressing
them as "you," namely, all the people in front of him, and he
proclaims the four beatitudes to the poor, those who are hungry
now, those who are hated and persecuted on account of the Son of

Man (vv. 2–22). He also announces four very stern admonitions to the rich, those who are full and laugh now, those who are praised by all (vv. 24–26). The people who have come "to hear him" no doubt feel that Jesus is addressing and questioning them. They cannot miss the repeated "you." They have to find out in what group Jesus is placing them. Jesus' words sound like an eschatological judgment which definitively encompasses the "now" of situations contrary to the kingdom of abundance and happiness or the future of irremediable need and overwhelming affliction.

God's Judgment

Jesus is clearly referring to real-life conditions: poverty and its consequences of hunger, misfortune, and persecution; wealth and its repercussions of satisfaction, laughter, and praises. It is also clear that in confronting them with the eschatological future inaugurated with him, Jesus is proclaiming the "Messianic inversion" of situations: those who hunger and weep now will find plenitude and happiness; those who are full and laugh now will feel hunger and affliction. It is not historical revenge but rather the judgment of God who uncovers the profound truth of human lives — concrete situations, aspirations, value systems, and lifestyles — in view of the proclamation of the salvation event and the reign of God.

It is therefore a judgment for conversion, a call to change our attitudes and situation in history, our aspirations and projects in view of the future kingdom that Jesus proclaims as already present and at work now. As Paul tells the Corinthians (1 Cor 15:17), faith in the resurrection of Jesus, without which our faith would be futile, is opening up human existence to a horizon of hope which transcends "this life" (v. 19). It provides us with a new key to understand and face situations and projects, to decide in what we place our ultimate trust: "trust in mere mortals and make mere flesh our strength" or "trust in the Lord" as expressed in the first reading (vv. 5 and 7).

The beatitudes and the woes of Jesus concerning such clear and concrete human situations constitute precise reference points to guide us on our journey without getting lost — and also to help us avoid being dazzled by worldly criteria and value systems, through the realities of this life, the "now" of our lives with the hope brought forth by the resurrection of Jesus Christ.

Seventh Sunday

A. Going beyond Precepts
Lv 19:1–2, 17–18; 1 Cor 3:16–23; Mt 5:38–48

The sermon on the mount is a challenge and a source of inspiration at the same time.

From Legalism to Love

Matthew has already presented various sayings of Jesus in which, to the justice codified by the law, he opposes a new practice, that of the kingdom ("unless your righteousness exceeds that of the scribes," 5:20). What are we to do now with those who seek to impose themselves upon us through some form of violence? Are we to respond in the same way, as common sense suggests or as it was established juridically by the law?

Jesus proposes three strong examples — striking on the cheek, the cloak, and the mandate — which are apparently renouncing any kind of resistance, but in reality they are attitudes inviting reflection on the part of the people involved in those situations. It is a time allowing us some distance and perhaps leading to a personal reencounter. The reason is the following: "give to everyone who begs from you" (v. 42). It is not a matter of adding new laws, new articles, new and more precise demands. That would imply staying with the mindset of the scribes and the Pharisees. As in the entire sermon on the mount, the question is to go one step farther, with a new life orientation, another way of evaluating our goods and our own lives. Everyone, including the aggressor, must be a temple of God, and we must recognize that (1 Cor 3:16). But in and of themselves, those precepts would not be viable and they would not allow any society to survive. What gives them meaning is the motivation which follows: love.

Whom and How Are We to Love?

The culminating point of the series of prescriptions proposed by Jesus is found in vv. 43 and 44. The law does not force us to hate our enemy, but Jesus eliminates all family, ideological, or national limitations: loving our enemies and praying for those who mistreat us go beyond every precept. This requirement (like all the previous suggestions) is based on the very example of God, the Father who considers everyone, the good and the evil, as his children (v. 45) — gratuitous love which is lived in the presence of God and words which are verified by Jesus' practice.

Quite simply, we are asked to be perfect and merciful like the Father (v. 48), holy like God, as we are told in Leviticus (19:2). An expression of this holiness will be our refusing to hate others (v. 17). Jesus dares to ask that as of now we share, as he himself does, the attitude of a God who is totally faithful, totally concerned for his children, a God who is totally good. Everything else flows from this.

B. Other People's Faith
Is 43:18–19, 21–22, 24–25; 2 Cor 1:18–22; Mk 2:1–12

Faith is to be lived in community. Our deficiencies can be remedied by other people's faith or that faith may help strengthen our own.

The Tenacity of Believers

This Sunday Mark presents us with a wonderful and curious scene against the backdrop of a controversy with the scribes and the Pharisees which occupies the whole second chapter. Once again in Capernaum, Jesus stirs up interest and causes different reactions. Some accept the promised and expected Messiah, while others reject him because he goes against their expectations and their current advantages.

Jesus is proclaiming the kingdom. Many people are present. Some of them are carrying a paralytic, but they are unable to reach the Lord. This does not stop them as they open the roof and, lowering the sick man, they put him in front of Jesus (vv. 2–4). The paralytic does not speak, he does not ask to be healed, but his friends' gesture is sufficient. Jesus is moved by "their faith" (v. 5), their solidarity, and, we might say, by their ingenuity. The Lord says to the man: "your sins are forgiven" (v. 5). The scribes who are constantly spying on Jesus become very upset, but they say nothing, thinking to themselves that Jesus is blaspheming (vv. 6–7).

Jesus reads their hearts and denounces their questioning (v. 8). To enable them to understand his message, Jesus tells the man to stand up and walk (v. 11). The faith of his friends has restored life to the body and spirit of the paralytic. The scribes have no interest in the sick man; they are merely watching Jesus. Because of his sensitivity to the paralytic's needs and to the boldness of his friends, the Lord bewilders the scribes. Their backbiting is counterbalanced by Jesus' clear and open gesture.

Something New Is Already Springing Forth

The scribes and, today, all those who hang on to formalism and who close their hearts, cling to the past. On the other hand, the God of our faith is always calling us to what is new. We need to discern the signs of the times, the newness which is already present and is now springing forth, but we have to perceive it (Is 43:18–19). The Lord is always ready to forgive, to blot out our past (v. 25). What we do with our lives from now on is what really matters.

But our language must always be clear. Ambiguities are foreign to the gospel. We cannot say yes and no out of fear or to avoid difficulties (2 Cor 1:18). Paul maintains that he always spoke clearly (v. 19). His message was always saying yes to God. So was the life of Jesus an amen to God, a yes to God's will. There is nothing pertaining to an ambivalent and false world in which religion is occasionally involved. The gifts of the Spirit that God has given us will guide our journey in the truth.

C. Being Friends with Our Enemies
1 Sm 26:2, 7–9, 12–13, 22–23; 1 Cor 15:45–49; Lk 6:27–38

The radical love which is required by the gospel has its origin in the love of God.

Like God the Father

This text from Luke also belongs to the sermon on the plain. The Lukan beatitudes reveal the gratuitous love of God for the least ones in history. This divine love is the root of the ethical demand which today's passage presents to us. Jesus speaks to the multitude in front of him (6:17 and 27), calling them to love unselfishly like the Father.

He starts with what seems most difficult: loving those who are our enemies (vv. 27 and 35) whether or not we are responsible for that. These enemies do not have to become our friends before we love them. The process is the other way around. Having people who disagree with us in life may be unpleasant, but it is unavoidable. The gospel asks something much more difficult than not having enemies (something which could be easily obtained on our own continent by saying nothing about injustices and human rights violations); we are asked to love them — making friends with people we consider as our enemies despite our discrepancies. Blessing them and praying for them are concrete ways of loving them (v. 28). It does not mean hiding reality, but rather not getting suffocated by it.

Like David

This demanding love must be translated into gestures: not responding inopportunely to an offense, giving what belongs to us (v. 29), including what we need (v. 30). The golden rule is found in God the Father's way: we have to be merciful like God (v. 36). God's love is not only for those who respond; its universality transcends not only national or racial boundaries but even the obstacles of our ungratefulness and of our sin (v. 35). Forgiveness is not an attitude for the weak or skeptical but rather the gesture of people who trust and believe that every person is able to change.

Forgiving means giving life. This is shown by Samuel's emotional account. Fiercely and unjustly persecuted by Saul, David finds his enemy defenseless, and yet he lets him live (1 Sm 16). This means that he is putting his own life at risk because Saul is looking for David to kill him. Thus David reveals his moral strength; he may have been physically frail because of his youth, but he has the steeled soul of a "man of heaven" (1 Cor 15), one who models his behavior on that of the God of heaven. Only the spiritually strong (v. 45), those who are convinced of their own opinions without dogmatism, are capable of giving life by loving and forgiving their enemies by becoming their friends.

Eighth Sunday

A. God or Wealth
Is 49:14–15; 1 Cor 4:1–5; Mt 6:24–34

We are continuing with the sermon on the mount. This time, the text brings us two central affirmations of Jesus' message.

The Danger of Idolatry

Contrary to what we commonly think, the risk of becoming idolatrous is a threat in every Christian life. In the Old Testament, prophets had already denounced it. The Lord points out this danger with unusual force: "you cannot serve God and wealth" (Mt 6:24). The word "money" translates the Aramaic *Mamonas,* unjustly obtained wealth used to oppress others and made into an idol. This is why we must make a choice. Jesus demands an exclusive option. The terms "love" and "hate" underscore the categorical nature of the decision.

In addition, Matthew uses the verb "to serve," which has a cultic connotation. We serve God but there is also the danger of serving wealth. Serving mammon amounts to converting it into an alternative for God, specifically because we can continue to profess that we adore God, when in truth and in practice we have given our lives over to money and to what derives from it. The alternative consists in choosing to serve one or the other. Idolatry is shown in terms of a concrete way of being, not in formal declarations.

The Kingdom and Righteousness

Matthew emphasizes this perspective in a beautiful passage of trust in providence based on the metaphor of the birds of the air and the lilies of the field (vv. 25–34). This is not a praise of fickleness but a call to freedom. Let us insist on the fact that trusting God, who loves us like a mother (Is 49:14–15), means placing our lives in the hands of God's provident care and being free to serve him and the poor. This is neither avoiding our own responsibilities nor despising human tasks and the necessary means of achieving them. On the contrary, Matthew's text insists on the need to look around (vv. 26 and 28), to be able to observe and discern what must be done. Thus, we will establish the priorities that will help us live without paralyzing anguish. The text insists: do not worry, do not strive needlessly (vv. 25, 27, 28, 31 and 32). Such an attitude prevents us from being free in the presence of all that is not essential.

This leads to the second central statement of this text: "Strive first for the kingdom of God and his righteousness" (Mt 6:33). The kingdom and righteousness: in a sense, this phrase summarizes the sermon on the mount. Welcoming the gift of the kingdom demands that we practice righteousness. This criterion "will disclose the purposes of the heart" (1 Cor 4:1–5). The grace of the kingdom has to produce our solidarity with others, especially with the poor and the needy.

B. New Wine in Fresh Wineskins
Hos 2:16–17, 21–22; 2 Cor 3:1–6; Mk 2:18–22

Our gospel for today concludes with this phrase. It has made a profound impact on Christian consciousness, which explains why it is so frequently quoted in everyday language.

The Newness of the Kingdom
Mark's text occurs in the middle of a harsh controversy with the Pharisees. The newness brought forth by the kingdom emerges from it. The dispute deals with fasting (v. 18). For John's disciples and also for the Pharisees (mentioned in Mk 2:16), fasting is an expression of repentance and penance. But the fast imposed on the people by the Pharisees is often a manifestation of a ritualistic and oppressive religion, the opposite of the religion of life and joy offered by Jesus. The basic reason for this is Jesus' presence. In the language of the prophets, the "bridegroom" (v. 19) designates God and the covenant is expressed in nuptial terms (see our first reading, Hosea's text). In its aspects of encounter and joy, the wedding feast is a symbol of the kingdom, as many gospel parables remind us.

The fact that Jesus' disciples do not fast indicates a rupture which is a characteristic of the kingdom. There is no room for patches (v. 21); they are useless, and new components will make the tear worse (v. 21). Reweaving our lives is the exigency of the kingdom. That implies leaving many things aside and opening up to the newness of Jesus' message.

Living Letters

We know Paul of Tarsus through his epistles. Here we have letters of a different type, one that Paul is especially fond of. He tells us that he does not inspire these letters. They come from Christ himself (2 Cor 3:3) and Paul contributes to the writing by his ministry with the people to whom he communicates the good news of Jesus. Differently from the letters we know, these are not written with paper and ink. In reality, it is the Spirit of the living God who is writing them, not on stone tablets as at Sinai but in people's hearts (v. 3). Those who have received Jesus' message are becoming letters communicating to others the "Spirit who gives life" (v. 5), living letters transmitting the love of the Lord. Accepting this love means allowing the Lord to write another epistle in our innermost hearts and to address it to the people we will encounter in the course of our lives.

These are also Paul's letters, and they will prevent us from being caught up in the letter which kills (v. 6). Because God is their author, we can trust these letters (vv. 4–5). They are love letters inviting us to a wedding (symbol of the covenant), to union "in righteousness and in justice, in steadfast love and mercy" (Hos 2:19). The practice of justice and love will enable us to know the Lord (v. 20). However, the road is not mapped out; every day we need to invent the creation of a just society in solidarity with people. This is why we cannot "put new wine in old wineskins" (Mk 2:22).

C. The Formation of the Disciples

Sir 27:4–7; 1 Cor 15:54–58; Lk 6:39–45

In Luke's sermon on the plain and in the sermon on the mount in Matthew's version, Jesus is presented as the teacher concerned about the good formation of the disciples who, in turn, are to be guides and teachers of others.

Fruits of Life or Death

The function of the disciples of Jesus does not end with their own formation. They are to guide and lead others. They are people who are sent and, as a result, witnesses who live in accordance with the faith to which they testify and who practice what they teach in their own lives. Hence Jesus' concern for the integral consistency of the disciples: a blind person cannot guide another blind person. If a person is blinded by inconsistencies, that person will not be able to correct and to arouse spiritual fidelity in the people who should be formed and encouraged (Lk 6:39). Disciples who do not convert the teaching they claim to accept and teach into life, "good fruit" (v. 43), are called hypocrites by Jesus, like the Pharisees who claim to be guides of the Jewish people. The fruits of our works manifest the goodness or the malice of the human heart, the truth or the lie of a disciple's word.

Works rather than words are the good or the evil which comes "out of the good treasure of the heart" (v. 45). Following the image used in Sirach (v. 6), Jesus compares the works with the fruits of the tree (vv. 43–44). Jesus' good work par excellence is giving life, victory over death. Death, the work of sin, has been definitively overcome by Jesus' resurrection. This is why we can flout death as Paul writes, invoking a text from Isaiah (1 Cor 15:55).

In today's world where life and death are entangled in a decisive combat — solidarity, justice, and peace against violence, injustice, and selfish individualism — it is easy to say on which side the disciples of Jesus have to be. The real difficulty is discerning the "good fruit," the truly effective work, overcoming fear and inertia, taking out of our hypocritical eyes the logs of the seemingly small daily inconsistencies of contempt, lack of solidarity, condemning consequences without denouncing their causes, etc. (Lk 6:42).

Consistency between Saying and Doing

Jesus requires that his disciples be transparent and consistent, the conditions of an authentic evangelizing testimony. The moral authority to proclaim the good news can only be based on the truth and consistency of our words, attitudes, and actions. Consistency is compelling. It is required of the church of all times if it is going to be faithful to its evangelizing vocation.

The "sting of sin" which causes death, as Paul states (1 Cor 15:56), is still hidden in the inconsistent conduct of many Christians. Paul invites the Corinthians and he also invites us "to be steadfast, immovable, always excelling in the work of the Lord"

(v. 58). Steadfastness in our practice, even in difficult and disconcerting times, builds up that moral authority so characteristic of Jesus. It is also required today to encourage and sustain those who weaken and succumb in the face of the apparent power of death. As believers in Jesus Christ's victory over death, "knowing that in the Lord our labor is not in vain" (v. 58), we owe a testimony of steadfastness and hope to society as a whole and especially to the most forsaken.

Ninth Sunday

A. Practice More Than Words
Dt 11:18, 26–28; Rom 3:21–25, 28; Mt 7:21–27

In concluding the lengthy teaching of the sermon on the mount, Jesus warns us about a frequent and dangerous distortion: reducing faith to knowledge and religious practices. Instead, we have to listen with our hearts and live according to God's will.

Building on Rocks

Salvation, or "entering the kingdom of heaven," according to the frequent expression in Matthew's gospel, "the righteousness of God," in Paul's letter to the Romans, consists as Jesus tells us in "doing the will of my Father in heaven." In his time and in our own as well, faith in God is often reduced to a strictly religious ambit separated from the tasks and responsibilities of daily life: the world of devotions or of the extraordinary and miraculous. However, Jesus forcefully rejects these as works of salvation: "I will declare to them: I never knew you; go away from me, you evildoers" (Mt 7:23). In other words, these actions may not coincide with God's will, which involves being agents of equality and justice. "Strive first for the kingdom of God and his righteousness" (Mt 6:33) as we read last Sunday. Establishing right and justice is the expression used by prophets in the Bible to designate the conduct God expects of believers. In his well-known text on the final judgment, Matthew himself identifies the fundamental criterion to define entry into the kingdom with concrete works of love for the needy.

Not taking this evangelical criterion into account is building "on sand" (v. 26), without foundation. The Lord invites us to build our lives "on rock" (v. 24) and the rock is God's will — his kingdom — of life, justice, and peace.

Faith in Jesus Christ

Authentic faith does not consist in a formal and superficial conforming to the words of the Bible. Deuteronomy situates faith at a deeper and more radical level of the human being: "putting these words in your heart and soul" (Dt 11:18) to meditate on them and follow them so that they may inspire and guide our daily conduct. This is the way we receive the "blessing" that God puts before us.

This "blessing," or the best word that God can say to humankind, is what Paul calls "the righteousness of God through Jesus Christ for those who believe" (Rom 3:22). Jesus Christ is the Word of God made flesh and poor for the salvation of all. In the faith which is lived in following Jesus, we welcome that word which makes us just and children, enabling us to put into practice the works of the will of God: justice and friendship in love. Therefore, faith in Jesus Christ is God's gift, which we first receive and then put into practice, not like those who obey the works of the law out of obligation but as children who do the will of the Father out of love.

B. Giving Life
Dt 5:12–15; 2 Cor 4:6–11; Mk 2:23–3:6

We have here another phase in the controversy with the Pharisees, a controversy which is becoming increasingly more demanding. The newness of the kingdom is found in the gift of life.

The True Sabbath

Once again, Jesus' disciples seem to violate the law, or rather the Pharisees' interpretation of the law (Mk 2:23–24). To their criticism Jesus responds by reminding them of an incident in the life of David, someone highly respected by the Jewish people. Besieged by Saul, David's companions entered the house of God and ate the bread of the priests (vv. 25–26). The message is clear: the hunger which is experienced takes priority over ritual prohibitions. Hunger reflects a need which puts human life in jeopardy. Formal precepts are at the service of life, all of life. This is why "the sabbath was made for humankind, not humankind for the sabbath" (v. 27). This is an extraordinary proclamation of freedom.

It reminds us of what is at stake in this controversy. The text from Deuteronomy clarifies the ultimate meaning of religious rules. We have to observe the sabbath, to rest (and make sure that others also rest), and to acknowledge that God is the source of our existence (v. 12). However, we must not forget the reason for this rule: the liberation from the slavery endured in Egypt (v. 15). In our surprise, we might wonder what one thing has to do with the other. The fact is that religious precepts cannot be new and subtle forms of slavery. On the contrary, they have to lead us to be free, free to love, as Paul would say.

Life or Death

With the following text, the controversy with the Pharisees takes on dramatic aspects. Mark carefully describes the episode. It happens in a synagogue on the sabbath (vv. 1–2). This is a very significant detail. Both the place and the day are sacred and the alleged violation of the law — this time not by the disciples but by Jesus himself — is more serious. The maliciousness of those who reject his witness does not frighten Jesus: he makes the man with a withered hand come forward, to the center. Everything is going to revolve around him and his health (v. 3). Then Jesus presents this probing dilemma to his adversaries: "Is it lawful to do good or to do harm on the sabbath, to save life or to kill?" (v. 4). Jesus does not ask them if it is lawful to work on the sabbath. They would have probably answered the question with a quick and perfunctory: no. Jesus goes straight to the point: the gift of life is the supreme rule. This disarms his listeners, who keep silent. They are unable to go beyond what is superficial and incidental.

This makes the Lord angry. The term is harsh, but harsher still are the hearts of those who distort the relationship with the Lord of life (v. 5) to the extent that the healing of the crippled man leads them to want to kill Jesus and even to conspire with their own enemies (v. 6). They refuse to accept that "the life of Jesus is made visible in our bodies" (2 Cor 4:10), in our bodies and not just in our souls. In a country and on a continent with so many physical and spiritual needs, where unjust deaths are a daily reality, these rich Markan texts have a lot to say to us about the authentic meaning of our following Jesus.

C. The Foreigner and the Widow
1 Kgs 8:41–43; Gal 1:1–2, 6–10; Lk 7:1–10

This Sunday's texts invite us to reflect on important aspects of salvation in Christ.

The Faith of the Marginalized Foreigner

The gospel of Luke relates one of Jesus' healings. As in all such cases, there is a strong relation between faith and life. This time, the beneficiary is a marginalized and humble person, a foreigner's servant (v. 2). In other words, the man belongs to one of the categories of the famous trilogy of the poor in the Old Testament: orphans, widows, and foreigners, people viewed as weak or discriminated against in the society of the time. The Lord praises the faith of the centurion, a pagan, and he gives it as an example to the Jews (v. 9). Previously, the man who humbly pleaded for his servant's health had told Jesus: "I am not worthy to have you come under my roof" (v. 6). The liturgy puts this simple formula on our lips as we prepare to receive the body and the blood of the Lord.

Life is God's gift; faith welcomes that grace. Here we do not have a relation of reward to merit but of grace to freedom, a grace emanating from a God who is sensitive to human pain. For without compassion (literally: feeling with), there can be no authentic gesture toward others. What motivates Jesus is not the carrying out of a duty or a function; instead it is his closeness to people. If we "are not deeply moved" by the situation in which the poor are living today, we will not know how to be in solidarity with them. Many discussions concerning the poor and their total liberation come from people approaching the matter as an ideological question rather than as a reality clamoring to God. Luke shows us Jesus' sensitivity in this regard.

Distorting the Gospel

The foreigner represents a type of poor, but there is also another dimension, namely, the universality of God's love, as evoked in the text of the book of Kings, our first reading. In the beginning, the Jews, a nationalistic people, did not allow pagans in God's salvific work. But the Lord is calling everyone to communion with him. The temple of believers must be open to "all the people of the earth" (v. 43). This is a dangerous temptation for those who belong to the church, the community of believers, to look with distrust on those who are not part of it. This attitude will always be challenged by the gesture of Jesus who proposes as a model to us the faith of a pagan, someone who humbly addresses Jesus out of love for another (his servant in this case).

Paul was the great apostle to the Gentiles. In his epistle to the Galatians, he fights the tendency to reduce the Lord's work to the members of the Jewish people. This is a powerful inclination, and the head of the apostles, Peter himself, gives in to it. In this epistle, Paul tells us how he had to fight for the universality of Christ's work (see chapter 2). For Paul, this is defending the true gospel (1:6–10). Paul knows that he has a message to communicate, but that does not give him ground to feel superior to others. Because he is convinced of what he has to proclaim, Paul is not afraid to confront the great themes and challenges of his time. He does not follow the easy way out by taking refuge among those who think like him; he does not keep silent when he has to speak; he does not use the gospel as a springboard to obtain a dubious social prestige (v. 10). He knows that this is not the way to be "a servant of Christ" (v. 10).

Tenth Sunday

A. The Kind of Mercy That Makes Faith Possible
Hos 6:3–6; Rom 4:18–25; Mt 9:9–13

The God of mercy always appears in disconcerting ways. God seems to delight in relying on what is the least adequate according to human judgment. He calls sinners like Matthew to be disciples, a couple, people already old like Abraham and Sarah, to be the parents of a great multitude. And God counts on us, weak as we are, to make the kingdom present.

Not the Righteous but Sinners

In the eyes of the self-righteous of Israel, there is something provocative in Jesus' practice: he "calls" those who should have remained outsiders because of their conduct, and he makes room for them. He calls Matthew and later he will call Zacchaeus, both publicans, that is to say, tax collectors, collaborators of the Romans and often swindlers of the people. For all these reasons, they are public sinners and justly despised. Moreover, Jesus does not hide this. Instead, he eats with them, and "many tax collectors and sinners were sitting with him and his disciples" (Mt 9:10). This must have occurred several times until it caused the scandalized reaction of the Pharisees mentioned several times in the gospels (Lk 15:2). In today's episode, the Pharisees are protesting to the disciples: "Why does your teacher eat with tax collectors and sinners?" (v. 11). Sharing a meal was a sign of acceptance and companionship. Doing this publicly with known sinners was truly unacceptable.

But for Jesus, as in the case of the miracles, this is an action revealing his identity as the prophet of the true God. Thus, he responds to his critics by using the text Hosea applies to God: "I desire mercy, not sacrifice" (Hos 6:6; see Mt 9:13). Welcoming sinners, the sick, the unworthy manifests the real universality of the offer of salvation which he is bringing. God's love is concretely universal in the expressed partiality and preference for the humanly unworthy and despicable. This is why Jesus adds: "I have come to call not the righteous but sinners" (v. 13). Here we should understand the "call" in the strong sense of summoning to the kingdom. Table fellowship with Jesus is a sign and a foretaste of the kingdom.

Hoping against Hope

Faith implies believing "against hope" (Rom 4:18) and human foresight. It is not the outcome of our reasoning and calculations. Faith situates us in another logic: that of God. Abraham believed "fully convinced that God was able to do what he had promised" (v. 21). God's promises of a new heaven and a new earth where life, justice, and peace will reign appear humanly remote to us and evoke our skepticism. Today we do need a faith as strong as that of Abraham, the father of believers, in order to believe in God and to take his promises seriously by preparing to accept them and assume them as the horizon and criterion to build our world according to these promises. Abraham "grew strong in his faith" (v. 20).

Our times are characterized by a certain weakness in our convictions and commitments. From us "who believe in him who raised Jesus our Lord from the dead" (Rom 4:24), it is right to expect a testimony of faith and strength to face the discouragement caused by so many dreams and projects that have failed. Strengthened by our faith in the God of life, we could offer to our brothers and sisters the liberating service of "hoping against hope."

B. We Believe and So We Speak
Gn 3:9–15; 2 Cor 4:13–5:1; Mk 3:20–35

We continue our reading of Mark. Today's text reminds us of the context of friendship of the kingdom and its proclamation.

Who Has Lost His Mind?

People follow Jesus with such enthusiasm that he does not have time to eat (v. 20). Jesus' criticism of the religious institutions established by those considering themselves authorized interpreters of the law preoccupy "his own" (v. 21) according to the literal translation of the text that many (including the Jerusalem Bible) translate by "his family." Be that as it may, they are people close to him, including those to whom he is related by blood. They are concerned by his disconcerting preaching and want to get him away from the crowd following him. They even fear he has gone out of his mind (v. 21). The reaction is harsh, but it makes us see how difficult it was then and still is now to accept Jesus' message. In our own time, Archbishop Romero's courage and evangelical spirit prompted the privileged of his country to spread the rumor, even in leaflets at the time of his funeral, that the archbishop was psychologically unbalanced. He was so devoted to the poor of El Salvador, however, that he didn't even have time to eat.

Opposition to Jesus' message is becoming more obstinate. He is accused of siding with those who oppose God (the term "Satan" means "adversary"). In two brief parables, Jesus proves how ridiculous the charge is (vv. 22–27) and he takes the offensive. God is always ready to forgive our sins and offenses, but rejecting the kingdom of life by alleging that the one proclaiming it is possessed by an evil spirit is a serious sin against the Holy Spirit (vv. 28–29). That type of behavior is neither occasional nor a fault; it is a premeditated and systematic attitude. It is a perversion of faith itself, and it expresses the intention of continuing with this attitude: a very serious sin, hence the mention of Adam's sin (see the reading from Genesis).

Jesus' Family

His mother and his brothers (that is, his close relatives) are looking for Jesus. The Lord takes advantage of that opportunity to clarify who belongs to his true family: the criterion consists in putting God's will into practice (vv. 31–35). That does not mean a rejection of family ties but a deepening of those ties. Mary's physical motherhood is inseparable from her acceptance of God's will. She freely welcomes the Son of God in her own body. In her, the woman and the believer become one. Here Mark does not mention the name of Mary (in fact he only mentions it once in his gospel; see 6:7). This discretion about the person whom a contemporary theologian calls "the first believer" emphasizes the content of Mary's faith: Jesus and putting God's will into practice.

That faith must be passed on. The experience of faith leads to our speaking about it. Inspired by a psalm, Paul says: "We believe and so we speak" (2 Cor 4:13). Speaking means making sure that our "inner nature" (v. 16), the "new person," is affirmed while our "outer nature" (v. 16), the "old person" who considers the kingdom as madness or something demonic, is torn down.

C. He Gave Him Back to His Mother
1 Kgs 17:17–24; Gal 1:11–19; Lk 7:11–17

The first reading and the gospel for this Sunday are closely related in theme. In both events the presence and the word of God become evident, and the identity of those who carry out God's word is clearly manifested.

He Was Moved to the Core

The particular aspects of the gospel account are worth observing. Jesus is walking with "his disciples and a large crowd" (v. 11). The widow is also accompanied by "a large crowd" (v. 12). Luke stresses the compassionate gesture of Jesus, who is called Lord

for the first time in this gospel: "When he saw her, he had compassion for her and said to her: Do not weep. Then he came
forward and touched the bier..." (vv. 13–14). The widow had
not asked for anything. In this case, as Mark often does, Luke
gives us the key which explains and provides the real meaning of
the actions which we commonly call miracles: "When he saw her,
he had compassion for her." Here Luke uses the same verb that
he uses to speak of the Samaritan's compassion (10:33), a verb
literally meaning "he was deeply stirred up." This is what Jesus
experiences when he sees the pain of the poor widow.

What matters here is not the prodigy, the superhuman power,
but rather the action which emanates from Jesus' merciful goodness in the presence of human suffering: compassion, consolation, closeness, personal and effective commitment — a goodness
which generates life and transforms the attitudes of those receiving it: "Young man, I say to you, rise! The dead man sat up and
began to speak" (vv. 14–15). Jesus' goodness is not merely a feeling; it is the power of life: it raises us up and makes us speak.
It is a goodness which has historical implications and effects. Besides, Luke does not forget a very human detail about Jesus: "He
gave him to his mother" (v. 15). Jesus is moved by the woman's
disconsolate weeping.

Today many mothers and many people among the poor also
accompany the physical or moral death of their young sons because they have been mistreated by hunger or premature death,
by the lack of work and opportunities, or because in their despair they have succumbed to drugs or violent ways. Today many
young people are paralyzed as if they were dead in the face of an
insecure future, finding no place in society and deprived of the
opportunity to speak up or be heard. Jesus' attitude is pointing
a way for the Christian community: the way of goodness which
leads to effective help, closeness, understanding, encouragement,
and stimulus to make them stand up, say what they have to say,
and walk with initiative with and among their people.

God's Visitation

Jesus' action, like that of Elijah, causes not only admiration but
gratitude and the praise of God. In the gospel, Jesus is not a thau-
maturge who is working wonders; he is "a great prophet" through
whom "God has looked favorably on his people" (Lk 7:16). The
actions in which Jesus efficaciously concretizes his goodness and

mercy toward those who are suffering reveal the kingdom of God's gratuitous goodness with his people. They are a credible gospel urging conversion to become daughters and sons of the Father of mercy. Just before our reading, in the sermon on the plain, Luke had mentioned Jesus' great invitation: "Be merciful, just as your Father is merciful" (Lk 6:36).

Also in the case of Elijah, his action of effective solidarity in restoring to life the child of the widow who had welcomed him into her home enables the woman to recognize that he is "a man of God and that the word of the Lord in your mouth is truth" (1 Kgs 17:24).

Like Paul, every Christian and the entire ecclesial community have been called by grace "to reveal his Son in me, so that I might proclaim him among the Gentiles" (Gal 1:16). Among a people who bury so many of their children daily there is no other way of announcing the good news of God's visitation in Jesus Christ and the truth of God's word than through mercy as the effective practice of solidarity and of life.

Eleventh Sunday

A. Proclaiming the Kingdom and Curing the Sick
Ex 19:2–6; Rom 5:6–11; Mt 9:36–10:8

The mission of the disciples prolongs and extends that of Jesus: proclaiming the good news of the kingdom of God to a people burdened by discouragement, suffering, and the absence of perspectives of salvation.

Mission and Compassion

Compassion is one of the qualities of Jesus which the evangelists often emphasize to characterize his unique way of coming close to those who suffer, and it also expresses his attitude vis-à-vis the collective suffering of his people.

The text we are considering today also mentions this attitude as the foundation of Jesus' evangelizing practice: proclaiming the kingdom and curing every disease and sickness: "When he saw the crowds, he had compassion for them, because they were harassed and helpless, like sheep without a shepherd" (Mt 9:36). It is impossible not to think of the real historical situation which the people were experiencing. Under the domination and the impoverishing plundering of the Roman empire, they are "harassed and helpless... without a shepherd" or a guide to open up horizons of salvation. Compassion is not pity, and it entails more than interest. It signifies sharing and making the sufferings and aspirations of others our own. Being compassionate is practicing solidarity.

Because it was an enormous and urgent task, Jesus summons the disciples so that they might "proclaim that the kingdom of heaven has come near" (10:7). From then on, the content of a disciple's vocation is clear: proclaiming the kingdom on the basis of daily commitment to establish life where it is lacking, where there is marginalization and a predominance of the spirit of injustice. In the face of such enormous shortages and sufferings afflicting and burdening the people in our society, the meaning of the mission, its urgency, and its vastness continue: proclaiming the kingdom and giving life. We have to discover the specific and effective ways to do that through discernment and our committed search, starting with the communities and the lucid analysis of concrete circumstances. For that search to be authentically pastoral, we must bear in mind two evangelical attitudes indicated by Jesus: trusting prayer to the Father, the "Lord of the harvest," and gratuitous surrender: "You received without payment; give without payment" (v. 8).

Gratuitousness and the Option for the Poor

In reality, salvation has been the totally gratuitous initiative of the love of God. Paul says so openly: "God proves his love for us in that while we still were sinners Christ died for us" (Rom 5:7). This is also the case of the covenant with the people of Israel, as we are told in the first reading: "You have seen... how I bore you on eagles' wings and brought you to myself" (Ex 19:4). God's liberating action converted them into his very own people.

Likewise, the church is called to be "God's people" and a "sacrament of salvation" for all humankind. Because its origin is in God's gratuitous love, the vocation of the church takes it out of being absorbed in its own internal affairs; it makes it go to the "harassed and helpless" of society. Being the church of Jesus necessarily leads it to a responsible option for the poor. That is the way the church will show its fidelity to the evangelizing and consoling mission received from the Lord and to the covenant.

B. The Humble Tree
Ez 17:22–24; 2 Cor 5:6–10; Mk 4:26–34

The parables are comparisons making the kingdom of God close and demanding.

The Lord Is at Work

Comparing means taking something known and familiar to translate a reality more difficult to grasp: "it is like...." People's daily life is the great source of Jesus' parables. The ones that Mark offers to us today present the kingdom of God in rural terms. The first parable opposes the power and richness of the soil with the toil of the farmers. Whatever they do, whether they sleep or are awake, "the seed sprouts and grows" (Mk 4:27). Within the seed, there is an inner force changing it first into grass, then a stalk, and finally wheat (v. 28). The people hearing the parable are perfectly aware of that process. With the wheat, you make bread, daily food essential to human life. Jesus uses the seed of life of the grain to communicate an essential element of the kingdom of God: it is a gift. God is the main farmer, and we are only his assistants. If we fail to understand that God takes the initiative, our own contribution is incorrectly situated.

Along with God, we will rejoice at the coming of harvest time (v. 29). This is the time of the Lord's judgment. On that day, all of us "will appear before the judgment seat of Christ" (2 Cor 5:10). Welcoming the kingdom, making its message of love, justice, and freedom ours, means acknowledging the power of God in our lives and acknowledging God as the artisan of history.

The Birds' Nests

The second parable deals with the apparent smallness of the kingdom. The great danger is that it may not appear visible to us. Once again, the comparison comes from the rural world. The mustard seed appears insignificant, yet it contains the potential of becoming a large tree. In its branches, the birds of the air will make their nests and seek the protection of its shade (Mk 4:31–32). The kingdom is like that; its beginnings do not announce all that is to come. At first, the kingdom is proclaimed in Galilee, of little value; its proclaimer frightens the powerful of his time, and they condemn him to an ignominious death, hoping that no one would remember what he had said and done. But the seed is sown in history and the tree keeps growing, always humble (Ez 17:24) yet vital and green.

Its fruits are found in testimonies like those of Sister Irene Mc-Cormack (a religious born in Australia). She did not come to Peru to be killed; she came to give her life, her friendship, her work, and her gestures to the poor, every day. She came from a rather peaceful country, without major problems, yet she was cruelly murdered in the midst of a people who increasingly have only their own death to express life, as Vallejo used to say. The Lord made the seed of the kingdom grow in Irene. When she would get up and go to bed, day and night, the kingdom was growing in her life with a power she herself may not have perceived. Her status as a woman and a religious, always marginalized, is a good representation of the insignificant mustard seed. Yet the Lord has converted her humility into a luxuriant tree which shades us and in which the preferential option for the poor makes its nest.

C. The Women Disciples
2 Sm 12:7–10, 13; Gal 2:16, 19–21; Lk 7:36–8:3

The reading of the gospel of Luke for this Sunday presents one of Jesus' most beautiful and eloquent gestures.

Love and Forgiveness

The respectful and, as a result, liberating defense by Jesus of the sinful and repentant woman before Simon the Pharisee may tell us more about the identity of Jesus and the forgiveness of God than all the wonderful parables on mercy that we find in Luke. Simon the Pharisee's bad thoughts about Jesus and the woman are disclosed ("if this man were a prophet, he would have known what kind of woman this is who is touching him," v. 39). Then Simon is brought to formulate an apparently impersonal judgment: the one "for whom a greater debt was canceled" (v. 43) will love more. With that premise, Jesus is able to explain to him that in the presence of God, human situations of just and sinners are profoundly altered. The woman, obviously "a public sinner" and thus socially despised and marginalized, becomes a model of conversion and of a repentant attitude because she welcomes the Lord's mysterious and gratuitous forgiveness. Thus Simon, the just Pharisee, becomes the one who is judged precisely by the expressive gestures of love of that anonymous woman. All that is known about her is that she is a "public sinner" and that "her many sins were forgiven" (v. 47).

Jesus' answer clarifies several points. The forgiveness comes gratuitously from God, from his merciful love which anticipates and is the motive of human repentance. The love shown by the woman expresses her accepting forgiveness. Just as the essence of sin consists in "despising God by doing what is evil in his sight" (2 Sm 12:9), conversion is shown through gratitude and love. Forgiveness is the work of God's gratuitous love, but once it is received it commits us to love (v. 47). God's forgiveness is not just a "let's wipe the slate clean"; instead it invites and empowers us to enter into a new relationship with God, based on love. God's forgiveness is liberating and it makes us free and capable of loving.

In the context of our violent and vindictive society, we should reflect more creatively on the effectiveness of pardon granted not as a sign of weakness and impotence but as an expression of a love which can generate new behaviors that respect the dignity of individuals and build up authentic peace and justice.

The Life of Christ in Us

Finally, Jesus confirms his identity, which Simon and the other guests have questioned. Yes, Jesus is a prophet and this is why he forgives sins and can tell the woman: "Your faith has saved you; go in peace" (v. 50). While others are keeping their doubts, the sinful woman believes in Jesus and she finds salvation. By her faith and her love, the woman has a bond with Jesus, and it is neither difficult nor foolish to imagine her among the women who accompany Jesus as disciples, along with the twelve (8:1–3). No one is excluded from following the Lord closely, either because of being a man or a woman, or because they have sinned.

Faith in Jesus Christ is what justifies human beings: "a person is justified through faith in Jesus Christ" (Gal 2:16) and faith situates human existence in a radically new dimension and depth. Paul expresses it in the following way: "It is no longer I who live but it is Christ who lives in me" (v. 20). Becoming disciples is

allowing ourselves to be won over by Jesus Christ's love, a love
which is the surrender of his life and making that present in our
daily gestures of love in the surrender of our own lives. Being
Christians is not a mystical experience; "it is Christ who lives in
me" actualized in our daily historical responsibility — the giving
of our lives — for a loving society based on new relationships of
justice which reconciles and builds up peace.

Twelfth Sunday

A. In Broad Daylight
Jer 20:10–13; Rom 5:12–15; Mt 10:26–33

On these Sundays of ordinary time, we are reading the gospel
of Matthew. One of his major themes is the following of Jesus.
Today's texts speak of the courage needed to do that.

Not Being Afraid

The tenth chapter of Matthew is dedicated to Jesus' disciples. The
Lord sends them on a mission and gives them guidelines to accomplish their task: the absolute nature of the kingdom, poverty
and steadfastness in proclaiming it. Our passage is situated in
this context. The proclamation of the gospel is no easy task; it
exposes its bearers to persecution and suspicion. The recent experience of the church in Latin America is a painful reminder of
this. But the Lord has forewarned us.

"Have no fear of them; for nothing is covered up that will
not be uncovered" (Mt 10:26). We have to say things in broad
daylight. The text repeats, "do not fear." Proclaiming the gospel
presupposes conviction and boldness. The evangelical message
uncovers all that is a rejection of God's will to love, the disguised
mistreatment of others, especially of the poor and the defenseless,
the lies in the religious justifications that some people offer in the
defense of their petty interests and privileges. This is why disciples have to be both frank and clear. The light of the evangelical
message does not allow us to take refuge in dark corners to hide
our fears and infidelities.

The Lord Liberates the Poor

God looks into our hearts. God disapproves of lies, however disguised they may be, and encourages those to whom he has committed his cause (Jer 20:12). These verses form part of an extraordinary text of Jeremiah. The prophet sees all his objections overcome by the love of God. Faced with the threats of his enemies, the anguished yet faithful prophet knows that the Lord will "deliver the life of the needy from the hands of evildoers" (20:13). And so he has to overcome his fears and proclaim God's word.

Jesus, the new Adam, through whom "grace abounded for the many" (Rom 5:15), identifies with the disciple who is to give an authentic and frank testimony of his message (Mt 10:32). For that same reason, Jesus will deny before the Father whoever "denies him before others" (v. 35). Before the countless injustices which are experienced today, before the verbiage of social lies aiming at covering them up, before attempts to use God instead of serving God, what should be our attitude? The ways of candidness and courage alone will make us proclaim Jesus who will, in turn, acknowledge us (v. 32).

B. Faith and Fear
Jb 38:1, 8–11; 2 Cor 5:14–17; Mk 4:35–41

God's gratuitous love is the source of our joy and of our courage to face the adversities and perplexities of our lives.

The Courage to Be Christians

The fourth chapter of Mark brings us a number of parables on the kingdom which conclude with the narrative of this Sunday's gospel. The kingdom of life and justice is a gift from the Lord. Having faith means welcoming that grace and making its demands our own. There is a subtle way of not believing, not trusting in the Lord: being afraid. It is subtle because it does not seem like rejection, but we have to look at things more in depth. In the passage we are reading today, fear is established as equal to lack of faith: "Why are you afraid? Have you still no faith?" (v. 40).

The corresponding text in Matthew mentions "little faith" (8:26). The gospel of Mark is often more biting, but it is the same idea in both cases. If there is faith, there is no fear. The harsh conditions in which the poor of the world are living, the violence present in the world, and the discouragement that this produces are serious challenges for the evangelizing task of the church and, therefore, for each one of us. Faced with this situation, some find reasons not to see reality as it is; in this way they try to escape from the commitments that a truly evangelical attitude demands. They are afraid of losing their present security — or their privileges — and they refuse to assume total availability to the Lord's will. Today's text reminds all of us that fear in the presence of the challenges of the gospel hides something very grave: a lack of faith.

Everything Is New

We tend to be afraid of what is new. We feel comfortable with our mediocrity, and we prefer to travel on known roads where those we encounter will greet us rather than question us. We are inclined to cover the message which is always life and newness in old frameworks. The principal norm of such an attitude seems to be our peace and tranquillity first, then the gospel demands.

But "if anyone is in Christ, there is a new creation: everything old has passed away ... everything has become new" (2 Cor 5:17). Being in Christ requires imagination and creativity placed at the service of others. Christians are people who constantly invent forms of loving, not in formal compliance of a duty but in terms of concrete persons, our neighbors, especially the most needy, today's poor and oppressed. This requires not being narrow-mindedly distracted by the problems we invent to avoid looking at inhuman reality face to face and to stay on grounds that do not question us. Paul says, "the love of Christ urges me on" (v. 14). Let us experience this same urgency.

The text from Job — we are at the start of a series of questions placed in the mouth of God — tells us that God's gratuitous love is present in the world order and that it gives meaning to everything. That love is the deepest source of our joy. But it is also always demanding that we be open to God and to the lives of others. If there is faith, there is no fear of difficulties and threats. Although there is no rest either, there is profound peace.

C. The Surrender of Life
Zec 12:10–11; Gal 3:26–29; Lk 9:18–24

In a Christian context, the cross expresses suffering, but it is the price for giving life. Christ's resurrection is precisely the confirmation of that will for life.

The Cost of Being Disciples

The beginning of Luke's ninth chapter relates that the disciples have been associated in Jesus' task. Now the Lord is asking them: "Who do the crowds say that I am?" (v. 18). It is not just a preparation for the question that will come later. In some way, the image that others have of Christ forms part of our own faith. Besides, it is the result of the testimony that we have given of the Lord. The answer is on the right track: people see Jesus in the line of the prophets (v. 19).

The second question is more direct: "But who do you say that I am?" The question elicits Peter's profession: You are "the Messiah of God" (v. 20). Then the Lord speaks of the rejection he will meet on the part of the leaders of his people. In the corresponding texts of Mark and Matthew, we are told that Peter resists accepting such a cost. Here, Luke simply indicates that Jesus' disciples will also experience the rejection of their own people. This is the meaning of taking up the cross daily (v. 23). The cross implies total surrender. Those who refuse it and seek to be on good terms with everyone or, what is worse, to use their Christian and ecclesial condition to enhance their image, lose their lives. The goal of a disciple, indeed, of the whole church, is service, not survival at any cost.

The Memory of God

The surrender of the Lord earns for us the gift of divine filiation. Daughters and sons are equal before the Father; there are no religious privileges. We know how far we are from this "there is no longer male or female" (Gal 3:28). The foundation of this equality and unity is in Jesus Christ. The cross and the resurrection create deep love relationships among human beings. And so does our own surrender as disciples that will make us see that every human life has the same value. What else can be the meaning of the preference for the poor, except placing on equal footing those that society strives to exclude and despise? This is the task of those who are "heirs according to the promise" (v. 29).

Bearing witness to the Lord, accepting to pay the price of being disciples in the areas of risk in today's world is to recall, as Bartolomé de Las Casas used to say, that "God has a vivid memory of the least and most forgotten people." This means that we have to affirm life wherever poverty and violence are sowing death. It also requires a spirit of forgiveness (Zec 12:10), not in terms of comfort and complicity in our attitudes but with trust in others, in their ability to react to inhuman and criminal actions.

Thirteenth Sunday

A. Apostles for Life
2 Kgs 4:8–11, 14–16; Rom 6:3–4, 8–11; Mt 10:37–42

The text of the gospel we are reading this Sunday is the conclusion of Jesus' instructions to the apostles sent on mission. They apply to all the baptized who are also sent to evangelize, to be missionaries as a consequence of their baptism.

Following Jesus with Love

"Whoever loves father or mother more than me is not worthy of me" (Mt 10:37). With these surprising words, Jesus makes it clear that discipleship entails a unique relationship of predilection and option for him. The family bond with father or mother, son or daughter, which Jesus considers natural and lofty, is not comparable to the love and free option for Jesus, the basis of following him as his disciples. The strong opposition that is established, very much in the Semitic style, can make us avoid what there is in common: love, love of our own people but also a demanding love of the Lord. Following his ways and his teachings (v. 38) supposes loving him and, as a result, it implies an act of freedom: love is found only in terms of freedom.

Although the disciples are given a body of teachings by their master, first and foremost they receive a mission, a meaning for their lives. This is why this mission takes precedence over all other bonds, which are superseded, not denied; rather they are configured in a new way by their fidelity to Jesus Christ and to his mission.

Living in Christ

Following Jesus implies friendship and communion with him. In this way discipleship, which involves taking up the cross of contradiction, is translated into surrender and unconditional service to the poor. For the disciple, it means finding life (v. 39) in an absolute and definitive way. The call of Jesus for unconditional discipleship is not a call to mutilation and negation but instead to the fullest realization and the joy of experiencing a new feeling in being incorporated in the new life of the risen Christ.

One of Paul's classical texts tells us about that life. Baptism incorporates us into the body of Christ. We make Jesus' journey our own. Like him we pass from death to life (Rom 6:3–4). This is our Passover, our passage. In this way, our lives are converted into "lives to God" (v. 10). Death to sin is death to selfishness, to our inability to welcome others. Matthew emphasizes the importance of this welcome: whoever welcomes someone sent by the Lord is welcoming the Lord himself (vv. 40–42). This identification of Jesus with his messengers is the answer to the primacy of God in the disciples' lives. This is what the Shunammite woman did. She did not belong to the chosen people, but she was able to acknowledge Elisha as "a holy man of God" (2 Kgs 4:9), and she welcomed him into her house. Life is union with Christ, the ability to love and to forgive; it is friendship, it can be the birth of a son (v. 16).

B. The Genuineness of Love
Wis 1:13–15; 2:23–24; 2 Cor 8:7–9, 13–15; Mk 5:21–43

Charity is love in terms of sharing. Jesus shows us the way.

From Anonymity to Identity

The leader of the synagogue is mentioned by name, an indication that there may have been a personal contact with him. Jairus is part of the social group which rejects Jesus, but he comes to the Lord as an individual. His daughter is dying, and he asks Jesus to make her well. We are not told what Jesus says, simply that Jairus goes with him (Mk 5:23–24).

A large crowd was also present. Mark inserts another episode, a beautiful and tender scene. A woman is suffering from a disease which, according to the categories of the time, signifies impurity. Moreover, she has spent all she had in trying to be healed (vv. 25–26). Marginalized for being a woman, for being sick, and for being poor, she humbly approaches Jesus; she does not even dare speak to him. Within herself, she thinks that perhaps by touching Jesus' clothes she will be cured without his being aware of it, as if she were trying to steal a miracle from him (vv. 27–28). Her plan proves successful. She touches Jesus' cloak, and she recovers her health. But the relationship with the Lord must always be personal, and the ensuing dialogue completes the meaning of the gesture.

"Who touched my clothes?" (v. 30). The disciples think this is a naive question, because with so many people pressing in, it could have been anyone. But Jesus knows what he is doing, and he gives the woman the opportunity to leave the anonymity to which she had been confined by the marginalization and contempt she was enduring. Jesus does not point her out among the crowd. She is the one who presents herself speaking "in fear and trembling." As the Lord welcomes her as a person who has dignity, she tells him "the whole truth" (v. 33). The Lord values her faith and her courage, telling her, "Your faith has made you well; go in peace" (v. 34). You have done it yourself by the trust you placed in me; now receive peace. He restores her physical health (she is healed) and her place in society (she comes out of her marginalized situation). To have faith is to have life.

God Did Not Make Death

The rest of the episode about Jairus's daughter deals with life. The girl has just died, and the matter seems closed (v. 35). But that does not stop Jesus. Faith is greater than death; in fact, faith is victory over death. Hence, Jesus' words to Jairus: "Do not fear" (v. 36). In the gospel, fear is the opposite of faith. Jesus does not seek the spectacular. On the contrary, he wants to minimize the importance of what he is about to do: "The child is not dead but sleeping" (v. 39). The Lord gives her life. She gets up and — a detail more significant than it seems — Jesus suggests that the girl be given something to eat. This forms part of every person's right to life.

Today the friends of death (Wis 1:16) deny that right to many people in the world. The texts of this Sunday remind us of the will for life that Jesus announces. Thus, before the needy who are suffering, Paul asks the Christians of Corinth to share what they have. With tact, he tells them that he is not giving them a command, he is simply suggesting a concrete gesture to prove "the genuineness of their love" (2 Cor 8:8). This sharing with those in need will bring about "a fair balance" (v. 14). This is what Jesus has done for the sick woman and for Jairus's daughter.

C. Freedom in the Spirit
1 Kgs 19:16, 19–21; Gal 5:1, 13–18; Lk 9:51–62

The common theme of the three readings is clearly discipleship and following Jesus. This involves a mission and a lifestyle that must be those of Jesus.

Three Disciples

Luke narrates Jesus' encounter with three people presented with the concrete possibility of following him as his disciples in a significant context: "as they were going along the road" (v. 57) and, even more precisely, on the way up to Jerusalem. Calling them to discipleship, Jesus has already resolutely decided to live faithfully his journey to the Father. "When the days drew near to be taken up, he set his face to go to Jerusalem" (v. 51). Jerusalem is not only a geographical indication; it is the place where Jesus' journey will meet its goal and completion: the passion, the resurrection, and the ascension. Going up to Jerusalem with determination expresses the free decision of his surrendering faithfully to the will of the Father.

The three encounters point to three aspects necessary for any experience of discipleship or of Christian life. The first one is the reference to Jesus: his person, his mission, and his lifestyle: "the Son of Man has nowhere to lay his head" (v. 58). Discipleship must be unconditional, without security. There are no places or times of refuge or vacation.

In the second place, discipleship does not mean only one condition or one personal lifestyle. It is a mission. A disciple is someone sent: "as for you, go and proclaim the kingdom" (v. 60). We would be totally wrong to claim we are Christians without becoming involved in the evangelizing project. The more intense our relationship and personal friendship with Jesus, the more they make us come out of ourselves to become witnesses and bearers of the kingdom for others.

Finally, Jesus' call is especially urgent. In the symbolic action of throwing his mantle over Elisha, Elijah calls him to become his disciple and servant, but he does allow him to take leave of his parents (1 Kgs 19:20). The urgency of the kingdom, which has already become present in Jesus, demands an immediate and decisive response, without delays or excuses: "No one who puts the hand to the plow and looks back is fit for the kingdom of God" (v. 62).

Free in Christ

The kingdom of God is received as a "gift," in total openness, and it involves all the dimensions and ambits of human life. In his love for all and preferentially for the poor, the Father urgently wants his salvation to penetrate and redeem everything and his kingdom to transform history in a radical way. Jesus' call to discipleship situates the explanation and the foundation of our response, which must be immediate and unconditional, in the salvific context of his mission.

On the other hand, the disciple's determined surrender is an experience of authentic freedom. "For freedom Christ has set us free" (Gal 5:1). For Paul, salvation is synonymous with liberation, but a liberation which makes us "through love become slaves to one another" (v. 13). It is a new way of living and understanding life and freedom: not "according to the flesh," which leads us to selfish closing in on ourselves and even to devouring others, but according to "the Spirit" (v. 16): the Spirit of God who is love, communion, solidarity, and justice. Following Jesus consistently, preparing for the kingdom, and living by the Spirit: this is the most transcendental and urgent option which the Lord continues to offer today to those who want to call themselves and really be Christians.

Fourteenth Sunday

A. Not to the Wise but to Infants
Zec 9:9–10; Rom 8:9, 11–13; Mt 11:25–30

The gospel of Matthew translates a profound ecclesial experience. This perspective helps us to understand his gospel.

The Addressees of Revelation

Today, we are reading a beautiful passage of this gospel. The context is one of prayer, thanksgiving, and the logical question: what is the reason for it? The expression "the wise and intelligent" (v. 25) designates the teachers of the law, the high priests and the scribes, that is to say, the minority holding social and religious power in Jesus' time. They are the ones who sit "on Moses' seat" (Mt 23:2) and who have taken over "the key of knowledge" (Lk 11:52). They are important religious, self-assured people who despise the marginalized and the poor. They consider themselves as the recipients of revelation and experts in its interpretation. By his statement, Jesus is challenging their authority.

On the other side, we have the "infants" (v. 25). The Greek term used by Matthew clearly denotes ignorance. They are "simple people," but not in the sense of being morally and spiritually humble. They are the simple, the ignorant people thought to be incapable of following the appropriate path on their own. They are people who need the guidance of the teachers of the law. The term "infants" is akin to the poor, hungry, afflicted, sinners, sick, sheep without shepherd, children, the "noninvited" mentioned in the gospel, a whole group of people, the "poor of the nation."

It is to them that revelation is first made known. Thus, the religious world of the time is undermined in its very basis: the privileged addressees of God's Word.

The Father's Gracious Will

We are not saying that ignorance is a virtue and that being wise is a flaw. Intelligent people are not necessarily conceited, and ignorant people are not always humble. The preference does not come primarily from moral or religious conditions but rather from a human situation in which God reveals himself, upsetting values and criteria. The despised of this world are those preferred by God, as Jesus Christ reveals to us (v. 27) — a good lesson for anyone trying to use the Lord's word unduly, a word which should lead us into service, not to the intoxication of power. This preference is rooted in God's gracious will, in his gratuitous love (v. 26). This is the motive of Jesus' thanksgiving.

The prayer of the Lord ("I thank you, Father," v. 25) is inviting us to do the same. God's free and gratuitous love is at the root of everything. From that perspective, we can understand that the Lord demands our commitment and solidarity with others. His "yoke is easy" (v. 30) because it is rooted in love, the love of Jesus who will come "humbly," not on a horse like the proud but riding the donkey of the poor (Zec 9:9). We will thus be prepared to live according to the Spirit of love and life rather than according to the flesh of sin and death (Rom 8:11–13).

B. No One Is a Prophet in His Homeland
Ez 2:2–5; 2 Cor 12:7–10; Mk 6:1–6

In our own lives, the Lord speaks to us through people in whom the word of God takes on human clothing. Today's texts present several cases of people sent by God.

Impudent and Stubborn People

Those sent by God are warned that in the course of their mission they will encounter "impudent and stubborn" (Ez 2:4) people who may not listen but at least "they shall know that there has been a prophet among them" (v. 5). Someone who speaks in God's name, this is the meaning of the Hebrew term *nabi*, which we translate by "prophet."

The prophet runs into the resistance of those who refuse to hear the word which invites them to leave their old security and to change their ways. The Son of God "was amazed at their unbelief" (Mk 6:6). The people of "his hometown" (v. 1) do not believe that one of their own can reveal the demands of God's love. "Is not this the carpenter, the son of Mary...and are not his sisters here with us?" (v. 3). They know him; therefore he cannot tell them anything new.

Puebla tells us about the "evangelizing potential of the poor." To the evangelical testimony of the poor of our country, the spiritual children of those who did not believe in Jesus will now say, "Are not these peasants who barely know how to speak Spanish? What can people who spend their lives complaining, not working, tell us?" We know them; therefore, we cannot expect anything from them.

Power in Weakness

The quality of a gospel proclamation cannot be measured by its immediate acceptance. What is of prime importance is the fidelity of those sent to the mission entrusted to them. Today's texts tell us about vocations: Ezekiel, Paul, and Jesus. God gives them a mission which is to be effective. But this effectiveness can take on surprising paths.

The weakness of those sent reveals the power of the Spirit present in them. The Lord shows his power in Paul's weakness (2 Cor 12:9). This has nothing to do with liking contrasts and paradoxes. This is the way of a loving and tender God who invites us but who does not crush us. The human weakness of those sent creates a space of freedom; their listeners may decide for or against them. They want the Lord to reveal himself only in grandiose actions and miracles; this would save them the trouble of discerning when and through whom the word is revealed.

For those who are sent, this is not easy. The "thorns in the flesh" (v. 7) are there to remind them that they are only people who are sent. We all ask that bad times pass quickly, and we do that more than three times (v. 8). We are especially hurt when the testimony — not without defects and omissions — we are trying to give is not understood. Yet, this helps us to return humbly to the sources of the entrusted task, to purify and correct the motives of our actions. Besides, as Paul tells us, it is when we appear weak that we are strong (v. 10).

C. Traveling Light
Is 66:10–14; Gal 6:14–18; Lk 10:1–12, 17–20

We continue to read the gospel of Luke. Starting with last Sunday, the texts belong to what Luke considers Jesus' journey to Jerusalem, the center of the religious and political power.

The Disciples' Freedom

We read in chapter 9 that during his Galilean ministry Jesus associates the twelve to his mission. Now, on his way to Jerusalem, Jesus is sharing his mission with the mysterious seventy-two disciples. We do not know much about them, but beyond the number (undoubtedly symbolic) their presence proves that the Lord's message is beginning to elicit demanding calls to fidelity. The instructions which Jesus gives them have inspired many missionary endeavors in the course of history, and they continue to be guidelines for us today.

These instructions have a central nucleus: the disciples' liberty. "Carry no purse, no bag, no sandals" (v. 4), in other words, do not trust your possessions, do not rely on power. Otherwise, you will not be able to be witnesses of peace (*shalom*), to accept to eat what is offered to you, and you will not know how to give life to others. In short, we will not be able to announce that the kingdom is at hand. To the extent that, as individual Christians and as church, we are attached and we are bound to the possessions and powers of this world, we are tempted by compromise and convenience. Then we attempt to preach a gospel which does not upset the powerful. The Lord knows that in Jerusalem the leaders of his people and the occupying power are going to reject him and mistreat him, but that does not make him renounce his freedom as the one sent by the Father. Instead, he is offering that same freedom to his disciples.

The New Creation

The age in which we live takes us to the root of our Christian being. Today, more than powerful means, we need great freedom to proclaim the reign of life, love, and justice. Our silence in the face of what is happening, our being bogged down in petty questions, the insipid and uncommitted calls to union without taking into account the diverse responsibilities and unjust inequalities, are all expressions of the fear of losing our privileges and of speaking clearly. Such attitudes show that our being settled in society, our baggage, weighs more than the gospel's demands.

Paul concludes his letter to the Galatians by proclaiming the reason of his great freedom as an apostle: Christ's cross. The cross was precisely the consequence of the freedom of Jesus, whose language was a clear yes and a clear no. "The new creation" (Gal

6:15) is the only thing that must count for us. If we know how to bring it forth, "it shall be known that the hand of the Lord is with his servants" (Is 66:14).

Fifteenth Sunday

A. The Effectiveness of the Word
Is 55:10–11; Rom 8:18–23; Mt 13:1–23

The heart of Jesus' message is the kingdom. The parables are a special way to help us know its significance.

Difficulty in Accepting the Kingdom

The thirteenth chapter occupies an important place in the gospel of Matthew. The preceding chapter dealt with the rejection of the mission of Jesus. In this chapter Matthew seeks to explain why some people can argue about and ignore the kingdom and others accept it. Today's passage brings us the most developed parable of this chapter. The two major groups of listeners of Matthew's gospel are present: the disciples and the Pharisees. Jesus explains to the former why the kingdom is not announced in a dazzling manner.

Jesus is speaking to great crowds (v. 2). He does not offer some mysterious teaching; instead he is addressing everyone. But certain conditions are required to understand the teaching. Four cases are presented. In the first three, the word is not accepted. On the contrary, in the last case, the result is good and varied (vv. 3–8). The failures of the seed are related to the difficult scenes of chapter 12, the lack of success comes from those refusing to hear the word. However, it is not all failure; the word is also welcomed and it gives fruit.

The parable is explained in the final part of our text. Very few parables have a commentary in the gospels. The disciples are concerned: why does Jesus speak in parables, they wonder (v. 10). The sharp phrases of the Lord's answer point to one thing: his preaching is rejected by those whose hearts have grown dull, namely, people who say one thing and do another: they are the Pharisees. They are actual people in Jesus' day. But in Matthew's gospel, Pharisaism is denounced as a danger for everyone hearing the word. In fact, it is a danger for disciples of all times: receiving the seed and failing to make it bear fruit.

Bread to Eat

Disciples are those in whom the word bears fruit, those who translate the kingdom of love into a permanent gesture of solidarity with others. Our worst and most subtle rejection of the kingdom is our pretending to accept it while denying it by our conduct: the parable and its explanation make this very clear. The power of the message is in God; if we welcome it, it will become nourishment in our lives, "bread to the eater" (Is 55:10). The church fulfills its role as a sign of the kingdom when it puts into practice the gospel of which it is the bearer. If it does not do that, it runs the risk of falling into the Pharisaism mentioned in Matthew's gospel. If we welcome the word in a consistent way, we will share "in the freedom of the glory of the children of God" (Rom 8:21). This is freedom to love, a profound experience of God in a commitment in solidarity with others. Disciples are and ought to be free people.

B. Prophesy and Poverty
Am 7:12–15; Eph 1:3–12; Mk 6:7–13

Christian life is lived on a daily basis, in what is ordinary, like the present liturgical season.

Trusting People, Not Money

A few chapters ago, Mark was telling us that Jesus established the twelve "to be with him and to be sent out to proclaim the message" (Mk 3:14). Now this is becoming a reality. Jesus is not well received in his hometown (Mk 6:1), and so he starts to teach in the neighboring villages. He seeks to complete his mission by sending his disciples to announce the good news. Going "two by two" (v. 7) is a traditional custom of the Jewish people to bring an important message. The Lord gives them instructions, the spirit of which continues to be essential for the bearers of the gospel.

The mission has to be carried out with simplicity and poverty. They are to wear sandals and carry a staff, "no bread, no bag, no money in their belts" (v. 8). Taking two tunics is a sign of wealth. Thus, the messengers of the kingdom are to travel light, taking only what is essential. In parallel texts, Matthew (10:9–15) and Luke (9:1–6) add or subtract a few things from the list. What matters is the meaning of the instruction, not the letter. Nothing must disturb the proclamation of the kingdom. It cannot be presented from the power and security which money or social position gives. We have to allow the gospel to appear in all its power. Jesus' followers will depend on the welcome given by those whom they address (v. 10) rather than on social advantages.

Not Being "Professionals"

The poverty of the messengers is a condition required by the message itself. If there is something difficult in the lives of Christians and of the church, it is precisely this. We tend to take precautions and security measures, to settle in and enjoy privileges which, paradoxically, may come in our society from the evangelizing task itself. But the Lord's call is permanent, and it brings us to the source and the meaning of the mission. Prophets have to confront this world's powers when they mistreat the people. If they do not listen, we will have to shake off the dust from our feet (Mk 6:11). Amos has a clear awareness that he is a message bearer. To the threat of expulsion he receives, he responds simply: "I am not a professional prophet ("I am no prophet, nor a prophet's son," 7:14). I am merely a member of this people, but I have received a responsibility from the Lord (the Lord said to me "Go, prophesy" v. 15). He fulfills his mission whether or not it pleases the powerful. In that task, he trusts only God, not money.

The mission we receive comes from an election "before the foundation of the world" (Eph 1:4). Being children of God is a grace as well as a responsibility for which we will have to account before God. Only a profound sense of God, the rejection of every social or economic privilege, an authentic personal poverty, a "nonprofessional" practice of our evangelizing role will enable us to give a testimony leading to conversion (Mk 6:12).

C. The Heart of the Gospel
Dt 30:10–14; Col 1:15–20; Lk 10:25–37

Today's texts bring us to the essence: faith in God is expressed through love.

Who Is My Neighbor?

This Sunday's readings are introduced by some apparently re-assuring words from Deuteronomy: "this command that I am commanding you today is not too hard for you, nor is it too far away" (v. 11). God does not require anything superhuman. In the final analysis, God asks only something very human, namely, as to love: first love "God with all your heart" (Dt 6:5) and immediately afterwards, love "your neighbor as yourself." The law and all the commandments are contained in this unique and encompassing love.

The lawyer questioning Jesus already knows that. The problem comes in terms of concretizing: "And who is my neighbor?" (Lk 10:29). If neighbor means one who is "nearby," how far does this proximity extend? With the parable of the Samaritan, Jesus does not respond with a complicated theory but with a simple comparison. The question has not been adequately posed. The condition of neighbor is not established by a previous situation of closeness based on kinship, friendship, or similar ideology. Instead, what makes us neighbors is our generous attending to people in need; this brings us close to them. Hence, Jesus' final question, this time adequately posed: "Which of these three, do you think, was a neighbor to the man who fell into the hands of the robbers?" The lawyer has to respond: "the one who showed him mercy" (vv. 36–37).

The focus given by Jesus to the love of our neighbor does not restrict the ability to love to the limits of what is close and known to us. Therefore, it is not according to the popular saying: "Charity begins at home." According to the gospel, charity begins with those who are suffering or in need, whether at home or elsewhere.

Go and Do Likewise

The parable makes other specific points. First of all, the love of neighbor is genuine human love moved at the sight of someone who is mistreated or injured. This is why love is concretized in an initiative which is an intelligent and effective action: the Samaritan personally bandages the man's wounds, takes him to an inn, and pays to have him well taken care of. Effectiveness is clearly required by authentic evangelical love of neighbor. Responding by doing anything to get out of trouble does not suffice. We have to do what a careful analysis of the need (personal, social, material, affective, etc.) demands as an appropriate response and solution for this need.

Love of neighbor, in the same degree as the love of God, of which it is an inseparable expression, is realized in practice. Addressing the lawyer, Jesus concludes with a categorical: "Go and do likewise" (v. 37). Love is verified in active solidarity, and thus the theoretical difficulty finds its specific solution. For that to happen, like the Samaritan we have to go out of our way and embrace the path of our neighbor.

Taking the love of neighbor as the criterion of Christian life, that is to say, being moved by the suffering and need of others and doing something constructive and effective about it, does not exceed our human strength (Dt 30:11). However, it is tremendously demanding, and it is the sign of the new life of God's children. Insertion into Christ and the grace of the one who is "head," "beginning," and "firstborn" (Col 1:18) make possible a new historical dynamism that can bring forth personal relationships and forms of social life founded on love-solidarity striving for the good of all, starting with a prioritized just solution for the needs of the weakest and most forgotten. The great Christian challenge to serve the cause of peace is to make the love of neighbor the efficacious instrument of historical and liberating transformation.

Sixteenth Sunday

A. The Kingdom and the Meaning of Human History
Wis 12:13, 16–19; Rom 8:26–27; Mt 13:24–43

As we have already mentioned, the thirteenth chapter of Matthew's gospel presents several parables on the kingdom. All of them emphasize that the presence of the kingdom in history involves a process. The kingdom does not arrive suddenly: we have to accept it, an acceptance which takes place in time.

Discernment

One of Matthew's frequent themes is that of judgment (Mt 7:21–23 and 25:31–46), that is, the time when things will be clear, when our lives will appear as we want to write them with our deeds. This is also the focus of the parable of the weeds. The disciples' request for an explanation underscores its importance (v. 36). This request also reminds us that the more incisive and definitive the message, the more difficulty we have in understanding it. In the end, there will be no evasions: those who say yes to the Lord and to others will enter the kingdom, and those who refuse to love by way of concrete deeds will be rejected (vv. 24–30). The Lord will search our hearts (Rom 8:27).

Wheat or weeds: there is no room for ambiguous or luke-warm positions. When we are confronted with violations of the most basic human rights, it is impossible to be merely spectators. Either we opt for life, beginning with the lives of the least and most insignificant people, or we are accomplices of death. The day of judgment is already shedding light on our lives now. The Lord is demanding and kind; he does not overwhelm us by his power (Wis 12:16).

But once again, the final stage will come only at the end of a process. The Lord does not suppress the weeds immediately; his call to conversion is ongoing. We are constantly called to be the wheat giving life.

From What Is Small

The beginning of the kingdom can be as tiny as a mustard seed. If we are not attentive to what its smallness contains, we run the risk of not appreciating it. On the contrary, if we make sure that good soil welcomes it and nourishes it, the seed will grow and become alive. It will also give life: the birds will make their nests there and new forms of life will be added (vv. 31–32). Time will bring things to maturity, yet everything will have started because we were able to discern the kingdom of heaven and the God of the kingdom in what seemed insignificant in human history. God is concealed behind the face of the poor. The kingdom slips out of the hands of those who pay attention only to the powerful of this world.

This is not just a matter of growth, but also of the transfor-mation of history. The kingdom is the yeast which leavens the dough, giving it new life. What appeared lifeless becomes alive; what was insipid acquires flavor. What seemed dead is trans-formed into nourishment; it gives life (v. 33). That transformation also requires time; it takes place gradually at a rhythm which we have to respect. The life which the yeast brings forth is always present, ready to change things from their roots, to transform what seems like insignificant dust into bread that is nourishing. Welcoming the yeast of the Lord's grace in our lives means accepting a transformation which makes us nourishment and service to our neighbor.

B. Like Sheep without a Shepherd
Jer 23:1–6; Eph 2:13–18; Mk 6:30–34

Last's Sunday gospel presented the mission which Jesus conferred on his disciples. The gospel text for today probes the theme of the shepherd, the person who has a responsibility toward others.

The "Poor of the Land"
After completing one stage of their task, the disciples gather around the Lord to assess what they have accomplished (Mk 6:30). Jesus invites them firmly and tenderly "to rest a while" (v. 31). Because of so many requests, "they had no leisure even to eat" (v. 31), as stated by Mark who is always attentive to that fact. This is a human aspect of the Lord which must be appreciated in all its simplicity and significance.

But as all those who take their pastoral work seriously know, there is no "deserted place" (v. 32) for people who have to bear witness to the gospel. People are coming from everywhere, even arriving ahead of the disciples at the place where they were going (v. 33). Once again, Mark presents Jesus' deeply human reaction. When he sees the crowds approaching, eager to hear the word, the Lord "had compassion for them" (v. 33). That is the end of the promised and deserved rest. Sensitive to the people who are "like sheep without a shepherd," the Lord "began to teach them many things" (v. 34).

These sheep, without a shepherd, are the poor of Palestine at the time. The "poor of the land," as they are called in the Bible, are considered ignorant and hopeless by the scribes and the Pharisees, poor because they are sinners, as the powerful and the leaders used to say. But Jesus looks after them first. He has come especially for those who are last according to society. Interrupting his legitimate rest, Jesus pays attention to them. No one is interested in them, yet they are the ones whom Jesus favors.

The Evil Shepherds

The text from Jeremiah shows us God rejecting shepherds who scatter instead of uniting, people who show no concern for the needs of those who are under their care. They have the responsibility of shepherds but they are not fulfilling their mission (Jer 23:2). Turning their backs on the people to whom they are sent, they use the privileges and honors with which they themselves have wanted to surround the responsibility the Lord has entrusted to them. Busy with "their evil doings" (v. 2), their schemings, they forget why they are where they are and they would not dream of shortening their rest to attend to the "poor of the land."

God's response is very swift. God himself will take up the task and, gathering the scattered sheep (v. 3), he will raise up new shepherds to care for them (v. 4). The model of these new shepherds will be the one sent by God to "execute justice and righteousness in the land" (v. 5). In the Bible, justice and righteousness express the will of God. This is the reason why the one sent will be called "Lord, our righteousness" (v. 6).

He will "create in himself one new humanity in place of the two, thus making peace" (Eph 2:15). As Christians, this is what we are called to do, to have compassion for (that is, "feel with") the poor, not to betray the mission the Lord confers upon us, to build a peace based on justice and thus to open for others "access in one Spirit to the Father" (Eph 2:18).

C. The Right to Be a Woman Disciple
Gn 18:1–10; Col 1:24–28; Lk 10:38–42

The mystery, hidden for generations and now revealed, is that God loves us freely and gratuitously. God's love is addressed to everyone without exception.

The Lady of the House

Luke has just told us that being a neighbor means going out of our way and approaching (getting close to) others (Lk 10:29–37). This time he presents a short and wonderful scene filled with an amazing content. Here we find two sisters with whom we are very familiar, thanks to John's gospel (chapters 11 and 12).

On his way to Jerusalem, Jesus is welcomed by Martha. In Aramaic (the language used by Jesus), her name means "the lady of the house." In fact, Luke specifies that Martha is the one who "welcomed him into her house" (v. 38). In doing so, in looking after Jesus, Martha makes him her neighbor. Then the text mentions Mary, who may have helped Martha in her tasks, but at that point Mary is sitting at the Lord's feet, listening to him. Showing interest in what a person has to say is also a way of welcoming that person. But the matter is not that simple. In Jesus' day, teachers of the law deemed that it was not the place of women to delve into the teachings of God's law. This was the task and the responsibility of men. With the Lord's approval, Mary is breaking that rule. Sitting at the Lord's feet (v. 39), she claims a right as a human person: to know directly, from the lips of Jesus, the "mystery that has been hidden throughout the ages" (Col 1:26), the right to be a disciple.

With the trust that friendship gives, Martha addresses a reproach to Jesus (v. 40). Affectionately, as indicated by repeating her name, Jesus criticizes her for being a prisoner of what she considers to be the proper role of a woman and lady of the house. Jesus calls her to break away from that concept situating a woman in a condition of a person confined to housework (v. 41). Like Mary, Martha must claim and fully occupy her place as a disciple of the Lord.

Few Things Are Necessary

This is not a question of Mary the contemplative opposed to Martha the active one (the parable of the Samaritan has just emphasized the importance of concrete gestures). In Christian life, both dimensions are essential. Jesus is responsive to Martha's attentions, but he brings her to see that she must not indefinitely overexert herself in such tasks. As a woman, she is also entitled to have other concerns.

Few things are necessary. To satisfy our hunger, we do not need to have a well-set table; what is essential suffices. In these matters, too, we have to "travel light"; otherwise our attention is distracted from what is really important. Mary has chosen "the better part": listening to the word of the Lord and bearing witness to it. House tasks must not suppress such interest. This is a woman's right which is still not fully recognized among us. By his words and deeds, Jesus liberates women from a concept which maintains them in a secondary role as mere housewives. The friendship, which always presupposes equality, of Jesus for Martha and Mary enables them to find themselves as persons: a lesson for us today.

Seventeenth Sunday

A. The Christian Scribe
1 Kgs 3:5–12; Rom 8:28–30; Mt 13:44–52

This is the conclusion of the parable chapter in Matthew's gospel. The author is leaving his own imprint in this conclusion.

The Absoluteness of the Kingdom

Two short parables underscore the unique value of the kingdom (vv. 44–46). Both the treasure and the pearl express what the kingdom must be for disciples: something absolute. Its demand is radical; everything else must be left behind or, rather, placed in relation to the kingdom, in other words, it must be relativized. Finding the "hidden treasure" or the "pearl" is not the outcome of calculated work. The parables suggest that it is something that happens by chance, a matter of luck. It is a simple way of reminding us that we are in the presence of something gratuitous, not something deserved. However, when the gift arrives, our response has to be selling all we have (vv. 44 and 45) in exchange for it.

Joy (v. 44) is the reaction which corresponds to the grace of the kingdom. Selling all we have does not mean doing that begrudgingly, as if it were a sacrifice. It should be a spontaneous gesture, something we do gladly because we have discovered something which gives meaning to our lives. Everything falls into place and acquires its own value when we start from the perspective of the kingdom. Being Christian, having a responsibility in the church, cannot be a pretext for presumption. No part of it is private property: it is a gift we receive from the Lord to be at the service of others.

Understanding to Discern What Is Right

The following parable takes up the theme of a previous parable in the same chapter (vv. 36–43). The gift of the kingdom calls us to discernment. In the presence of the kingdom, people are divided into those who welcome it and those who refuse to accept it. Once again, there is nothing in between. We need "understanding to discern what is right" (1 Kgs 3:12). We need discernment to perceive that "all things work together for good for those who love God" (Rom 8:28).

After indicating what the kingdom is like, the Lord will ask his followers: "Have you understood this?" (Mt 13:51). In other words, Jesus is referring to all the comparisons he has presented. Jesus praises the Christian scribe for his affirmative answer. The scribe has been able to discern and to encounter the treasure of the kingdom in his life, discipleship. In his life, he strives to fulfill the will of love revealed by the kingdom. Because he puts the Lord's designs into practice, he is able to understand God's teachings and to "bring out of his treasure what is new and what is old" (v. 52). The evangelist who is constantly asking that our words and our actions be in harmony, Matthew himself is an example of a Christian scribe (v. 52). He is someone who knows Jesus' message from within because he has first lived it. Hence, his words do not sound hollow, as is so often the case in the church when we forget to ask God: "Give me an understanding mind to govern your people" (1 Kgs 3:9).

B. More Sharing Than Multiplying
2 Kgs 4:42–44; Eph 4:1–6; Jn 6:1–15

The word of God is bread which nourishes but bread is also the word of God.

The Word of the Bread

Jesus' gestures are called signs in John's gospel, signs indeed because they refer to something more profound, to what is signified. These gestures draw a large crowd (Jn 6:1–2). Jesus is with his disciples, and he sees the people preoccupied by the hunger they must feel. Perhaps with too much common sense, Philip points out that they do not have enough money to buy bread, two hundred denarii would not be enough (a denarius was a day's wage for a laborer; see v. 7). Thanks to a boy, Andrew timidly indicates that they do have something, though it seems insufficient. It is not much, five loaves and two fish (vv. 8–9). It is really very little, but we have to know how to give from our poverty. Jesus works through his disciples, asking them to make the people sit down on the grass. There are about five thousand present. Making the people sit down (we are told three times that they sat down) means treating them as free persons and with dignity, not like servants, forced to eat standing and hurriedly to be at their master's disposal. The Lord takes the few loaves they have; he gives thanks and distributes the loaves (v. 11). We are not told that he multiplies the loaves. Yet there is enough for everyone because of the boundless love inspiring the gesture. All the people are satisfied.

In the first reading, we learn that Elijah has done the same thing. He also asks his servant to feed the people and receives the same answer: it is not sufficient. The prophet repeats the command. All the people eat, and they even have some leftovers. Sharing bread is expressing the love of God; it is the word of God. In these days of neoliberal economy, the number of people excluded from the system is growing, people who have no part in it or in its benefits. They are expendable; in fact, they are an obstacle for the proper functioning of the economy. We say that there are no possibilities, or very few, of satisfying their most basic needs. The invitation to know how to share must prompt us to build a society that does not exclude anyone.

Life Is Communion

According to John, all the people eat and there is food left over. Love always means abundance. The fragments fill twelve baskets. This is a significant number: twelve refers to the twelve tribes of Israel, to the twelve apostles, to the entire people (Jn 6:12–13). But the people misunderstand; they do not see what they should have seen in Jesus (v. 15). They need time to understand. Gradually, the signs of the Lord will become clearer to them, but for the time being Jesus withdraws. Remaining are Jesus' loving gesture in sharing the bread and our mission to continue that gesture throughout history with all people. The twelve baskets set on the grass are calling us to continue Jesus' deed.

Paul clarifies the meaning of the Lord's message. The love of God, revealed in Jesus, forms us into one body, one hope (Eph

4:1–6). This implies mutual service in the different parts of the body. Therefore we have to ask ourselves: as Christians, are we ready for this in our torn-apart world? However little we may have, are we willing to share? Sharing bread is the word of life.

C. Teaching How to Pray
Gn 18:20–32; Col 2:12–14; Lk 11:1–13

The readings for this Sunday invite us to reflect on the dimension of praying in Christian life, an attitude of trust in God, the kind Father always ready to listen to his children.

Praying to Our Father

Luke delights in frequently presenting Jesus praying. In all the decisive moments of Jesus' life, Luke never forgets to point this out. Jesus' frequent prayer and his unique way of starting it, "Abba, Father," is the best sign of the content of his spirituality as a filial experience. It is trust and surrender to the Father and his will, even in the paradoxically darkest situations. Jesus' last words before his death, "Father, into your hands I commend my spirit," are a succinct summary of his daily surrender.

It is not surprising, therefore, that the disciples who have observed Jesus want to learn: "Lord, teach us to pray, as John taught his disciples" (v. 1). Jesus is a spiritual master precisely because he also shares his own prayer with his disciples. The content of this prayer is what we call the Our Father. Luke presents a shorter version than Matthew's with a few variations. He keeps the initial invocation "Father" and the five basic petitions. In prayer, we must ask that "your kingdom come" and become a reality for us with all its consequences: daily bread, forgiveness, and victory over temptation. The Our Father is the norm and guide of all Christian prayer. When what we ask for is not part of these petitions, that means we are neither praying to the Father nor praying as Jesus has taught us.

The Open Door

With the short parable of the "persistent friend" and the advice accompanying it — "Ask and it will be given you; search and you will find; knock and the door will be opened for you" (v. 9) — Jesus indicates an important aspect of prayer. It must be constant and persistent, not so much because God needs to be convinced but because in this way we freely show our sole trust in the Father in the midst of our needs. The Father's door is always open for us (v. 7). This is why the first reading shows us Abraham insisting with the Lord and interceding for the inhabitants of Sodom and Gomorrah with bold and trusting freedom, and God generously grants his request (Gn 18:23–32).

Finally, starting with a comparison ("you, who are evil") and using a process widespread in rabbinical reasoning going from the least to the most important, Jesus categorically proclaims the ultimate motivation of trusting prayer: "how much more will the heavenly Father give the Holy Spirit to those who ask him" (Lk 11:13). Differently from us who are "evil," the heavenly Father is good and gives us not only "good things" but his great gift: the Holy Spirit. Paul says to the Colossians, the love of the Father "made you alive together with him, when he forgave us all our trespasses" (Col 2:13). In the grace of his love and the abundance of his revelation, God's gift far surpasses what we do not even dare to ask for.

Eighteenth Sunday

A. Sharing Bread
Is 55:1–3; Rom 8:35, 37–39; Mt 14:13–21

Matthew offers us two versions of what is called the multiplication of the loaves. Today's gospel presents the first one, which corresponds better to the parallel texts in the other three gospels.

Listening and Eating

To speak about bread is to speak of daily nourishment in its most basic and necessary aspect. We learn this from the first words of our lives as children. At the same time, as we also know, there is not bread on every table. Many people live a cruel experience of hunger from an early age. The Bible shows us a tender God who is attentive to our fundamental needs.

On the day of the Lord, no one will lack nourishment. At that time, all our needs will be fully met. In fact, as Isaiah tells us, no one will have to pay to eat: "Come, buy wine and milk without money and without price" (v. 1). In satisfying this vital need, money is useless, and it even perverts the process. Utopia? Maybe, though not in the sense of something illusory and deceitful but rather as a project in history which upsets the present order. What is abnormal is having to pay — and still worse, not have the money to pay for it — for something to which we are fully entitled.

Be that as it may, Isaiah's passage clearly reminds us that God's promises are promises of life, a life which should be lived in delight. Thus, the Lord invites us to listen and eat well, to delight in "rich food" (v. 2). As John Paul II said to a million hungry people in Villa El Salvador (Lima), every person is entitled to having bread on the table, including "you that have no money" (v. 1).

Being Companions

Matthew's text reiterates this will for life. Jesus has compassion for those who are suffering from lack of bread. God does not desire hunger. Oftentimes hunger expresses situations in which the right to life is trampled upon. Jesus makes those who have followed him his companions; in other words, he shares bread with them. This is what the term "companion" means. "Taking the loaves... he gave them to the disciples and the disciples gave them to the crowds" (v. 19). The Lord is inviting us to do just that, to share our bread, to make the poor, and indeed every person, our companions in the journey to the Father, sisters and brothers in the project of building a more human, just, and loving society. Before the constant deterioration of the conditions of life of so many people today, that project becomes more urgent and more realistic contrary to what we may think in our resignation and skepticism.

In this way, nothing will be able to separate us from the "love of God in Christ Jesus our Lord" (Rom 8:39). It is that love which impels us to encounter others.

B. The Works God Wants
Ex 16:2–4, 12–15; Eph 4:17, 20–24; Jn 6:24–35

Knowing God involves a long process which requires profound fidelity to avoid fears and the temptation not to go all the way.

The Bread of Life

John's sixth chapter begins with the account of the multiplication of the loaves. Today's text probes the depth of the meaning of this gesture of Jesus. As usual for John, this is a "sign" which points to more universal realities (Jn 6:26). The Lord's actions express the gratuitous love of God. The entire passage focuses on the theme of the works.

People are looking for Jesus but the Lord wants them to understand the totality of his message on which God the Father has set his seal (v. 27). The people are open to this teaching. At first, they may have followed Jesus only because he was giving them the food they needed, yet they were willing to perform the works demanded by God (v. 28). Jesus makes them see that this has to start by believing in him "whom God has sent" (v. 29). This is the work that God wants: faith in Christ; from that faith all the other works receive their full meaning. Then the Lord presents himself as "the bread of life" (v. 35), of all of life. The manna in the wilderness which their ancestors had eaten (vv. 31–32) and the food that they receive from the hands of Jesus are works, "signs" that express the bread which "gives life to the world" (v. 33). We have to believe in him. The rest of chapter 6 revolves around that idea.

The Fear of Freedom

The journey to the God of life is not an easy task. We tend to get lost along the way and we are discouraged by the efforts we have to make. On their way to the promised land, at one point the Jewish people turned against Moses (Ex 16:2). Their difficulties made them yearn for a mediocre but familiar existence. Freedom frightened them, and they wanted to go back to the security of oppression and mistreatment. This is the temptation of every believer. This is why Jesus repeats to his disciples: "Do not be afraid" (Jn 6:20).

Fear characterizes the "old self" (Eph 4:22). The circumstances in which we live may be stormy, perhaps we feel that the ground under our feet is slipping away, the forces of death seem to have the upper hand and, as the Bible says, we think that evil people are about to asphyxiate the just. In spite of this, if we do not want to head for our own destruction (v. 22), we have to accept being renewed in the Spirit (v. 23). Although we may not see the way clearly, God is working so that we may clothe ourselves with the "new self" (v. 24) and continue to hope.

The works of Jesus enable us to know that God is life. Our own works will make others know that believing in God means not being afraid and that it is necessary to continue on the journey to the promise of freedom and life.

C. The Kingdom Is First
Eccl 1:2, 2:21–23; Col 3:1–5, 9–11; Lk 12:13–21

We always have to establish priorities in our lives. Today's texts remind us of the criteria to follow.

Greed Is Idolatry

This text is found only in Luke. There are no parallels in Mark or Matthew. The passage begins abruptly. Jesus has just given important explanations of his message to a crowd (Lk 12:1). Suddenly someone asks him a question often formulated to a religious authority (v. 13). Jesus refuses to take sides because this is not his field (v. 14) but he does go to the core of the matter: one should guard against becoming a prisoner of greed and of endless ambition (v. 15). Referring to greed, Luke brings us the same term that Paul uses in our second reading. He calls greed "idolatry" (Col 3:5; see also Eph 5:5). In fact, idolatry consists in putting our trust in, giving our lives to something or someone other than God.

The text of Luke rises against that would-be security or, more exactly, against that inversion of values. This is why Luke relates a parable intended to illustrate what is said in verse 15. The heart of these lines is made up of a monologue, and this is significant. It deals with a rich man absorbed in his thoughts and very pleased with the outcome of his crops. Not only does he put his trust in his possessions, but he is ready to use them exclusively for his own benefit. He says to himself: "relax, eat, drink, and be merry" (v. 19).

The intervention of God makes the man see how foolish and misguided his plans are. There is no reference to the man's destiny in the afterlife. The parable does not claim that his riches bring him eternal condemnation; this is not the point here. What is at stake is a question of priorities and of the meaning of life. There is a rejection of the accumulation of riches for oneself because this is not in accordance with God's will of selfless and generous love (v. 21).

Centering Our Lives on Christ

The first readings for today also deal with priorities. The letter to the Colossians advises us to set our minds "on things that are above, not on things that are on earth" (v. 2). What is above is Christ and his message. Christ must be the center of our lives; this is what "setting our minds" means. In order to do that, we have to strip off "the old self with its practices" (v. 9). The old self, present in us, is that part of us which does not know the testimony and the teaching of the Lord, and as a result confuses its goals and the meaning of life, becoming absorbed in self and personal benefits.

The text invites us to clothe ourselves "with the new self which is being renewed in knowledge" (v. 10). This involves a process, an ongoing renewal expressed in works, in the same way as the old self was expressed in works (v. 12). For that new self, "Christ is all in all" (v. 11). Everything else is "vanity of vanities" (Eccl 1:2). Likewise, the author of Ecclesiastes invites us to have discernment to put order in our lives. Human beings fully realize themselves in solidarity with others. On the contrary, they are diminished as persons and as believers if their purposes do not go beyond self-satisfaction. Striving for the kingdom and welcoming it liberate us from a paltry and diminished worldview and allow us to journey with ease in the realm of love and generosity.

Nineteenth Sunday

A. Jesus Is Coming to Our Encounter
1 Kgs 19:9, 11–13; Rom 9:1–6; Mt 14:22–33

We often wonder where we can encounter God. But in fact it is God who comes to our encounter. The readings for this Sunday allude to the mountain, the storm, the gentle breeze as possible situations revealing God. The gospel shows us that even in our moments of "little faith" the Lord responds to our call by making himself present.

Take Heart, It Is I

Matthew's account emphasizes a contrast between Jesus praying alone on the mountain, the traditional attitude and place of encounter with God, and the disciples sailing across the lake in a storm in the middle of the night. "By this time the boat battered by the waves was far from the land, for the wind was against them" (v. 24), expressions symbolizing the insecurity and the disturbance which make a peaceful encounter with the Lord difficult.

In the middle of the night, Jesus "came walking toward them on the sea" (v. 25). The disciples who were not expecting him in that way "were terrified, saying, 'It is a ghost!' And they cried out in fear" (v. 26). In his confusion, Peter even dares ask for a proof — "Lord, if it is you, command me to come to you on the water" (v. 28) — without realizing that there is no proof for faith in the presence of God without our own commitment and risk taking. The objective of Jesus' presence is not to remove the difficulties of life and the darkness of situations but rather to offer trust to move forward in the midst of them: "Take heart, it is I; do not be afraid" (v. 27). The proximity of Jesus and of his word requires our faith to recognize him as the savior.

This is why, midway between reproaching and encouraging him, Jesus says to Peter: "you of little faith, why did you doubt?" (v. 31). As an incentive for us, this "little faith" does not invalidate our condition as disciples. It does allow us to open up to the full recognition of the Lord's presence: "And those in the boat worshiped him saying, Truly you are the Son of God" (v. 33).

A Gentle Breeze

Even for the disciples, faith is a process open to more in-depth encounters with the Lord. It is really essential not to pigeonhole the forms of God's presence and passing in our lives. The first reading refers to what God has told Elijah: "Go out and stand on the mountain before the Lord, for the Lord is about to pass by" (v. 11). However, God is neither in the great wind, nor in the earthquake, nor in the fire, circumstances of the known theophanies in the Bible; rather God is in a tiny whispering sound (1 Kgs 19:11–12). There are no circumstances or situations which are closed to the experience of God. There is only one seeming prerequisite: getting out of ourselves and standing before God to discover his passing in our lives and in the events of reality. This passing can be as discreet as a gentle breeze which is neither overpowering nor crushing.

In the second reading (Rom 9:1–5), Paul deplores that his compatriots, who have received so many signs of God's presence — such as the filial adoption, the glory, the covenants, the law, the worship, the promises and the patriarchs — do not recognize Christ, who was announced and prefigured in those signs. All of salvation history was pointing to Christ, and he is the key for reading and understanding God's passing in history. This is what we strive to do when we gather as a community to examine the events of our lives in the light of faith: to discern the footprints of the Lord in order to follow him more closely.

B. The Humanity of Jesus
1 Kgs 19:4–8; Eph 4:30–5:2; Jn 6:41–51

The gospel reading continues to present this essential text from John's sixth chapter.

Everyone Is Called to Be a Disciple

The discourse — the controversy — of Capernaum continues. After sharing the loaves, Jesus reveals he is the "bread of life," a demanding life which requires faith in his message. As they have already done before, some of his listeners react, but this time they do not dare speak out loud: "they began to complain" (Jn 6:41). They do not accept Jesus as the bread that has come down from heaven, and they murmur as their ancestors, complaining about the lack of food (Ex 15–17), had done in the desert. The term used here involves a nuance of unbelief. Their major argument is the humanity of Jesus; he is just the son of Joseph (v. 42). John insists on this aspect: "The Word became flesh" (1:14). The one sent by God is a man who belongs to history. The unbelief of the leaders of the Jews is still present among us. We prefer to believe in a God who belongs to another world or who is present only in our inner hearts but who does not question us through others, especially through the most needy.

Jesus rejects their murmuring, but he does not enter into discussion on his own origin. He specifies the way and the meaning of belief in him which is a grace of God. The impulse comes from the Father and the result is eternal life, the resurrection (vv. 43–44). While on the journey, we have to accept to be taught. These lines refer to Is 54:13 about an oracle addressed to Jerusalem: "All your children shall be taught by the Lord." John eliminates "your children." The disciples, those who are taught, are not bound to a single nation: "they shall all be taught by God" (v. 45). This is a reaffirmation of the universality of Jesus' message; what he passes on to us is what he has learned from the Father (v. 46).

Abiding in Love

Following Jesus and believing in him mean having eternal life as of now. It is the life of communion uniting the Father with the Son (v. 47). Jesus is the bread of that life (v. 48). He nourishes it by his testimony, his teaching, and in the surrender of his life. Death does not put an end to it, as had happened to those who had been nourished by the manna in the wilderness (vv. 49–50). The bread of life liberates us from death. What gives us life is the flesh of Jesus, his body that will endure death on the cross. Thus, what causes the unbelief of the representatives of the people (in John, this is the meaning of the term "the Jews"), the humanity of Jesus, is instead the subject of faith and the source of life.

That humanity of Jesus must lead us to appreciate concrete and historical situations of hunger and thirst within the gift of eternal life (1 Kgs 19:4–8). Communion in the body of Jesus makes us brothers and sisters of everyone; we have to create a community of equals among ourselves, people who by forgiving one another are giving life to one another (Eph 4:30–32). If we give life, life in all its forms and expressions, and only then, will we be "imitators of God." In the Peruvian and Latin American church of these days, we have wonderful and painful examples that giving life can mean giving our own lives (5:1–2).

C. Faith and Hope Embrace
Wis 18:6–9; Heb 11:1–2, 8–19; Lk 12:32–48

Faith is not always an easy experience based on obvious security. The three readings for this Sunday invite us to examine the meaning we give to faith and to the foundations supporting it.

The Assurance of Things Hoped For

There are times when darkness and insecurity seem to be over-whelming believers. On occasions, circumstances are especially difficult and demanding for our faith. Fidelity to the word of God and following Jesus turn out to be arduous.

As the letter to the Hebrews reminds us, "faith is the assurance of things hoped for, the conviction of things not seen" (Heb 11:1). Faith is neither the possession of the goal nor certainty based on things that are evident. Instead, as in Abraham's case, it is obedience to God's call, trust to set out on the journey "without knowing where he was going" (v. 8), relying solely on the fidelity of God making the promise. But the ultimate objective of the promise, the definitive homeland of complete and joyful communion with the Father goes beyond all the provisional realizations of the journey. Referring to people whose faith the author praises, the text says: "they died in the faith, without having received the promises but from a distance they saw and greeted them" (v. 13). However, faith gives encouragement to believers and sufficient strength to live the dark present with fidelity. In speaking about Moses further on, that same letter to the Hebrews makes it very clear: "By faith...he persevered as though he saw him who is invisible" (v. 27).

In the gospel text, Jesus promises the kingdom that the Father delights in giving to his disciples, the "little flock" (v. 32). The road is not free from difficulties but it is the committed word of God, the assurance to journey without fear, that is to say, to believe the promise. But precisely because it is a promise, it is not a present and a tangible reality. The coming of the Son of Man as Lord and Savior is not a verifiable quantity. But while he is coming, while he appears as if he were absent from history, Jesus is calling us to be vigilant and to be prepared for his coming unexpectedly, "doing what was wanted" (v. 47). In the meantime, faith consists in living in active hope what is promised in fullness at the coming of the Lord.

Promise and Communion

Faith in God's promises, in the kingdom, implies a commitment to take responsibility for history so that the word pledged by God may leave its mark of salvific effectiveness on our reality. Faith does not give believers guidelines to live more tranquilly and comfortably. Knowing the will of God gives us greater responsibility to the Lord: "From everyone to whom much has been given, much will be required" (v. 48).

But according to the parable of Jesus, faith is not only the experience of a life in tension because of demands and commitments. In the end, it is an experience of plenitude and communion (v. 37). Faith leads to a communion of goal and destiny with the Lord because it started with his call. At the origin and the conclusion of a life of faith, we find the promise and the fullness granted by the Lord. The book of Wisdom points this out: "you called us to yourself and glorified us" (18:8). While we are on the journey, fidelity, consistency, and trust are required of us. In our present difficult and dark times, even though we are "looking at them from a distance," we must not lose sight of these promises. Because they come from God, they carry the assurance of their realization and they strengthen our hope.

Twentieth Sunday

A. No One Is Excluded
Is 56:1, 6–7; Rom 11:13–15, 29–32; Mt 15:21–28

Everything indicates that the gospel of Matthew comes from a Christian community with a strong Jewish influence. This is why the relationship with the pagan world is an important and significant theme of this gospel.

To All the Nations
Today's texts raise a question concerning the universality of the proclamation of the kingdom. It would be erroneous to think that the matter has been resolved in the course of history. In our text, the geographical reference is charged with theological intent. The dialogue between the Phoenician (or Canaanite) woman occurs on pagan soil: "the district of Tyre and Sidon" (Mt 15:21). The presence of Jesus outside the boundaries of his people is significant. The dialogue is harsh. The Lord seems to resist the woman's plea, claiming that "he was sent only to the lost sheep of the house of Israel" (v. 24). What is relevant, however, is that in the

end, Jesus grants her request. This is the thrust of his message. Despite what many were thinking when this gospel was being written, the gospel of Jesus is also addressed to the Gentiles.

This openness is a central Matthean theme (28:19). This is also a point which Paul emphasizes in chapters 9 and 11 of his epistle to the Romans, with one admonition: if the Jews cannot consider themselves privileged, the Gentiles should not either. All are equal before God. The first reading mentions the universal perspective already emerging in the prophets. Because the house of God is a "house of prayer" (Is 56:7), it is a house for all peoples.

Matthew's ecclesial experience leads him to affirm the universality of Jesus' message. Gradually, the Jews who formed part of his community come to open up to that perspective. Today we must not think we are exempt from a narrow-minded mentality in terms of the outreach of Christian faith. We are often inclined to feel as if we were private owners of the gospel and to identify our customs and cultures with Jesus' message. As a result, we are denying the right to live the gospel from the perspective of other cultural worlds. It is one thing to believe with conviction and another to exclude people who do not think like us.

A Spiritual Struggle

In the context of the controversy between exclusivism and universalism, we are witnessing a dialogue between Jesus and the Canaanite woman, a dialogue which involves other aspects. It is impossible not to be moved by the woman's humility and disarming obstinacy. She already knows something about Jesus since she calls him "Son of David" (v. 22). Matthew shows the woman shouting (v. 22). She is so persistent that the disciples beg the Lord to get rid of her. But Jesus starts a dialogue not devoid of sharp words. Before Jesus' negative answer, in keeping with the commonly held opinion of the Jewish world, the woman keeps insisting. This is followed by another less harsh rejection. But the woman is not intimidated, and she boldly uses the argument just presented to her to reiterate her request.

Jesus, who has led this instructive dialogue, gives in to the humility of the woman who has firmly resisted his negative answer. In fact, Jesus acknowledges the faith of the pagan woman (v. 48) with admiration and joy. The Lord presents her as a model to believers, especially to those who, in the worst possible aberrations, look with contempt at people who do not share their religious opinions. We cannot pursue our spiritual struggle if we do not accept that everything comes from God.

B. Sharing Life
Prv 9:1–6; Eph 5:15–20; Jn 6:51–59

The gift of Christ's body and blood sheds light on the previous verses of John's sixth chapter, which we are reading these Sundays.

Teaching in the Synagogue

Teaching in the Capernaum synagogue, Jesus goes back to the theme of the bread and presents himself as the bread of life. While the controversy continues, Jesus expands his teaching. Those who want to follow him and to receive the gift of life must be in close union with him. They have to be in communion with the sign that expresses Jesus' death and resurrection and communicates his life because it is an effective sign (vv. 51–53). Because of this communion, the Lord will raise them up "on the last day" (v. 54). The sacramental bond becomes personal union: "Those who eat my flesh and drink my blood abide in me, and I in them" (v. 56). These words are reminiscent of the words used by John to refer to the intimate bond between the Father and the Son. This union is the foundation of our own union.

Jesus is speaking in the synagogue, saying to those present that "the bread that came down from heaven" is not like the bread that their ancestors ate in the wilderness "and they died." On the contrary, the one who "eats this bread will live forever" (v. 58). Communion in the body and blood of Christ means adopting as our own the meaning the Lord sought to give to his life and surrender. It is appropriating his commitment to proclaim the gospel.

Redeeming Time

We are invited to the banquet of "Sagacity," Wisdom in other versions. Wisdom is very active; she has not only invited, she has also built her house and set her table (Prv 9:1–2). She says to the people invited to the carefully planned banquet: "Come, eat of my bread and drink of the wine that I have mixed. Lay aside immaturity and live and walk in the way of insight" (vv. 5–6); this is the way that allows us to discern what is good, just, and wise.

In the letter to the Ephesians we find a strong presence of the perspective found in the so-called sapiential books. Our text is warning the Ephesians not to live "as unwise people but as wise" (v. 15), with maturity and insight. "The days are evil," but wisdom consists in confronting them, "making the most of the time [*kairos*]" (v. 16). This *kairos* is the propitious time filled with possibilities for believers. These evil days must not paralyze us. We have to discern and pay attention to their values. Literally, the term translated by "making the most of" means "redeeming." This is really the point, "redeeming the present time." Whatever interpretation we give to the expression (also found in Col 4:5), one thing is clear: Jesus' followers are given time in order to carry out good works. But to do that, we have to understand "what the will of God is" (v. 17). The opposite of this would be wasting time, and, in the words of the book of Proverbs, it would mean accepting the banquet of "the foolish woman" (9:13–18).

The banquet of the Lord redeems our time. It prevents human history from becoming engulfed in selfishness, sin, and death without hope. Taking part in that banquet helps us to discern the meaning of life in our circumstances because we are "filled with the Spirit" (Eph 5:18). This is one more reason to give "thanks to God the Father at all times and for everything in the name of our Lord Jesus Christ" (v. 20).

C. Genuine Peace
Jer 38:4–6, 8–10; Heb 12:1–4; Lk 12:49–53

Scripture repeatedly reminds us that the proclamation of the love of God will always shock the powerful of this world.

Going to the Roots

The twelfth chapter of Luke's gospel offers advice and warnings to the disciples. Jesus is continuing his way up to Jerusalem, opposition to his mission is becoming more aggressive, and, foreseeing the outcome, the Lord warns his followers. The text for this Sunday is written in paradoxical terms. It is a way of approaching a complex and controversial reality.

Jesus is the messenger of peace, a profound and lasting peace, not mere rest or, even less, a label on an empty container. The peace in question implies justice, respect for other people's rights, especially the rights of the most defenseless, "the poor and the oppressed" as the bishops insisted at Puebla. The proclamation of that peace runs into the opposition of those taking advantage of an unjust social order. Self-centeredness, with its consequences, rejects the call to friendship based on our condition as daughters and sons of God. This is what the Lord points out to his disciples. His message is one of peace, but because of it he will suffer a baptism by fire (Lk 3:16); he will be plunged into pain and death. Jesus does not seek that, but it is what he encounters and accepts: the price that he has to pay already places him under stress (Lk 12:49–50).

Peace is the fruit of love, the result of an authentic communion which eliminates the causes of divisions and mistreatments among people. To some people — in good or in bad faith — to point out the motives of the lack of solidarity and justice will appear as seeking to cause divisions. In fact, some prefer not to see the origin of evils because it would question their present privileges. Jesus is aware that his proclamation of the kingdom is disclosing a reality in which divisions are unfortunately already present. He seeks to eliminate them by going to their cause: the lack of concrete and committed love. This requires an option for or against the Lord (vv. 51–53).

A Prophet's Tribulations

The church fathers have often presented Jeremiah as prefiguring Christ. In today's text we are told that officials intended to put him to death because he had followed God's command. The officials of weak King Zedekiah see the prophet as a traitor to the nation (Jer 38:4). Like many people today, they prefer not to tell the truth. They allege that those telling the truth are creating the situation they denounce. This is the worst of lies.

The divisions are neither caused by Jeremiah nor by Jesus. Both are striving to eliminate them. They neither hide the truth nor secretly play with their mission to announce the word of God. They want real reconciliation. They are not seeking to be appreciated by all, to receive honors and rewards from the powerful. Regardless of what anyone says, we must give testimony to all the demands of God's love as we "look to Jesus" (Heb 12:2).

Twenty-First Sunday

A. Authority Is Service
Is 22:19–23; Rom 11:33–36; Mt 16:13–20

The Lord understands his mission and that of his followers in terms of service, not as a way of imposing themselves on others.

Recognizing the Messiah

This passage from Matthew's gospel brings us an important profession of faith of the disciples in Peter's words. It is no accident that it takes place in Caesarea Philippi, namely, in Gentile territory. With this subtle point, Matthew (see also Mk 8:27) wants to indicate the universal nature of the mission of Jesus, the Messiah. The Son of God has come to announce his Father's love for everyone and in a special way for the poorest, to all the nations of the world.

To the first question that Jesus addresses to his disciples — "Who do people say that the Son of Man is?" (v. 13) — they answer that the people think he is a prophet (v. 14). That is a fairly good answer. In fact, Jesus is situated in the great prophetic line of Israel, which is why he does not separate the love of God from the practice of righteousness. In the sermon on the mount we read, "Strive first for the kingdom of God and his righteousness and all these things will be given to you as well" (Mt 6:33). Those who have heard and seen Jesus have understood something important in thinking of Jesus as a prophet.

But this is not enough. Jesus' second question is much more direct and blunt: "But who do you say that I am?" (v. 15). The question is still valid now: who is Jesus for us today? We might be surprised if we had the courage to answer. Is Christ really the dynamic and demanding center of our lives? Or does our answer about his identity show an anemic affirmation without any impact on our daily lives? Peter's answer was not a mere formula: "You are the Messiah, the Son of the living God" (v. 15). It requires a conduct rooted in the decision to follow the Lord's footsteps in terms of his love for the marginalized and the insignificant people of history and in terms of his service to the neediest.

Servant and Apostle

The authority that Jesus gives to Peter is situated in that context, the context of the Son of God who lays down his life for others. It is not a power to dominate but to serve. Peter understands that, and thus he refers to himself as "servant and apostle" (2 Pet 1:1), and he advises everyone "to serve one another with whatever gift each of you has received" (1 Pet 4:10). The text from Isaiah (22:20–23) makes the same appeal to us. In giving authority to Eliakim, the Lord asked him "to be a father to the inhabitants of Jerusalem" (v. 21). According to the Old (First) Testament, a ruler's mission is "to establish righteousness and justice" like a loving father who wants his children to live. It is only in that context that it makes sense for the Lord to give him the "key of the house of David" (v. 22). This is the will of the one whose "judgments are unsearchable and whose ways are inscrutable" (Rom 11:33). Every Christian life has its source in the contemplation of God's mystery.

B. To Whom Can We Go?
Jos 24:1–2, 15–17, 18; Eph 5:21–32; Jn 6:61–70

We are concluding the reading of the rich and lengthy sixth chapter of John's gospel. After having presented himself as the bread of life, the Lord starts to reveal to his disciples that this will cause opposition that will lead to his death.

The Spirit Is Life

The disciples find "this teaching difficult" (Jn 6:60), and they are frightened by the price that has to be paid to proclaim life. They do not dare say that directly to the Lord. Like many of us in similar circumstances, they express their fear and resistance under their breath (v. 61). Then the Lord moves one step further in his teaching even though it means that some of his followers are going to walk away.

Jesus opposes the spirit, which is life and power, to the "flesh," which means death and cowardice in the Bible (v. 62). He does not oppose it to the body, as many of us tend to think because we are marked by the distinction between body and soul that we inherited from Greek philosophy. Once again Jesus says that his words "are spirit and life" (v. 62). Believing in them means accepting life; rejecting them is, in some way, delivering Jesus to death (v. 64). This is what Judas will do (he is mentioned in v. 71). Later, like Judas, many will do the same. They are those who, although they form part of Christ's disciples, do not feel challenged by injustice, the exploitation and mistreatment of others, especially of the most dispossessed. They are the Judas of history because their conduct is a betrayal of Jesus and his teaching. Jesus' words will expose them.

Choose Today

The Lord's demanding teaching causes "many of his disciples" to abandon him (v. 66). Following Jesus entails conditions not accepted by all. It is better to face the matter clearly than to pretend we are listening to God if we are not concerned about putting God's instructions into practice.

This is what Joshua says to his people: "if you are unwilling to serve the Lord, choose this day whom you will serve" (Jos 24:15). Serving God involves solidarity with God's chosen ones: the least among the people. The people being thus challenged choose the Lord who liberated them from "slavery in Egypt" (v. 17). "Choose this day" unequivocally and without delay. This is particularly difficult in our own days when we experience situations of cruel violence which destroy innocent lives. We have to be convinced that it is impossible to build anything solid on poverty and injustice.

Serving the Lord of life is extremely difficult and demanding. Before the magnitude of the task or the hostility that we encounter, we are going to be tempted to walk away. Let us ask the Father to make our response to Jesus the same as Peter's: "To whom can we go? You have the words of eternal life. We have come to believe and know that you are the Holy One of God" (v. 69).

C. Entering through the Door
Is 66:18–21; Heb 12:5–7, 11–13; Lk 13:22–30

The salvation of the God who is revealed in the Bible is not just for a few; it is open to everyone. This is the great lesson taught by the readings for this Sunday.

The Narrow Door

The gospel begins with the question from one of Jesus' listeners: "Lord, will only a few be saved?" (v. 23). The question can be understood in terms of numbers, but Jesus does not take it that way. His answer is as direct as it is seemingly disconcerting: "strive to enter through the narrow door" (v. 24). Salvation passes through the narrow door. A key to understand Jesus' answer is found at the beginning of the text reminding us that Jesus is making his way to Jerusalem (v. 22). In the gospels, the way to Jerusalem expresses Jesus' determination to fulfill faithfully his Father's mission to proclaim and practice the good news to its ultimate consequences. The listener's question and Jesus' answer take place in that context, on the way up to Jerusalem.

The narrow door is clearly restrictive not in reference to people but in terms of the "right" to be saved. Salvation does not come from a mere physical closeness to Jesus (vv. 26–27). It is not enough to have eaten and to have drunk with him or to have listened to him in the public squares. It is not the consequence of belonging to a specific people either, in this case, the Jewish people (v. 28). The text does not say it, but in fidelity to the spirit of Jesus' answer we could add that salvation is not limited to one race or one culture. Salvation comes when we accept Jesus and start to follow him. This is the narrow door, the only door to life, and it is a demanding entrance. At times, it may be painful, like the discipline mentioned in Hebrews, "but later it yields the peaceful fruit of righteousness" (12:11).

The Wide-Open Door

Thus, the narrow door becomes a wide-open door, open to all without exclusivism. This is emphasized in Isaiah's text with the Lord saying: "I am coming to gather all nations and tongues" (v. 18). The narrow door or the following of Christ must be placed in relation with openness to universality, to all nations. All are invited to follow the way of Jesus.

All are invited but the invitation means following the way of Jesus. Openness to universality does not water down the content of the invitation. Hence, the reference at the end of the text: "some are last who will be first" and "some are first who will be last" (Lk 13:30). The immediate context of this phrase is not the same as in Matthew (19:30 and 20:16). Here it points to the relation of the Jewish people with other nations. We can also think that the narrow door is precisely the entrance door of the multitude to the table of the banquet of the kingdom.

Twenty-Second Sunday

A. Becoming a Disciple Again
Jer 20:7–9; Rom 12:1–2; Mt 16:21–27

It is not easy to be a disciple of Jesus, but the call to follow him is permanent.

Following Jesus

Last Sunday's text presented Peter's profession of faith, his acknowledging Jesus as "the Messiah, the Son of the living God" (Mt 16:16). But now the situation is changing. The Lord reveals to his disciples the difficulties he is going to encounter with the leaders of his people. The three groups mentioned in the text, the elders and the chief priests (mostly Sadducees) and the scribes (mostly Pharisees), will have Jesus arrested and condemned to death. The Sanhedrin was the highest authority of the Jewish people in those days (v. 21).

Peter refuses to accept what is revealed by Jesus. He is not willing to pay such a price to follow him. His praxis does not agree with his theory. He recognizes Jesus as the Christ (the Messiah), but, shocked by what Jesus announces, Peter withdraws. The Lord responds emphatically. Some translations have Jesus say: "get out of my sight, Satan" (16:22), but Jesus is literally saying: "get behind me [this is the meaning of the Greek term used by Matthew], Satan." There is a strong rejection of Peter's reaction, but at the same time Jesus is telling Peter to take up his place as a disciple again, a place which calls him to get behind Jesus in order to follow him and not be an obstacle in his way. In other words, Jesus' strong rejection of Peter also contains forgiveness of his error. Jesus believes that Peter is able to conduct himself as a disciple again and to walk in his footsteps. Even though Jesus disagrees with Peter, he trusts his return.

Discerning the Will of God

Jesus' reaction contains both firmness and welcome. The Lord knows that discipleship involves a process. We learn to be consistent rather than to profess one thing and do something else. It is not easy to put the gospel into practice, but it must be done and this is demonstrated in our works. The need to be consistent is increasingly more urgent. Our solidarity with those who are suffering will prove our belief in him who has come that we "may have life and have it abundantly" (10:10) in the words of John's gospel.

Following Jesus, allowing God to entice us today (Jer 20:7) must lead us to speak clearly and not to settle with palliatives. It is not a matter of creating problems but rather of acknowledging their presence and saying that they have to be solved on the basis of the needs of the poor. Many people will not like such words and actions. We will be tempted to keep quiet (Jer 20:9) or to avoid problems for ourselves like Peter. But the Lord always expects us to know how to discern his will (Rom 12:2), not to separate the love of God from the love of neighbor, especially the poor, and to come back again and again to our places as disciples.

B. Caring for Orphans
Dt 4:1–2, 6–8; Jas 1:17–18, 20–22, 27; Mk 7:1–8, 14–15, 21–23

If faith in God is not expressed in loving gestures toward others, it is devoid of content.

Clean Hands

Jesus' controversy with the Pharisees is marked by the opposition between a formal, exterior religion and the real, interior demands of the kingdom of God. The disciples have started to free themselves from those religious precepts, and the Pharisees take advantage of this opportunity to situate Jesus outside of what they consider the tradition of his people (Mk 7:1–5). The Lord responds precisely by relying on tradition, the authentic tradition represented by the prophet Isaiah. Thus, he situates himself in the great prophetic perspective: what God wants is conversion of the heart rather than words and purely formal attitudes. The demands of these attitudes do not come from God; they have been invented to avoid the real demands (vv. 7–8). Jesus goes beyond this scolding. He speaks out loud to the crowd so that all may know about the easy and hypocritical religion that the Pharisees are proclaiming (vv. 14–15). Defilement has nothing to do with not washing our hands. Instead, it comes from harming others, forgetting their needs and believing that we are "clean."

This appeal of the Lord is still fully valid. The gospels indicate Pharisaism as a risk for every believer. We also see it among us and within ourselves. One way to water down the gospel is to transform it into a series of formal rules which need to be observed only externally. Those who do that or try to do it look with contempt at those who, in their judgment, do not comply with these rules. Often the poor consider themselves "sinners" because they live in a complex and confused world without being able to follow what Jesus calls "human precepts" (v. 6) in agreement with Isaiah. These norms characterize Christians who are arrogant, devoid of compassion, people whose hands are clean because they have no hands, as the poet Péguy used to say.

Pure Religion

True cleanliness consists in putting the word of God into practice (Dt 4:1; Jas 1:22) — a word of love, a gift of God from whom all things come (Jas 1:17). It demands of us concrete gestures toward others: caring for orphans and widows (v. 27); visiting the victims of poverty, exploitation, and oblivion; opting for a just and human order and against what causes deaths, "disappearances" and sufferings.

Miguel Company, Michael Tomaszek, Zbigniew Strzalkowski,* friends and brothers in hope, came to our country to "care for orphans," not to wash their hands of the problem. This is the reason why they went to Chimbote and to Pariacoto, to show their solidarity with the poor and to proclaim the God of life. They

---

*The last two were priests assassinated by terrorists of Sendero Luminoso. The first, also a priest, survived a similar assassination attempt (these events took place in August 1991).

were assassinated — in Miguel's case, there was an assassination attempt — for taking care of the orphans and for not forgetting the concrete needs of the poor. The surrender of their lives takes us far away from all formalism.

C. Loving Freely
Sir 3:17–18, 20, 28–29; Heb 12:18–19, 22–24; Lk 14:1, 7–14

Important people of the time did not view Jesus as an amenable person, and today's important people do not either.

Without Looking for a Reward

The Lord is invited to eat at the house of one of the leaders of the Pharisees. However, their intention is not sharing but setting a trap. They want to watch his conduct closely (Lk 14:1). Those who are resisting Jesus' message would like to find eventual weaknesses to attack him. Jesus shocks them by healing people on the sabbath, and then he leaves them speechless (vv. 2–6).

In addition, upon seeing that the guests are looking for places of honor (it must have been a relatively important meal), Jesus tells them a parable with a pointed message. The parable communicates the central message of his preaching: "all who exalt themselves will be humbled and those who humble themselves will be exalted" (v. 11). The last will be first. This is what has been called the messianic inversion: in the perspective of the kingdom, the despised and insignificant come first.

As followers of Jesus, as church, we must bear that in mind. Being Christian or being a church dignitary is not a mundane honor and even less a sinecure. Because it is so easy to fall into this trap in our society, we have to be particularly careful. Jesus' criticism of the Pharisees (Lk 11:43) continues to be valid.

Revelation to the Humble

The people who are ambushing the Lord to find him at fault will not have anything to complain about. They are receiving what they deserve; Jesus continues to pull the rug from under their feet. He suggests that they do not invite (he was invited by them) their "friends" or "relatives" or "rich neighbors" or any others who might be able to invite them in return (v. 12). Instead, they should invite "the poor, the crippled, the lame, and the blind"

(v. 13). Let us observe in passing that the list is dealing with the marginalized. Because of the seriousness of their illness, they are even considered as sinners by those claiming to be righteous. These people have no way of returning the favor, and this is why they should be invited. Gratuitous love sets the example in "the city of the living God" (Heb 12:22). The parable which follows in Luke (vv. 15–24) takes up the list in question and underscores the gratuitous nature of the kingdom addressed to the insignificant.

This is the God who "reveals his secrets to the humble" (Sir 3:20). We will find the same idea in Mt 11:25 because this is the Father's gracious will, as we are told in this gospel. Those who seek places of honor, those who feel important, those who do everything out of their love of power and positions of honor will not be invited to the banquet of the kingdom. They will not "find support" (Sir 3:31). They have already received their reward.

Twenty-Third Sunday

A. Fraternal Correction
Ez 33:7–9; Rom 13:8–10; Mt 18:15–20

The gospels communicate the experience of faith of the Christian communities to which the authors who give their names to these books belong.

Regaining a Member of the Church

The gospel of Matthew stresses this aspect in a special, clear, and demanding way. At every step of the Matthean text, we find the experience of a community with its successes, its difficulties, its norms, its conflicts, and its hopes. Thus, the central theme of this gospel deals with discipleship, in other words, following Christ. The passage we are reading today is a clear example of the ecclesial experience which forms the background of Matthew's gospel.

Here we are dealing with the proper behavior toward members of the community who have sinned, namely, those who have failed in their role as disciples of Jesus. Matthew suggests that the member at fault be corrected by another member and that he or she be reminded of the evangelical demands. The purpose of this correction is clear: to invite that person to convert, to return to the way of the followers of the Lord (v. 15). If this does not happen, then other members of the community must be called. This will add to the objectivity and firmness of the suggested attitude (v. 16). Lastly, the church, the assembly of the disciples, has to take care of the matter (v. 17). Being Christian presupposes a determined behavior. The kingdom, which is the heart of Christ's message, entails ethical demands for those who are committed to live and announce it. The community is responsible for the fidelity of its members to the Father's will for life. Love requires us to pay attention to another member's errors. We have to warn others so that they may "turn from their ways" (Ez 33:9).

Fulfilling the Law

We are undoubtedly in the presence of a delicate matter which is difficult to handle. However, it is a strong reminder of the necessary requirements to belong to the ecclesial assembly in an authentic and responsible way. For example, in today's world, people who are, in one way or another, accomplices or even authors of situations of poverty and death of so many and who pretend, at the same time, to be Christians have to be called to task by the community of the disciples of the One who proclaims the kingdom of life to all and especially to the neediest and the oppressed. If the community does not do that, it distances itself from what the Lord demands and becomes lukewarm and mediocre.

The last verses of Matthew's passage, as well as the text from Romans 13:8–10, make us see the profound meaning of this apparent harshness. The correction in question has to be done lovingly. The context is clearly communitarian. It is the context of a church which prays and addresses the Father as the foundation of its being and doing, with the confidence that the Lord is in our midst (vv. 19–20). The ultimate reason of that rigor toward another member, a rigor that we often avoid because of our cowardice, is love of neighbor. Paul tells us that the practice of love is "the fulfilling of the law" (v. 10). Love of neighbor involves demands which challenge our apathy and our desire to avoid problems.

B. False Criteria
Is 35:4–7; Jas 2:1–5; Mk 7:31–37

Jesus, the itinerant preacher from Galilee, crosses the borders of
his people and brings the good news to pagan lands (Mk 7:24
and 31).

The Tongue of the Speechless Will Sing

The Markan passage easily lends itself to a figurative interpretation: the Lord is opening up our minds, and he enables us to
speak adequately about him. We are dealing with a valid and ben-
eficial meaning for our lives as Christians. However, this must not
make us forget the original and literal meaning: a deaf and mute
man starts to hear and to speak. The text preserves an Aramaic
term, *Ephphatha* (v. 34), referring to events which the author remembers and which astound the people witnessing the healing
(v. 37).

We are dealing with a physical reality compounded by a social reality. In fact, in the mentality of the time, deafness and
muteness (probably from birth) are among the afflictions which
are viewed as punishment. Those suffering from them are seen
as sinners or perhaps children of sinners (see the case of the
man born blind in John 9). By opening the ears and releasing the
tongue of the man brought to him (vv. 32–35), Jesus brings him
back to health and the man is no longer sick. At the same time,
Jesus reintegrates him into society, giving him back his religious
rights, and the man ceases to be marginalized.

A community of people open to the word must show solidarity
with those who suffer physically and socially. Like marginalization and exploitation, hunger and sickness are incompatible with
God's will for life. The good news is life, as the text of Isaiah also
reminds us. "The eyes of the blind shall be opened; the ears of
the deaf shall be unstopped; then the lame shall leap like a deer
and the tongue of the speechless sing for joy" (35:5–6).

Showing No Favoritism

Believing in the God of life is demanding. James speaks to us
from his ecclesial experience. He presents his "supposition" (2:2)
with a detail proving this comes from something he has experienced. In the Christian community, there are people who are not
aware of all that is implied in being a follower of the one who

said: "the last shall be first." They maintain the categories of the world and give the first places in the church to those who are also first in society because they are powerful and they wear fine clothes (vv. 2–3). On the contrary, they treat the poor, those in dirty and perhaps smelly clothes, with contempt. This is the very opposite of what the Lord requires.

The epistle of James is particularly sensitive to God's preference for people who are insignificant. Those who make distinctions are accused of proceeding with "evil thoughts" (v. 4), that is to say, thoughts opposed to the truth of Jesus. The simple but demanding text from James continues to challenge us. Among ourselves, do good names, economic and social status, and "fine clothes" continue to carry weight and have a voice that are denied to the poor? We cannot build a church, sign of the kingdom of life, if we show favoritism.

C. The Requirements for Discipleship
Wis 9:13–19; Phlm 9:10, 12–17; Lk 14:25–33

The gospel for this Sunday undoubtedly brings us one of the "harsh" texts of the gospel. It is not easy to understand what Jesus wants to tell us at first glance.

What Disciples Have "to Hate"
The Lukan text starts by affirming that following Jesus entails "hating" what is closest and dearest to us: our families (v. 26). This is a very powerful text. In order to understand it, we must point out that Jesus' use of the verb "to hate" is a semitism, a way of speaking that is typical of the cultural milieu of Jesus. At the time, the meaning of "hating" would have been equivalent to "postponing" or putting in second place. In this sense, we are not asked to cultivate hatred toward our loved ones. Instead, in the light of the requirements of following Jesus, we are asked to relativize even our most natural and legitimate loves. Nothing and no one can compete with the demands of following Jesus. What our relationship with the people we cherish the most requires must be seen in the light of our faith in Jesus. This is the significance of the term "hate" in our text.

The requested (and specified) "hating" is a necessary condition to carry the cross. Carrying the cross is actually another way of speaking of following Jesus. In Luke, the aspect of the daily practice of carrying the cross always stands out (v. 27). Carrying the cross and following Jesus' way are a daily process involving fidelity and making many decisions.

Calculating the Cost

Luke uses other images to help us understand the seriousness and the depth which must characterize our Christian commitment. The way of faith is like someone who wants to build a tower (v. 28). It is also like a king who wants to wage war against another king (v. 31). In both instances, it is necessary to calculate the cost. Figuring out the cost does not mean reducing Christian life to a kind of quantitative accounting of means and money. This is not the case. Instead, the text invites us to reflect on the cost, the demands of a life of faith. If we think that faith in Jesus is not going to affect our lives profoundly, even our daily lives, we have failed to understand what discipleship really demands. Hence, the need to calculate the cost or to assess what discipleship means in the gospel.

The text ends (v. 33) with a typically Lukan note: giving up all our possessions. The desire to accumulate possessions, wealth, and power is the great enemy of Christian life. This is why the cost of discipleship implies giving up our search for wealth. Nothing can interfere with following Jesus.

Thus we will be prepared to welcome others like brothers and sisters. Welcoming with love is the theme of the beautiful letter of Paul to Philemon, a letter which is not always well understood. Paul is asking him to welcome Onesimus "as you would welcome me" (v. 17). But he goes further still telling Philemon that he is sure "that he will do even more than I say" (v. 21). Gratuitous love knows no limits. This is helpful in setting our paths right (Wis 9:18).

Twenty-Fourth Sunday

A. Settling Accounts
Sir 27:33–28:9; Rom 14:7–9; Mt 18:21–35

The heart of biblical revelation is God's gratuitous love. This has to be the norm of our relationship with others.

Forgiveness Is Always Gratuitous

Matthew's eighteenth chapter contains a series of instructions for the daily life of the Christian community. Forgiveness is one of them. Peter wants to know how often we should forgive (v. 21). The Lord situates the question within a much broader horizon: we must always forgive. That is the meaning of the mysterious expression "seventy-seven times" (v. 22). There may also be an allusion — taking the opposite position — to Genesis 4:24. There are no limits; love is not compatible with obligations that can be counted. Mutual forgiveness builds up the community and it implies our trusting people.

Jesus' statement is illustrated in one of the most beautiful parables in the gospels, one found only in Matthew. The "settling accounts" (v. 23) will vanish before God's justice based on gratuitous love. At the servant's request, the king forgives the debt. "Ten thousand talents" (v. 24) constitutes a fabulous sum that cannot be repaid (something like the foreign debt of the poor countries). This is why the slave's promise is merely an attempt to move the Lord (v. 26). The king's forgiveness is totally gratuitous; he forgives simply "out of pity" (v. 27), out of love, not because he expects some day to receive what is owed to him.

Do Not Hold Grudges against Your Neighbor

The conduct of the slave is the exact opposite of the Lord's action. The fellow slave barely owes him a hundred denarii (a denarius was the day's wage for a laborer), an amount that can be easily repaid, but the debtor's plea is not heeded. The "wicked slave" (v. 32) has not learned the lesson. According to a strict justice, he can send the debtor to jail, but the king has just shown him another kind of justice based on gratuitous love that asks for nothing in return. This justice considers people for what they are rather than for what they have.

The God of Jesus loves because he is good. In the presence of this boundless love, people's merits are secondary. Those who believe in this God must love in the same way. The love of God is the model of our conduct. The Lord is always ready to renew his covenant (Sir 28:7) which implies that we must also open our hearts to others. In the presence of gratuitous love, the question "how often should I forgive" (Mt 18:21) loses its meaning. There is nothing more demanding than the gratuitous and boundless love of the one who is "Lord of both the dead and the living" (Rom 14:9).

In the presence of the sufferings of this world's poor beaten down by merciless economic liberalism, in the presence of unprecedented and cruel conflicts, profound appeals for justice are emerging, a justice which goes beyond what is legal in order to reach the most fundamental rights of human beings. Loving gratuitously as God loves us brings justice to the root and fullness of its demands.

B. The Price of Discipleship
Is 50:5–9; Jas 2:14–18; Mk 8:27–35

Faith is expressed in works, in concrete gestures of love. This is a central theme of the biblical message.

Who Is Christ for Us?

This is a key text of the gospel of Mark. The scene takes place on the way to pagan territories (Caesarea Philippi), an indication suggesting the universal outreach of the dialogue which follows (Mk 8:27). Jesus takes the initiative and asks those who have heard and have seen him what idea they have of him. The question has a certain rhythm as it occurs in two phases. First, Jesus is interested in what people think of him (v. 27). Shortly before that, the disciples had returned from an evangelization mission (Mk 6:6–13) and thus, the question is also: what testimony have you given of me? According to the answer, people situate Jesus in the line of the prophets (Elijah, John the Baptist). There is no mention of an alleged political messianism (v. 28). For the people, Jesus is rooted in the great prophetic tradition. This is an interesting perception.

The second question is more challenging and more probing: "But who do you say that I am?" (v. 29). They are the ones who have followed Jesus and listened to him for some time. The question is asked of the group and Peter answers in the name of all: "You are the Messiah" (v. 29). Not just a prophet, Jesus is God's anointed one, the Christ. But the dialogue does not stop here. Jesus announces that he will be rejected by the powerful of his people, a rejection which will lead to his death. This is too much for Peter, who refuses to accept the difficulty involved in the mission of Jesus. The Lord reprimands Peter for his attitude: "get out of my sight, Satan" (v. 33), according to some translations. It would be more exact and more literal to say: "get behind me," which is the same as saying, come back to your place as a disciple and do not be an obstacle (Satan) in my way. Therefore, Jesus' reproach already includes his will to forgive. He believes that Peter is able to take up his position as a disciple again and to be Jesus' follower. Jesus rejects the stance of Peter, not the person. On the contrary, Jesus makes Peter see that, in spite of everything, he still trusts him.

Faith without Works Is Dead

Peter had no difficulty in recognizing Jesus as the Christ. What he did not accept was the price that had to be paid to be a disciple (vv. 34–35). There is a "Peter side" in each one of us, our resistance to follow Jesus in practice. However, it is an integral part of our faith in him. A profession of faith which does not include discipleship is incomplete. Orthodoxy, correct opinion, demands orthopraxis, namely, a behavior which is in harmony with the opinion expressed. In the final analysis, our faith in Christ is at stake in our daily following of Jesus, in our works (Jas 2:14–18), and in our making Jesus' way our own. The Lord will forgive our faults along the way, but he continues to call us to total fidelity which must be translated into solidarity with others, especially with the poor and the forgotten. The surrender "to the extreme" of so many people in Peru and in Latin America makes us see the cost of being disciples (see the suffering servant of Isaiah 50).

C. One for Ninety-Nine
Ex 32:7–11, 13–14; 1 Tm 1:12–17; Lk 15:1–32

The texts for this Sunday speak to us of the love of God, a love conditioned neither by our kind words nor even by our righteous conduct. This gratuitous love of God anticipates our gestures.

A Missionary Perspective

The passage from Luke brings us three parables on the tenderness of God. According to some experts, they make this chapter the heart of the third gospel. The evangelist underlines two central ideas: the initiative of God and his joy in encountering what was far away. Let us not forget that the narratives seek to make things clear to those who are censuring Jesus because of his interest in public sinners (who are, therefore, despised) and because of his friendship with them (Lk 15:1–3).

Looking for the lost sheep, the lost drachma, running to meet the returning son, all that implies leaving what we already have. It does not mean neglect or a lack of consideration. To the protest of the son who stayed with him, the father responds: "you are always with me and all that is mine is yours." The father's solicitude for the son who left the paternal home shows his concern for the one who needs him the most (vv. 15–31). It also means not limiting ourselves to conserving but going toward what is uncertain. This is the missionary impulse without which the church is not a faithful sign of the kingdom in history. We are always threatened by our tendency to withdraw within ourselves to feel protected. Counting our religious treasures over and over reveals a kind of spiritual avarice. It is a form of worshiping the golden calf and of refusing the demands of the living God (Ex 32:7–8).

Survival is not decisive for the church but service is. This means opening up to confrontation, finding new ways to proclaim the gospel, not being afraid of leaving the safety of our homes (and of social prestige) in order to go humbly through the streets and public squares to find those who do not consider themselves as Christians, or perhaps, those who left the church because of the countertestimony given by the pettiness or the dogmatism of so many believers.

The Joy of the Reencounter

The gratuitousness of God's love is the central focus of his plan and the source of his joy. In the three parables, the encounter implies forgiveness and joy. Paul has experienced forgiveness in his life. He who had been "a persecutor and a man of violence" (1 Tm 1:13) is considered "worthy" to assume a ministry addressed to those who are far away.

Joy is not found in withdrawing. It is found in mission, in our ability to welcome those who, for one reason or another, are not part of us. Forgiving means giving life and also receiving it (Lk 15:24), hence, the rejoicing. It means converting those who are far away into our brothers and sisters, as is requested in the parable of the Samaritan. We deprive ourselves of this rejoicing in the Spirit when, confined in our fears and resentments, we do not go out to learn from others what there is to learn, to forgive what has to be forgiven, and to respect what must be respected — in other words, when we prefer the ninety-nine to the one "sheep" which makes more demands on us.

Twenty-Fifth Sunday

A. Avoiding the "Evil Eye"
Is 55:6–9; Phil 1:20, 24–27; Mt 20:1–6

Today's text contains a parable found only in Matthew and undoubtedly one of the most eloquent of the entire gospel.

The Eleventh Hour

The text goes to the heart of Jesus' message: the free and gratuitous love of the Father. The full wage which the owner decides to pay to the laborers who come to work at the end of the day, at the eleventh hour (vv. 11–12), causes the reaction of those who had been there since the morning. The equal treatment seems unjust to them. The landowner rejects their accusation: "Did you not agree with me for the usual daily wage? Take what belongs to you and go" (vv. 13–14).

God's justice is over and above the formality of human justice. It takes into account the greater needs of people, of those who are "standing idle in the marketplace" (v. 3) against their will because no one has hired them. Nevertheless, the workers of the eleventh hour have the same right to work as the first laborers and the right for them and their families to live from that work. In a world like ours, with most of the population underemployed or unemployed, the right to work is a manifestation of the right to life, as John Paul II strongly reminded us in his encyclical *On Human Work*. This fundamental human right is not respected when a society and its legal order do not provide full employment for its people in the name of economic laws which coincide only with the profit and privilege of a few.

Your Ways Are Not My Ways

There is still more in this parable. The Lord says: "I choose to give to this last the same as I give you." Then he asks in an incisive way: "Are you envious because I am generous?" (vv. 14–15). This is the heart of the matter. The literal expression "is your eye evil..." is revealing. This is the kind of look which turns reality into stone, not leaving room for anything new or for generosity as it attempts to place limits on God's goodness. It is the "evil eye" looking around to defend our own interests, what makes us erect walls to protect our property even though it might mean poverty for others. It is the kind of look which makes us think that what is just for others is unjust for us if it affects our privileges. Not looking with an "evil eye" is a requisite for believers in the good God. If we avoid greed, we will put into practice what Paul recommends to the Philippians: "live your life in a manner worthy of the gospel of Christ" (1:27).

The God of biblical revelation does not demand observance merely of legal and formal justice. God's love, and what it demands of us, goes beyond these boundaries and moves generously and freely to look for those whom society marginalizes and oppresses. Isaiah tells us that the Lord's ways are not our ways (55:8). We have to be open at all times to the newness and creativity of God's love. Gratuitousness does not belong to the realm of what is arbitrary or superfluous. What is gratuitous does not contradict or disdain the quest for justice. On the contrary, it gives justice its true meaning. There is nothing more demanding than gratuitous love.

B. I Have Come to Serve
Wis 2:12–20; Jas 3:16–4:3; Mk 9:30–37

Jesus announces for the second time that the hostility which his proclamation of the kingdom encounters among the powerful of his time will lead him to death.

Who Is the Greatest?

Mark is the evangelist who reminds us most often of how difficult it was for the apostles to believe in Jesus and to accept the demands of discipleship. Mark says, "They did not understand what he was saying and they were afraid to ask him" (9:32). Jesus intends to help them take the final leap, asking them: "What were you arguing about on the way?" (v. 33). In spite of that, the disciples "were silent, for on the way they had argued with one another who was the greatest" (v. 34). Being close companions of a master followed by the crowds is already a matter of prestige for these humble inhabitants of Galilee. In the midst of their confusion, now they are wondering what their position will be in the change that Jesus is promising. Moreover, each one of them is coveting the best place (see Jas 4:2).

They have actually understood that the Lord is advocating a transformation of the religious order. What is grave is that even in that realm, ambition for prestige and power can exist. It is not necessary to believe in a temporal kingdom to fall into this attitude. We see that daily in our midst. The pursuit of honors, the desire to be the center of decisions, self-complacency in the authority entrusted to us, all these are temptations which are found in the church itself. It is a major perversion of the message of the Lord reminding us once again that the mark of disciples consists in being "the last of all and the servant of all" (v. 35).

Without Hypocrisy

In a prophetic gesture, Jesus takes a little child, that is to say, someone whom adults do not value, and he affirms his identification with the child (v. 36). Whoever welcomes an insignificant child welcomes him and his father (v. 37). The text reminds us of the famous passage in Matthew 25:31ff. Being the servant of all must begin with being the servant of the last ones in society.

This is the wisdom "which comes from above" (Jas 3:17). It is not just an interior attitude but must be translated into "good fruits" (v. 17). These are the fruits of "righteousness," the result of the actions of those who make peace (v. 18), in other words, the *shalom* of God which means life and integrity. This is what the wisdom of the Lord's disciples has to be, without the hypocrisy (v. 17) of those who speak about serving when, in fact, they exercise authority for their own benefit.

This attitude will meet with all kinds of resistance. People who are accustomed to greed will wage war on those who attempt to live that way (Jas 4:2). Those who do not exercise authority as service but instead as an instrument of power and domination will subject believers "to insult and torture" (Wis 2:19). They will doubt the veracity of their words and deeds (v. 17) testing them "to find out how gentle they are and make trial of their forbearance" (v. 19). They will even condemn them "to a shameful death" (v. 20). This is what happens to Jesus at the hands of those who abuse their power, even with alleged religious justifications. To them, the Lord opposes the testimony of his way of understanding authority as a service. The Lord invites all of us, without exception, to follow his own example.

C. God or Money
Am 8:4–7; 1 Tm 2:1–8; Lk 16:1–13

The gospel offers us a difficult but essential text to understand Jesus' and the evangelist's attitude with regard to material goods.

A Shrewd Administrator?

Our perplexity before the parable comes from the master's praise of the administrator who is literally called a "dishonest manager" in the text itself (v. 8). The matter gets worse with the commentary which follows (vv. 9–13). There, literally speaking, the subject is also "*mammon* [money], dishonest wealth" (v. 9), and Jesus tells us to make friends for ourselves by means of this wealth.

How can improper behavior be a model for Jesus' disciples? Our text causes headaches for biblical scholars. One interpretation, which partially resolves the difficulties, consists in saying that in reducing the debts the administrator has only limited himself to eliminating his own percentage (rather high according to the customs of the time) from the amount owed (vv. 5–7).

Should that be the case, there would be no theft but only a far-sighted and opportune renunciation to what he was entitled to. But in that case, why speak of dishonesty? Others soften the term (*adikia* in Greek), saying that in verse 8, it merely means something obtained by ruse or deceit. Thus, according to that viewpoint, we would have a shrewd man planning his schemes rather than a real violator of the law. But we would still have to work out the meaning of the word "dishonest" associated with wealth (v. 9).

Imagination and Congeniality

There is another way to interpret the text without having to minimize the seriousness of the fault committed by the administrator. What is being praised (v. 8) and what, with great freedom of spirit, Jesus proposes for our imitation (v. 9) is not the fraud, which is censured, but instead, the shrewdness with which this man, a child "of this age" (v. 8), has proceeded. The "children of light" (v. 8) must imitate the administrator's astuteness, not his dishonesty. The fact that the man has used his ability for inappropriate causes does not take away from the inventiveness which he has shown. The Lord's disciples must have that kind of imagination in order to place it at the service of other goals: the proclamation of the gospel.

With that interpretation the text appears extremely bold and demanding. In addition, this interpretation can be reinforced if we turn to a perspective whose presence in the gospels easily escapes us even though it carries a powerful message. We are referring to irony. We can read verses 9–12 from that perspective. Jesus' followers must not be austere and certainly even less unpleasant preachers of the gospel. We have to be imaginative and able to make friends. No one can deny the pertinence or the validity of the advice, especially if we think of the lack of joy that so many Christians manifest and their constant propensity to criticize and to attract attention. The irony consists in proposing someone who has acted badly as a model of conduct, and the irony even allows us to take advantage of such behavior. Irony always makes our outlook more complex and sharper.

On the other hand, there is no doubt whatsoever about Luke's rejection of dishonest wealth and its consequences. In order to leave no doubt, the passage ends with a categorical statement: "you cannot serve God and wealth [*mammon*]" (v. 13). A fundamental option has to be made. Not choosing means trampling on the poor (see Amos 8:4). Being clear in our option will help us in giving testimony at "the right time" (1 Tm 2:6).

Today we are starting to read Luke's sixteenth chapter, which contains radical and crucial demands. It was fitting at the beginning to keep in mind that we have to know how to present these requisites in a creative and clever way. And why not in a congenial way, too?

Twenty-Sixth Sunday

A. Which of the Two?
Ez 18:25–28; Phil 2:1–11; Mt 21:28–32

Christ shows us the way to accept the will of the Father in our lives.

The Way of Righteousness

Jesus is in Jerusalem. Time is running out. The hostility of those who are rejecting his message is intensifying. Today's parable is simple and challenging. Before making his comparison, the Lord asks for the opinion of his listeners. They are the ones who will decide (Mt 21:28). Let us just indicate that the order in which the behavior of the two sons is presented dismisses an interpretation which would identify the first son with the people of Israel and the second with the church (vv. 28–30). It is not a matter of chronology. What is at stake is something more profound and more permanent in the life of a believer: doing the will of the Father.

The account is terse. We are not given reasons for the two forms of behavior; they are merely described. In spite of his initial reservation, the first son does the will of the Father (v. 29). Although he says no in words, his action ends up by saying yes. On the contrary, the second son is a liar: he accepts in theory what he rejects in practice (v. 30). He is not consistent. Following Jesus is a matter of practice which determines our destiny before God. Doing takes precedence over saying. Jesus' question leaves no room to escape and it demands discernment: "which of the two did the will of his father?" (v. 31). It is not enough to answer: "the first." Those who are listening to Jesus know they are being challenged: with which one of the two do you identify? Which do you think is the way of righteousness?

Emptying Ourselves

The same question is addressed to us: do we belong to those who think it is enough to say yes, Lord (Mt 7:21), to enter the kingdom? Complying with formalities, even religious ones, has its advantages. When we follow the dominant rules of society, we avoid problems for ourselves and we are well thought of. But this is not the justice of which Jesus speaks. We are told with audacity that those who claim to be good observers of the law will be preceded in the kingdom by those whom they consider as the law's greatest violators: publicans and prostitutes, the public sinners (v. 31). This is one of the Lord's harshest statements, but it situates us in the realm of the justice that the kingdom requires: putting into practice the will of the Father who loves every person and especially the most needy and despised. Ezekiel tells us (v. 27) to do "what is lawful and right." All of us, without exception, must constantly convert to this righteousness which is life (v. 28). This mandate is the judge of our lives. In the presence of this, it seems clear that only arrogance can make us believe that we are "righteous" and throw doubts on the behavior and beliefs of those who do not agree with us.

To do the will of the Father, the Lord shows us the way of humility: "he emptied himself taking the form of a slave" (Phil 2:7). He left every privilege behind. Our condition as Christians, our responsibility in the church, must not lead to "conceit" (v. 3) and haughtiness but rather to solidarity. In this way alone will there be authentic "sharing in the Spirit" (v. 1). The beautiful canticle of Philippians reminds us that immersion in history is the path which the Son of God has taken to make us his friends.

B. Everyone Has to Be a Prophet
Nm 11:25–29; Jas 5:1–6; Mk 9:38–48

The message of Jesus frees us also from feeling we are the only ones representing him in this world.

Without Any Form of Sectarianism

The Markan passage is situated in a broad context in which the group close to Jesus opposes those who, though they are outsiders, are also following him (9:33–37). The disciples feel they are the sole recipients of Jesus' mission, and they want to prevent others who do not pay attention to them (9:38) from acting in his name. The Lord rejects this undue ill will toward people who do not belong to his circle of followers. His grace and his power are present beyond his closest disciples (v. 39). Then Jesus gives them a guideline for discernment in the future: "whoever is not against us is for us" (v. 40). This broad criterion challenges the disciples' tendency to feel they are the sole owners of the message of Jesus. This continues to challenge us today. The resentment which the Lord detects continues to be ours toward people who do not belong to the church or who do not form part of our own group within the church.

Whoever gives life (giving a cup of water, see v. 41) will be rewarded. It does not mean that what we think is not important. However, it should be underlined that the essence of following Jesus is found in the way we live love. The disciples' ambition to be Jesus' only followers is a stumbling block which can drive away "these little ones" who are opposed to the "great ones" of Jesus' immediate circle (v. 42). The text rejects the self-centeredness of those who feel they are the exclusive owners of the message. However, nothing places limits on the love and the grace of God. The text also condemns every form of sectarianism of groups within the community itself proclaiming to be the only interpreters of the evangelical teaching. Jesus frees us from our pettiness.

Entering Life

The following verses of Mark's text establish an interesting equation between life and the kingdom of God. Entering life (v. 43) is the same as entering the kingdom (v. 47). It is a precise and clear way of saying it.

The first reading helps us to emphasize a few guidelines of Mark's message. Joshua, Moses' assistant, asks him to forbid others from prophesying. On the contrary, Moses considers that all the Lord's people should be prophets, that is to say, they should speak in the name of God. There are no restrictions.

Joshua's envy is the same as the envy of Jesus' disciples. What is important is to receive "the spirit of the Lord" (Nm 11:29), namely, life.

James presents the "counterprophets," those who announce life but who bring about death through their selfishness as rich people, their mistreatment and oppression of the poor. The expression "a day of slaughter" (v. 5) may be referring to judgment day — the judgment of a God who loves the poor in a special way and who calls everyone, without exception, to be witnesses to life.

C. The Anonymous Rich Man
Am 6:1, 4–7; 1 Tm 6:11–16; Lk 16:19–31

Luke, Paul's companion, is very sensitive to poverty. Both he and Paul denounce the greed for money.

Lovers of Money

The parable, found only in Luke, is addressed to the Pharisees and to all those who, like them, are "lovers of money" (Lk 16:14). The parable is in a chapter dedicated to the theme of wealth, and it forms a powerful commentary to two basic affirmations of this gospel: "blessed are you who are poor" (6:20) and "woe to you who are rich" (6:24). The text for today has two very clear parts.

The first part (vv. 19–26) tells us about the reversal of situations between the poor man, Lazarus, and the rich man locked in his selfishness. This is the only case in which a person in a parable is given a name. In addition, here the person named is the poor man, someone who is generally anonymous in history. On the other hand, the rich man, the important character (who must have had a prestigious name) is unnamed in the parable. We would be wrong to think that it is an inconsequential detail. The proof of the surprise this causes to readers of this gospel lies in the odd custom of assigning a name to the rich man as well, but, in fact, he is not named in the text. He has been called Dives, which is the translation of the Latin word for rich. When the story is read from the perspective of the kingdom, an inversion occurs. Those who according to criteria of power and social prestige are the most important are anonymous before God. Those who are considered insignificant and nameless are the ones who have value for the God of the kingdom.

Consequently, the passage is inviting us to change our ways of seeing things. The gospel tells us in countless ways that the last will be first. They should also be first in our commitment, in our building up the church, and in our establishing a new society — a society and church made up of people like Lazarus who are despised now by those who, according to the parable, do not deserve to have a name.

The Root of All Evils

The second part (vv. 27–31) of the parable leaves no room for doubt. To the unnamed rich man's attempt to allege the ignorance of his peers as the reason for the indifference to the plight of poor Lazarus, "Father Abraham" (v. 29) categorically answers that they have the word of God to listen to. In spite of the clarity of the gospel message, today we also look for subterfuges or ask for miracles in order to avoid the gospel demands.

Those who ignore the poor (Am 6:4) are rejected by the Lord. Paul gives us the reason for such a behavior: "the love of money is a root of all kinds of evil" (1 Tm 6:10). Greed leads us to place in money and in the various forms of power flowing from it the trust which should only be in God. This is why Paul calls it idolatry and the poor are victims of this perverse worship. This is a danger which threatens everyone, including those who claim to believe in the God of Jesus Christ. Whatever our position in the church may be, Paul is inviting all of us "to pursue righteousness" (v. 11) in order to keep the commandment given to us without spot or blame (v. 14). This conduct — and its consequences — is separated by a great chasm (Lk 16:26) from the conduct censured in the nameless and heartless rich man.

Twenty-Seventh Sunday

A. The Murderous Tenants
Is 5:1–7; Phil 4:6–9; Mt 21:33–43

We continue to read the final parables on the kingdom in the gospel of Matthew.

The Fruits of the Kingdom

This parable of Matthew is known as the parable of the murderous tenants. As we will see, the name is accurate not only because we have the murder of the landowner's son. The parable deals with a vineyard which has not given any fruit. The people in charge of it, the tenants, react violently to the owner's messengers sent to collect the fruit of their work (v. 35).

What are the fruits in question? This is a key question for the meaning of the text. The reference (at times literal) to the passage of Isaiah which is presented in today's first reading will help us give an appropriate answer. In this song of the vineyard, Isaiah tells us that from what had been planted (that is to say, Israel), the Lord "expected justice, but saw bloodshed; righteousness, but heard a cry" (Is 5:7). The establishment of justice and righteousness is one of God's major mandates in the Old Testament. In addition, this is a way of expressing fidelity to the covenant between God and his people. The God of life and love wants justice to rule in the midst of his people and he wants the rights of everyone, especially the poorest, to be respected. These are the fruits that the vineyard, which the Lord planted and cared for, should have produced.

Injustice and Murder

This is the essence of the parable we are considering. The tenants have not practiced justice and they have not established righteousness. Worse yet, they have committed murders and there are complaints about their mistreatments and extortions. In the Bible, oppression of the poor is frequently presented as homicide. Therefore it is not surprising that the tenants react to those sent by the Lord with the same contempt for other people's lives as they show in their daily behavior. Thus the tenants are not only murderers because they kill the messengers, or even the son, but because they despoil the poor and violate their rights. They are murderers from the moment they fail to produce the fruits of justice which the Lord requires, and as a result the kingdom of God will go to someone else. These are powerful expressions. Yet we are witnessing this in our own times in the situation of people asking for a fundamental right: the right to eat.

The Matthean text alludes to the rejection of Jesus' preaching by the leaders of Israel (vv. 42–43). But it brings us to ask

ourselves also if there is not some kind of complicity with the
murderous tenants in our daily lives. We can ask ourselves, for
example: what role does the establishment of justice and righteousness play for us? What are our fruits? A few chapters later,
the gospel of Matthew will tell us that failing to feed the poor
is the same as denying Christ himself, which means condemning
the poor and Christ to death. Being Christian is precisely the opposite; it is giving life. This is what the gospel requires, and if we
put it into practice, the God of peace will be with us (Phil 4:6–9).

B. Equal before God
Gn 2:18–24; Heb 2:9–11; Mk 10:2–16

The central theme of the texts for this Sunday is the significance
of the human couple in biblical revelation.

The Human Couple

Once again the Pharisees are attempting to place Jesus in contradiction with the religious laws of their time. They have witnessed
Jesus' attitudes which show that he values women, and for that
reason, to test him, they ask: "Is it lawful for a man to divorce
his wife?" (Mk 10:2). They know that it is lawful, but perhaps
this time Jesus will be trapped. The Lord refutes this pretense
and, with authority, explains to them the reason behind Moses'
precept ("because of your hardness of heart," v. 5). But more im-
portantly, Jesus goes to the heart of the matter by referring back
to the "beginning of creation" (v. 6).

Women are not things; they are not part of men's patrimony.
They are persons. Marriage is the union of equal beings who are
primarily identified in terms of their orientation to God. Jesus establishes his position by referring to the two accounts of creation.
Thus, the gospel sends us back to Genesis.

Beings for God

The first chapters of Genesis bring us two narratives of the creation of man and of woman. The first corresponds to the so-called
priestly tradition and the second to the Yahwist tradition. The
initial version underlines the fundamental equality of man and
woman: "So God created humankind in his image, in the image
of God he created them; male and female he created them" (Gn

1:27) (quoted in Mk 10:6). Both have been equally created in the image of God and in relation with him.

The second Genesis account (the only one mentioned in the first reading) speaks of the woman as the helper of the man, stressing complementarity more than equality. "The Lord God said: It is not good that the man should be alone; I will make him a helper as his partner" (2:18).

The central message of these texts is that both man and woman are beings for God, and they are equal before him; this is their basic feature. At the same time, they are also one for the other. Man and woman are created in God's image, and this seals their relationship. Equality is the foundation of complementarity, and the latter does not make sense without the former. This is a partnership based on love, and there can be love only between equals. In Jesus, we are all brothers and sisters (Heb 2:11). This Sunday's texts are a powerful reminder of this equality between women and men without which there cannot be a healthy, human, and Christian life in a couple. These texts reject the would-be male superiority and the "machismo" which are so rooted in our cultural mindsets and which frequently lead to treating women with insulting discrimination.

Considering all other conditions in which so many families live today in the context of these readings, let us say that we are challenged by the demand of a new sharing of responsibilities, based on respect and equality between spouses. Men and women have been equally created in the image of the God of life, and based on that they are to enrich one another.

C. What We Have to Do
Hb 1:2–3, 2:2–4; 2 Tm 1:6–8, 13–14; Lk 17:5–10

The readings for this Sunday deal with the theme of the gratuitousness of faith in an original way.

Increase Our Faith

The gospel starts with a petition from the apostles. Experiencing the need to have a deeper faith, they want to increase their trust in the Lord: "increase our faith" (Lk 17:5). Jesus' answer is a bit surprising. He does not respond directly to the apostles' plea. Instead, he speaks to them about faith and its power to accom-

plish great things, especially from a small beginning, from a faith
which is like a mustard seed (v. 6). What Jesus seems to be saying is that what counts is not having more or less faith but rather
having a strong faith and putting it into practice. We strengthen
faith by practicing it. It is like saying that we learn to love by loving. We learn to believe by believing. Faith cannot be increased
independently from putting it into practice.

To put it differently, there is no path to faith other than discipleship. There is no short-cut to faith. There is only one way, the
way of Jesus. This is the way we are called to follow. It is a difficult
path in the midst of growing poverty and contempt for the human
rights of people harassed in so many ways, people whom we
attempt to deceive with illusions of nonexistent sources of water.

Truly Useful Servants

The second part of today's gospel presents the theme of faith
as a gift. The comparison is seemingly harsh. The servant who
does what he or she is supposed to do deserves no special thanks
from the master (vv. 7–9). In the first place, complying with the
requirements of the faith commitment is not a question of our
own merit. This is why it is not only possible but necessary to
admit that we are "useless servants" or, as some translations say,
"worthless slaves" (v. 10). In saying this, there is a strong affirmation that, first and foremost, faith is a gift. Our capacity to
live that faith, to do what we ought to do (v. 10) is also a grace.
Therefore, the statement about the "uselessness" of the "worthless slaves" is in perfect accord with deeply committed faith. A
life of faith is always a gift which we receive to the extent that we
love God and others.

Consequently and paradoxically, truly useful servants are precisely those who admit they are "worthless." The emphasis on
"worthless" (according to the terms used in this text) seeks to
enhance (in a clearly Hebrew expression) the gratuitousness of
faith. Paul is very aware of this since he received the grace which
led him to go from persecutor to disciple (1 Tm 1:14). Only those
who live this gift and acknowledge it can be bearers of the gratuity of God's love to others. In this way, they can be truly useful
in the work of the kingdom. They are in sharp contrast with
those who show off as teachers without giving the testimony
of love mentioned in the letter to Timothy (vv. 6–7). They contrast with those who, being useless (in the common sense of the

word), consider themselves useful and even indispensable. Solidarity, honesty, and truth must be a disciple's attributes. Life is the reward of those who have faith (Hb 2:4).

Twenty-Eighth Sunday

A. People Not Invited to the Banquet
Is 25:6–10; Phil 4:12–14, 19–20; Mt 22:1–4

In the Bible, the banquet is a frequent image to express the eschatological event — the reign of God — in which God gives himself freely and definitively.

Gratuitousness Favors the Poor

In his narrative Matthew seems to have juxtaposed two parables: the parable of the guests and that of the man not wearing the wedding robe. Undoubtedly, both parables deal with being invited to the kingdom. For a long time it was thought that the unworthy guests referred to the people of Israel who did not welcome the prophets. But there seems to be a better and more consistent interpretation: identifying the unworthy with the people's leaders who benefited from their knowledge of the law in addition to their social rank. They were the ones who had "farms," "businesses," or interests which they placed ahead of the invitation to the kingdom. Moreover, they mistreated the servants. Obviously, "those invited were not worthy" (v. 8).

The invitation to the kingdom is irrevocable and is always open. But its addressees must be sought in another (social) place: "Go therefore into the main streets and invite everyone you find to the wedding banquet" (v. 9). These are the places of people who have no home, no steady employment, or no businesses in the city, the poor and the outcasts, those considered as ignorant and sinful by the religious leaders of the people. In a parallel text, Luke is even more direct and specific: "invite the poor, the crippled, the lame and the blind" (Lk 14:21). Those are the historical addressees of the messianic endeavor, just as Jesus himself responds to those sent by John the Baptist to ask about his identity. Matthew adds that in the main streets they "gathered all whom they found, both bad and good; so the wedding hall was filled with guests" (v. 10) — "bad and good" in that order to make clear that people are not invited because of their merits but rather because of the gratuitous goodness of God toward the poor, the last, and sinners. This grace transforms the "uninvited" into the privileged addressees of the banquet and the kingdom. Being in solidarity with the last and serving them can convert us into guests seated at the same table with the uninvited.

Waiting in Hope and Commitment

In Matthew (it is different in Luke's parallel text), the parable continues with another theme. Someone presents himself without a wedding robe. Accepting the invitation to the kingdom requires a certain practical behavior to which the image of the robe is referring (v. 11).

As the prophecy of Isaiah promises, the perspective of the kingdom consists in our salvific communion with God, source of fulfillment and joy: "this is our God; we have waited for him, so that he might save us. Let us be glad and rejoice in his salvation" (25:9). That will be the definitive victory over death and tears: "he will swallow up death forever. Then the Lord will wipe away the tears from all faces and the disgrace of his people he will take away from all the earth" (v. 8).

The hope of salvation relativizes the value of every other good. That is the experience of Paul who knows "what it is to have little and to have plenty" and how to live in different circumstances: eating well or going hungry, having plenty or being in need (Phil 4:12). Eschatological hope is vibrant and committed hope to transform God's promises into anticipated historical reality and to do that for a fundamental reason: "I can do all things through him who strengthens me" (v. 13).

B. The Eye of a Needle
Wis 7:7–11; Heb 4:12–13; Mk 10:17–30

The word of the Lord exposes us before God's eyes and our own.

On a Journey

The image of the journey is central in the gospel of Mark (Mk 10:17). We are dealing with the theme of following Jesus. This is the meaning of the question addressed to the person whom Matthew calls only "the young man" (19:22). For Mark (and Luke), he seems to have been an older man who asks how to inherit life (Mk 10:17). Jesus begins by referring to God whose goodness is at the root of everything. This is a way of summarizing the first part of the commandments. Then Jesus immediately spells out what corresponds to the second part with an important addition (found only in Mark): "you shall not defraud" (v. 19). The phrase is like a summary of the list just mentioned, the minimum requirement for believers. The rich man simply says, without any arrogance, that he has kept all these precepts (v. 20). This was the conviction of the learned of the time: it is possible to observe the law in its entirety.

However, following Jesus is much more demanding. Lovingly, Jesus invites the man to become one of his followers. In addition to giving up his wealth, the man must give it to the poor and the needy. This will enable him to follow Jesus (v. 21). It is not enough to respect justice in our personal attitudes; we have to go to the root of evil, to the basis of injustice: the desire to accumulate wealth. But giving up his possessions proves to be too difficult for the man. Like many of us, he prefers to live his faith resigned to comfortable mediocrity (v. 22). He does believe but not that much. We profess our faith in God although we refuse to put God's will into practice. Jesus takes advantage of the opportunity to make things very clear to his disciples: attachment to money and to the power it provides is a major obstacle to entering the kingdom (v. 23). The following comparison is rigorous. Some have tried to water it down alleging, for example, that in the city there was a small door called "the eye of the needle." Thus, all a camel had to do was to bend over to be able to go through.

A Two-Edged Sword

The disciples, on the other hand, understand the message perfectly well. The whole matter seems next to impossible for them. To go through the eye of a needle means placing all our trust in God and not in wealth. It is not easy either personally or as church to accept this challenge and, like the disciples, with would-be realism, we wonder: "Then, who can be saved?" (v. 26). We allege that money gives us security and that it enables us to be effective. The Lord reminds us that our capacity to believe in God alone is a grace (v. 27).

As the community of disciples, as church, we have to renounce the security that money and power give. This amounts to having the "spirit of wisdom" (Wis 7:7), allowing wisdom to be our light (v. 10). We are led to wisdom by God's word, the edge of which cuts through our ties to all human prestige. Before the word, nothing is hidden; all our complicities appear very clearly (Heb 4:12–13). As believers and as church, are we capable of passing through the eye of a needle?

C. A Good Samaritan
2 Kgs 5:14–17; 2 Tm 2:8–13; Lk 17:11–19

Remembering people means having them present, not as if they belonged to a dead past but rather as people who are close to us and alive.

True Purification

Once again we have a text that is found only in Luke. Juggling with geography because there is a Samaritan in the story, the evangelist states that Jesus is on his way to Jerusalem going through Samaria. He meets a group of ten lepers who ask him to have mercy on them (v. 12). They address Jesus as "Master" (v. 13), a title which Luke puts only on the lips of the disciples. This might make us think that the lepers, even in the marginal situation to which their disease confines them, are considered as followers of the Lord. Be that as it may, the fact is that they are seeking physical health but also want to rejoin the social group from which their affliction separates them. Leprosy makes them impure, and this is why they are keeping their distance from Jesus and his companions (v. 12). In keeping with the laws of the time, Jesus sends them to the priests so that they may verify the cleansing he is going to work in them (v. 14).

There are other similar narratives in the gospels, but here we find something which Luke wants to emphasize. There is a detail which is sometimes overlooked: it so happens that one of the lepers is a Samaritan (v. 16) and therefore someone who is looked down upon by the Jewish people, though not by Jesus, who shows no partiality. On the contrary, Jesus prefers marginalized and insignificant people. Luke, who shows such sensitivity to the poor, does the same with the Samaritans (see the parable of the good

Samaritan). These lepers have accepted a Samaritan among them; pain has brought them together. However, the Samaritan is the only one who comes back to give thanks. Considered inferior and half pagan, he is the only one who opens his heart to the Lord (v. 15) and thus expresses the real content of purity. The clean of heart are not those who observe rules and appear irreproachable but rather those who are consistent and act with humility, according to the gratuitous love they have received.

Remembering Jesus Christ

In this text, the Samaritan is the one who remembers Jesus — a grateful man, doubly marginalized as a leper and as a "foreigner" (v. 18, literally belonging to a different race). Thus, on the way to Jerusalem where he will be killed at the hands of the defenders of formal purity, Jesus gives life: "your faith has made you well." The grateful Samaritan has to get up and go on his way (v. 19). Having been able to recognize the love of God, from that moment on he must give freely what he has received freely.

Remembering Jesus Christ as Paul asks us to do (2 Tm 2:8) implies our embracing Jesus' testimony of love without legal or religious boundaries (let us think of those, in our own time, who are in the same situation as lepers were in Jesus' time). We must also embrace Jesus' preference for the poor and the despised. Today's texts tell us that we will not be able to do that if we live complacently simply because we are Christians and we are important in our society or in the church. Giving thanks, like this good Samaritan, means being pure of heart, which is a prerequisite for acknowledging that "there is no other god except the Lord" (2 Kgs 5:17).

Twenty-Ninth Sunday

A. Against the Power of Money
Is 45:1, 4–6; 1 Thes 1:1–5; Mt 22:15–21

This time Matthew brings us a very well known and often explained passage. However, its interpretation is frequently sketchy and often inadequate.

Attachment to Money

The opposition between Jesus and the Pharisees is mounting. The following chapter of Matthew's gospel will present the climax of this controversy. Today's text serves as a preparation for that moment. The Pharisees, nationalistic Jews, make a pact with their traditional enemies, the followers of Herod, a collaborator of the Romans and, therefore, a traitor to his people (v. 16). Now together they are facing their greatest opponent: Jesus, who has come to proclaim the reign of God and the role which the poor, despised by the Pharisees, have in it. This is why they join forces; together they go to see Jesus. With fastidious words they are trying to make him stumble before the political power exercised by those who tyrannize their people.

"Is it lawful to pay taxes to the emperor [Caesar] or not?" (v. 17), they ask Jesus. His answer starts by unmasking them: "Why are you putting me to the test, you hypocrites?" (v. 18). Things must be clear. Jesus is not fooled by the feigned praises they address to him. Then Jesus asks them to show him a coin, a denarius. According to the gospels, Jesus never touches the coin personally. Looking at the inscription on the coin, Jesus tells them: "give to the emperor the things that are the emperor's and to God the things that are God's" (v. 21). This statement is sometimes taken as a teaching about the distinction between two powers, political and religious. Yet the text we are considering points to something more profound. As usual, Jesus does not accept being caught within the limits of the question that is formulated.

There Is No Other God

The Pharisees are speaking about "paying taxes" to Caesar. Jesus is speaking of "giving" the coin back to Caesar. These are two different things (in the original Greek, the verbs used express it clearly). The denarius shows an inscription with the head of its owner. The money belongs to the Roman oppressor. In the Pharisees' question, there is a possible insinuation of not paying the tax and thus of their keeping the money for themselves. Their would-be nationalism does not go farther. Jesus is going to the root: it is necessary to eradicate all dependency on money. It is not only a question of breaking with the political dominion of the emperor; it is necessary to break with the oppression which comes from the attachment to money and its possibilities of exploiting others. Jesus tells them to give the coin back to Caesar and to be liberated from money (mammon, see Mt 6:24). Only then will they be able to worship the true God and to give him what belongs to him.

If we are not freed from the power of money, we will not be able to grasp what we are told in Isaiah's text: "I am the Lord and there is no other" (45:6). In these days, many events have made us feel the power of wealth. Jesus is inviting us to give back to Caesar his means of exploiting and forgetting others, to rid ourselves of the oppressive power of money and to recognize the persuasive presence of the Holy Spirit among us (1 Thes 1:5).

B. Serving and Giving Life
Is 53:10–11; Heb 4:14–16; Mk 10:35–45

The section of Mark's gospel from 8:22 to 10:52 contains a series of instructions on discipleship. The texts for these final Sundays are taken from this section. Today's text emphasizes a key point.

The Disciples' Road

In the section to which we have just alluded on several occasions, Mark mentions that Jesus and his disciples "were on the road" (10:32). Following the Lord means starting on the way. By using this classic biblical expression, the evangelist wants to communicate to us what he understands by discipleship. It involves a journey in which we move forward and backward, clearly and in darkness. Mark has a keen awareness of the complexities of the process. Incorruptible, he frequently makes us see the deficiencies of the disciples' faith.

Two of Jesus' closest disciples show their confusion when they say to him: "grant us to sit, one at your right hand and one at your left, in your glory" (v. 37). The Lord responds by asking them if, like himself, they will be able to pay the price of suffering and death (the "cup" and the "baptism") to announce the kingdom of life (vv. 39–40). This statement of Jesus had already caused Peter's initial rejection (8:31–32). What Christ, the "suffering servant" (Is 53:10–11), proposes to his followers (Mk 10:39–40) is surrender to others, not personal glory.

The Meaning of Power

The other disciples get angry with James and John, not because they misunderstand the meaning of Jesus' message but rather because they have come forward to ask for what, in reality, they are all looking for (v. 41). As a matter of fact, it is not easy to understand what accepting the kingdom entails. One of the serious perversions of discipleship consists in believing that our condition as Christians or our responsibilities in the church give us power as "tyrants" (v. 42), lording it over others — in other words, personal glory according to the predominant categories among the great of our society (v. 42).

Jesus, the Messiah, reverses the prevailing order. Seeking to make his disciples move forward on the journey they have started, he teaches them that the great one is the servant and the first one is "the slave of all" (vv. 43–44). This is the messianic inversion which, as we know, forms a central element of the evangelical message. This begins with the Lord himself who, having become one of us (Heb 4:14–16), has not come to be served but to serve.

Serving does not mean that we passively accept that things continue as they are. Serving implies initiative and creativity, knowledge and efforts to build a human, just, and loving world. What the gospel rejects is power as domination, the desire to be recognized as "leaders." It does not reject power that is understood as effective solidarity. In our own days, the hunger which two-thirds of humanity are experiencing and the constant violation of human rights by authoritarian governments, make it urgent for us to place what we are and what we have at the service of the marginalized and to transform today's injustice and exclusion of the many.

C. A God Who Is Listening
Ex 17:8–13; 2 Tm 3:14–4:2; Lk 18:1–8

Luke is the evangelist who most insists on the place of prayer in the life of Jesus, and also on the disciples' need to pray always (we find a similar emphasis in Paul's letters).

God Will Certainly Listen

Today's brief parable selects a fascinating case to show the efficacy of prayer and to teach the disciples "the need to pray always and not to lose heart" (v. 1). We are all perfectly aware that Jesus' time does not have a monopoly on unjust judges and widows seeking justice without obtaining it. In our text, the widow achieves her objective because of her persistent insistence in the same way as the inopportune friend of another parable (Lk 11:5–8), an anecdote which enables Jesus to state "ask and it will be given to you...everyone who asks receives" (vv. 9–10) — a statement of faith, the profound conviction that someone is listening and attentive to our needs and our crying out. In the first reading, Moses is presented in a very colorful scene as a model of perseverance in prayer. In this he is supported by his people (Ex 17:12).

But what is really paradoxical is the conclusion of our parable. We move from the unjust judge to God who will certainly listen to his chosen people when they cry to him "day and night" (18:7) even if, at times, he seems to delay. We find insistent, perhaps desperate crying out, clamors for justice to the good and merciful Lord as the last resort. The same thing happens in Moses' prayer: with his people in deadly straits, with his hands held up, he is appealing to God for his people (Ex 17:11–12). A prayer in dire need, this is what so many of our poor and mistreated people are experiencing, often with the same deep faith.

Will There Be Faith?

The God who brings about justice, his swift answer, praying without losing heart, all these are aspects of an eschatological atmosphere as it is presented in the text which immediately precedes this one (17:22–37). And it is even more evident in the final question of our text, a tragic evocation of the coming of the Son of Man: "will there be faith on earth?" (v. 8). Faith is not automatic, nor is it given forever if it is not nourished. Faith grows and matures through prayer as well as through the practice of the justice that is asked of God. Faith is a gift and it is also a task.

The letter to Timothy contains a significant text: scripture shows us the path of a life of faith; it trains us in "righteousness" (3:16). Thus, we will be equipped for "every good work" (v. 17). If faith is a task, it involves a fundamental requirement to proclaim the word "whether the time is favorable or unfavorable" (4:2), without fears and with the conviction that the word can enlighten every person's life.

Thirtieth Sunday

A. Love Your Neighbor as Yourself
Ex 22:20–27; 1 Thes 1:5–10; Mt 22:34–40

The essence of Matthew's message in the twenty-second chapter is contained in these verses: love of God and love of neighbor are inseparable.

One Love or Two?

Jesus answers the Pharisees who want to put him to the test (Mt 22:37–40) that love of God and love of neighbor are two fundamental dimensions of the gospel of Christ. Some of the tensions we are experiencing in the church have their root in a biased way of interpreting the relation between these two commandments. Some people emphasize the love of God in a way that makes the relationship with neighbors appear secondary and added to what is really important. From that perspective, it is difficult to understand the relevance of the historical commitment of Christians or the demands of the poor, what the Bible calls orphans, widows, and aliens (Ex 22:20–26).

On the other hand, other people suggest that being Christian is manifested more or less exclusively in our commitment and solidarity with others. Without a doubt, this is important for believers. But we are running the risk that prayer, celebration, knowing and savoring the word of God, vital expressions of the gratuitous world in which our relationship with the Lord is situated, lose their full meaning and reduce their outreach.

This is why if we want only to keep one of these loves, we lose both. People who pretend to seek God while they have no interest in their neighbors will not find the God of the Bible. Perhaps they will come to a prime mover of existence. On the other hand, gratuitousness is not only the ambit of our encounter with God, it is also the ambit of the mutual encounter with one another.

Where Will the Poor Sleep?

It is not difficult to reconcile these two demands in theory. The real problem arises at the practical level. The Exodus text helps us face it by reminding us that it is necessary to be concretely concerned: "if you take your neighbor's cloak ... in what else shall that person sleep" (22:27). Is this our situation? Are we concerned about knowing what the poor of our country will wear and where they will spend the night? Will they have a roof over their heads? Will they sleep on the floor, on a mat, or in a bed? Will they have a house, or land from which they will be soon expelled? Being Christians in Peru today means feeling challenged by these questions. This is where the two loves blend. Asking on what the poor will sleep is important to God: "If your neighbor cries out to me, I will listen, for I am compassionate" (Ex 22:27). Believing in "the living and true God" (1 Thes 1:9) leads us to be compassionate too. "Feeling with" the poor will lead us to encounter God.

The quotation from Leviticus 19:18, "you shall love your neighbor as yourself" (Mt 22:39), indicates a Hebrew way of speaking that establishes an equation between "yourself" and "your family." Loving our neighbors as ourselves means loving them as if they were members of our family, as if they were our own. It is a call to a nationalistic people to welcome strangers as if they belonged to their own household.

Those who have no place to sleep must be loved as if they were members of our families. Making every effort so that they may have a home is living our love of God. And we all know what such a commitment means in Peru, in this country of the "homeless." In fact, "on these two commandments hang all the law and the prophets" (Mt 22:40).

B. Salvation and Compassion
Jer 31:7–9; Heb 5:1–6; Mk 10:46–52

Today the gospel of Mark brings us a vivid, tender, and very meaningful account in spite of its apparent simplicity.

On the Way to Jerusalem

In an important dialogue of Jesus with Peter (Mk 8), the Lord announces he will have to undergo great suffering and die at the hands of the leaders of his people. This will take place in Jerusalem, the center of religious power and also economic and political power. The Lord is on his way to Jerusalem, where the definitive confrontation will occur.

As they are leaving the historical city of Jericho, they encounter a blind beggar, a man who is poor on two accounts. He is sitting by the roadside. Mark has preserved the name of that person who is insignificant in the eyes of his contemporaries: Bartimaeus (10:46). Later, he may have become a member of the Christian community formed by the Jews of Palestine. The beggar Bartimaeus greets Jesus the Galilean as the Son of David (v. 47). By doing so, this poor man anticipates the enthusiastic welcome given by the inhabitants of Jerusalem to the Messiah (Mk 11:10). This welcome will be one of the causes of Jesus' arrest and execution. The blind man sees what others are not able to perceive. Acknowledging Jesus as the Christ comes from the insignificant people of society, from those who are by the roadside, from people that some try to silence (v. 38).

Knowing How to Listen

The beggar keeps on calling, and he invokes the compassion of one who is sensitive to human needs because he has been "chosen from among mortals" (Heb 5:1). The Lord who has a foreboding of his death in Jerusalem has time for the beggar. He does not impose his will hurriedly; instead Jesus wants to listen and he asks him: "What do you want me to do for you?" (v. 51). Jesus has come to reveal the love of a Father to us (Jer 31:9) not to impose dictatorial orders. The poor, the insignificant are not mere objects of our generosity or assistance, not even of our charity. They are subjects with their own desires and rights.

Today when we are facing the tragic urgency of the world's poor, we can easily deceive ourselves into pretending we know what suits them better than they do. In all human relationships, and helping another is a form of relationship, we have to respect other persons and recognize their rights. We have to give what we have, but in order to do that we must also be attentive to what others experience as their needs.

The blind man is not begging for alms. He is asking for health and for life. His request is trusting and quick: "he sprang up and came to Jesus" (v. 50). His request is also affectionate as he calls Jesus, "my teacher" (v. 51). The Lord restores his sight and declares him saved or, to be more accurate, he tells the man that his faith, his trust in him, is what has given him life, what has made him well (v. 52). Bartimaeus takes his place as a new disciple and, no longer sitting by the roadside, he starts to follow Jesus on the way which will lead him to the cross and the resurrection. In these painful but rich times in Latin America, many people like Bartimaeus are no longer sitting by the roadside; they are springing up to come to the Lord, the friend of life.

C. The Cries of the Poor
Sir 35:12–14, 16–18; 2 Tm 4:6–8, 16–18; Lk 18:9–14

The texts for this Sunday present two important themes: Pharisaism and solidarity with the poor. Keeping in mind the road which leads to the kingdom will make us clearly see the contrast between the two.

Believing We Are Righteous

The parable of the Pharisee and the tax collector is one of the best known in the gospels. Once again, we have a text unique to Luke. In the gospels the Pharisees are not only the historical people Jesus had to face; Pharisaism is also presented as the permanent temptation of Christians. In this parable, for example, the Lord makes us see that being disciples must not lead us to conceit or to contempt for others.

Pharisaism consists in feeling justified and pure, different from others (Lk 18:11) on the basis of the formal observance of religious precepts (v. 12). In the gospels, the Pharisees are those who say one thing and do another; they are the hypocrites. This inconsistency is present in the behavior of many Christians, and it is a dangerous possibility for all of us who belong to the church. What the Lord requires of his church is an attitude of humility and service, a church which is not afraid of admitting its sinfulness and which lives the love and forgiveness of God as a grace (v. 13). The parable is a strong warning against the pride of believers. To their surprise, the people they despise (self-righteous Jews considered publicans as public sinners) receive God's favor (v. 14). No one escapes from this slap on the wrist.

A Race toward the Kingdom

A merely formal religious practice is not supported by openness and commitment to others. Taking the presence of Jesus into account means remembering the consistency of his life. He proclaimed the kingdom, he prayed, he read scripture, and, at the same time, he gave life to everything around him and was especially sensitive to the poor and the insignificant. Imitating the Lord means starting the race toward the kingdom (2 Tm 4). In that process, we have to remember that God cannot be bribed by our offering sacrifices to him (Sir 35:14) — sacrifices in compliance with the norms of worship but unjust because they do not take into account "the cries of the poor" who will not rest "until they reach God" (v. 21). Jesus has come to reveal to us a God who "listens to the prayers of those who are wronged" (v. 16) because he is a God who is just and wants justice. He is a God who rejects those who, pretending to be close to him, despise those whom God prefers. This contempt leads them away from the God whom they claim to be following.

These texts set us free from our pretended security. They remind us that there are no exclusive owners of the truth and ethics and they call us to live our Christian faith with humility as we learn from other persons and commit ourselves to the least members of society.

Thirty-First Sunday

A. The Greatest among You Will Be Your Servant
Mal 1:14, 2:2, 8–10; 1 Thes 2:7–9, 13; Mt 23:1–12

Jesus' exhortation "the greatest among you will be your servant" gives us the key to understand the admonitions addressed to the priests (first reading) and to the "scribes and Pharisees" (gospel), as well as the testimony which Paul gives about his own behavior at the service of the communities (second reading).

One Father: The One in Heaven

Matthew's text brings us a harsh controversy with the Pharisees. Jesus forewarns the people who are interested in hearing his words and the disciples not to take Jewish religious leaders as their models "because they do not practice what they teach" (v. 3). He questions their desire to appear important and to enjoy privileges in society. As the prophet Malachi had warned the priests of his day, the only meaning of their function is "to listen and lay it to heart to give glory to my name, says the Lord of hosts" (2:2). Giving glory to God means listening and putting his will into practice as the only absolute. Jesus had been the model of that: the meaning of his life was to do his Father's will in everything and to accomplish the signs of his reign. This is the reason why Jesus, the Christ, is the only teacher to acknowledge and to follow. For the same reason, Jesus recommends this to his disciples: "call no one your father on earth, for you have one Father — the one in heaven" (v. 9).

People who are granted a function or a responsibility in the community must carry it out with humility rather than considering themselves the center or the absolute reference for others. They must be the ones who, by their words, their attitudes, and their consistent behavior, remember who is the only Teacher and the only Father. Jesus summarizes this saying, "the greatest among you will be your servant" (v. 11). This is neither a rejection of the specific function of direction nor does it suggest that being great is bad. However, it does point out that such people should be the first to serve as something new, inspired by Jesus' own example.

Evangelizing with Love

In his first letter to the Thessalonians, Paul confesses that he exercises his apostolate with the love of a mother "tenderly caring for her own children" (v. 7). He does not pretend to be a master who teaches authoritatively but one who gives the gospel by giving himself without sparing his "labor and toil." Evangelizing is not laying heavy burdens "on the shoulders of the people" (Mt 23:4) but rather, first of all, giving oneself. We truly proclaim what we live only with consistency and joy. Prior to any evangelizing technique or methodology, what is required is the testimony of a "pure, upright, and blameless conduct" (v. 10) and the service of the word offered with love and humility. In this way, the word will be received "not as a human word but as what it really is, God's word, which is also at work in you believers" (1 Thes 2:13).

The gospel of the Lord can be communicated and proclaimed

with love only by way of generous surrender and humble service. The Lord wants us to be witnesses and servants of the word, people who listen and take the glory of his name to heart. As Saint Irenaeus said in the second century, the glory of God is men and women who are fully alive.

B. Keeping in Our Hearts
Dt 6:2–6; Heb 7:23–28; Mk 12:28–34

The memory of believers who know they are loved corresponds to the memory of God who forgets no one.

God Alone

In the controversy with the Sadducees, Jesus has just stated that the biblical God "is God not of the dead but of the living" (Mk 12:27). A scribe (no doubt a Pharisee) asks him a question debated among the learned: "Which commandment is the first of all?" (v. 28). As usual, Jesus' answer becomes a challenge. There is not one major commandment, there are two of them: love of God and love of neighbor. But both are preceded (only in Mark, not in the parallel texts of Matthew or Luke) by a statement (taken from Deuteronomy) which is found as the beginning of all: "The Lord God is one" (Dt 6:4; Mk 12:29). The two loves mentioned flow from this principle, which is why they are inseparable since they have a common source.

Biblical faith (on whose tradition Jesus relies) is a process through which we acknowledge God as the absolute in our lives. God is not something abstract but someone whom we must love "with all our mind and with all our strength" (Mk 12:30). This is the reason for the categorical rejection of all forms of idolatry that we find in the Bible. As we know, idolatry means putting our trust in someone other than God. This is a danger for all believers.

Not long ago we celebrated the four hundredth anniversary of the death of Saint John of the Cross. A mystic and a poet, his historical context was very different from ours. He was not directly concerned about many of the problems which afflict us now when we try to live our faith in God in the midst of the poverty and injustice experienced by the vast majority of men and women. However, he was the bearer of a universal message to which we must also be sensitive from the context of our own reality: all we need is God. Nothing must veil God's face to us. Power and money are idols denounced in the Bible. In a subtle way, so can be our commitment to justice, our social analyses, or our theological task when they entice us to stop on our journey to God, a journey which must never stop. In his context and in his own way, John of the Cross gives witness that "the Lord our God is one."

Love Your Neighbor as Yourself

Precisely because the presence of God is so unique, our neighbors are important to us. Loving another derives from the same principle. It is the other commandment mentioned by Jesus. It is not an addition and it is not optional. Its roots are also in the one God, a God who loves everyone, a God who remembers everyone. Loving God means that we make people who are important to God also important to us. Keeping God's word in our hearts (Dt 6:6) is expressed by loving those whom God loves. In the biblical mentality, love your neighbor "as yourself" (Lv 19:18; Mk 12:31) means as your own family, your own people. It means loving strangers with the same intensity and solidarity as if they were members of our family.

The scribe understands that. He even senses that this is what gives meaning to worship, which would be empty otherwise. The Lord approves the man's opinion (v. 34). But, however appropriate this opinion may be, it is not enough, it is necessary to put it into practice. Everything indicates that for the scribe and also for us, it is easier to speak correctly than to act in harmony with what we say.

C. Loving the Living
Wis 11:22–12:2; 2 Thes 1:11–2:2; Lk 19:1–10

The gospel for this Sunday offers us one of Luke's most delightful narratives: the story of Zacchaeus, the tax collector.

The Rich Man

One of the first details provided by the Lukan text refers to the fact that Zacchaeus was a chief publican and he was rich (v. 1). He is not, therefore, just anyone, but the chief tax collector, and he is looked down upon by Jews because of his collaboration with the ruling Romans. Zacchaeus is undoubtedly a rich man who handles money. The presence of Jesus becomes a challenge to him. But the gospel does not tell us the motives Zacchaeus has to see Jesus. It mentions only his enthusiasm and the efforts of this man, short in stature — hence his climbing a sycamore tree (vv. 3–4) — to see Jesus.

From his place in the tree, Zacchaeus receives the call of Jesus: come down because I must stay at your house today (v. 5). At once, Zacchaeus hurries down the tree and welcomes Jesus (v. 6). Jesus enters Zacchaeus's house, but the story makes it very clear that Jesus is the one who invites Zacchaeus to open the door. The initiative comes from Jesus. Zacchaeus answers Jesus' invitation and, rising to his feet, responds by promising to give half of his possessions to the poor and to pay back those who have been victimized by his zeal for profit and his collaboration with the occupying Romans (v. 8). Jesus' presence has an impact on Zacchaeus's lifestyle: he starts to give and to share.

No One Is Excluded

The narrative shows that Jesus also addresses the rich. No one is excluded from the call to participate in the kingdom. But Jesus' call to the rich man is an invitation for him to cease to be rich, to cease to hoard for himself. The gospel underscores the fact that Zacchaeus is a tax collector, in other words, someone despised by Jewish society. The kingdom is also for those who are not socially well considered. Jesus does not exclude anyone. If people are excluded from the kingdom, it is because they have excluded themselves. Jesus' intention is always to save, especially to save those who are lost (v. 10).

The text also questions the true kinship with Abraham. Being a child of Abraham — and here we can appropriately add being a child of God and brother or sister of Jesus — is not a matter of blood, race, or culture. Kinship is the fruit of practice; it is a response to a call (2 Thes 1:11): sharing and living as a brother or sister of others. This is why Jesus recognizes this publican as a son of Abraham, a son of Abraham standing firm. Zacchaeus is called to love the living, as the book of Wisdom beautifully puts it (11:26). The God of our faith is the one who always forgives and who wants all people to put their trust in him (Wis 12:2).

Thirty-Second Sunday

A. A Sincere Desire for Instruction
Wis 6:12–20; 1 Thes 4:13–14; Mt 25:1–13

The parables from the last chapters of Matthew sharpen the perception of God at work in history. The gift of eternal life in Jesus judges our lives.

Lord, Lord

The parable refers to the way weddings were conducted in Jesus' time. At a given moment, the bridegroom would arrive and go in with all the guests and the celebration would start. Matthew's gospel, always permeated by ecclesial experience, presents the Christian community as the ten bridesmaids waiting for the bridegroom. It includes foolish and wise people (vv. 1–4). On various occasions, Matthew points out the differences and even the divisions which are present in the church. The bridegroom's delay will reveal the situation. At first, all the bridesmaids do the same thing: they fall asleep (v. 5). That fact is not censured in this passage. This is not the focus. What does count is that some bridesmaids have brought oil with them and the others have not. Therefore, they find themselves in different situations when the bridegroom appears (vv. 8–9).

Here the bridegroom is an allegorical reference to the Lord. His arrival is a judgment which separates the waters. Those who have heard his message and put it to work will have a share in the kingdom: "those who were ready went with him into the wedding banquet" (v. 10). To those who have not made the gospel the norm of their lives or, perhaps more correctly, who have only accepted it formally, the Lord will say: "I do not know you" (v. 12). The meaning of the phrase is the rejection of those who pretend to be what they are not. Those who have not lived as authentic followers of Jesus are saying "Lord, Lord, open to us" (v. 11). This expression is reminiscent of what was said in Mt 7:21: "Not everyone who says to me, 'Lord, Lord,' will enter the kingdom of heaven." To those who are believers in words only, the Lord will also say: "I never knew you; go away from me" (7:23).

Keeping Awake

The passage concludes with a call to be alert, to pay attention to the gospel demands (v. 13). Vigilance is nourished by hope. Paul reminds us that the basis of this hope is the conviction that Jesus has risen from the dead. A life imprisoned by death leads to sadness (1 Thes 4:13). Hope makes us leap over this barrier. Believing in the resurrection is affirming a life which knows no temporal or historical limits. Dying in Jesus (v. 14) is giving one's life in love as Jesus has done. God will take to himself those who have done that (v. 14). Eternal life starts here and now; otherwise it would not be eternal. First and foremost, however, it is a gift from the Lord.

The Bible invites us to have a sincere desire for instruction, for the joyful knowledge of God. That is wisdom, and it is marked by love (Wis 6:18). This is why wisdom "leads to the kingdom" (v. 20). Wisdom will assist us in discernment required in Matthew's text. It will not allow us to say we are Jesus' disciples if we do not put his message into practice.

B. Knowing How to See
1 Kgs 17:10–16; Heb 9:24–28; Mk 12:38–44

Jesus is already in Jerusalem. There he will be arrested and executed. Before that he will announce his good news in the city dominated by people who refuse to hear it.

Ostentation and Spoliation

The controversy with religious leaders of the people takes a dangerous turn for Jesus. The Lord denounces their taste for ostentation and honors (Mk 12:38–39). But what is at stake is not only something frivolous, because their ostentation is based on their despoiling the poor: "they devour widows' houses" (v. 40). The trilogy of the poor is well known in the Old Testament: widows, orphans, and aliens, or defenseless people whose lives are very harsh.

In this Markan passage and also in the passage from 1 Kings, the widow represents the poor, the insignificant people. The few things they have are devoured by those who should be their spiritual guides, those who say long prayers "for the sake of appearance" (v. 40). They will be judged more severely than others because of this iniquitous robbery (v. 40). The Lord rejects all use of religious prerogatives (which exist only to serve) in order to obtain the first places and to be surrounded by honors. And he calls all of us to examine ourselves in this respect.

The Widow's Mite

Then Mark immediately relates a simple episode. Jesus is going to the temple, the heart of the religious, economic, and political power of Jerusalem. Jesus sits down "opposite the treasury" (v. 41) and he starts to watch how believers going to the temple put their money in the treasury (v. 41). The temple was very large and Jesus, seemingly by himself (v. 43), selects a spot that will enable him to see what he cannot see from any other position. This may be the main teaching of the text.

The rich are putting in large sums. On the contrary, "a poor widow" puts in "two small copper coins" (v. 42). This is not a casual fact for this keen observer who sees beyond appearances. His reading of reality comes from the message of the kingdom which he proclaims and from the perspective in which he has placed himself. The teacher will make his disciples see the significance of what is taking place. What the "poor widow" has done seems insignificant to a people not enlightened by faith, who are outside the pulse of history, but for Jesus her two coins are worth more than all the alms of the rich (v. 43).

The reason for this is clear: the rich are giving out of their abundance, but the widow "out of her poverty has put in everything she had, all she had to live on" (v. 44). The widow of Zarephath had done the same with the prophet Elijah (1 Kgs 17:10–16) — not out of abundance but out of her need. In his encyclical *Sollicitudo Rei Socialis* (no. 31), John Paul II invites us to do the same. Christ gave his life for us (Heb 9:24–28) and disciples must not be above the master.

This is the foundation of solidarity. It is not a type of assistance which is humiliating but rather a commitment which is encouraging, a surrender, an interchange among equals. In order to perceive this, it is necessary to know how to see, which implies selecting our vantage point to observe reality.

C. A God of the Living, Not of the Dead
2 Mc 7:1–2, 9–14; 2 Thes 2:16–3:5; Lk 20:27–38

Today's texts speak to us of the gift of life, eternal life which is expressed in our belief in the resurrection.

A Being for Life

For the first time in Luke's gospel, the Sadducees appear on the scene. They are part of a group recruited among the upper echelons of priests and laity. They are more important because of their influence, their wealth, and their ties with Roman authorities than because of their numbers. Enemies of the Pharisees, they end up joining them to oppose Jesus, whose preaching of the kingdom is undermining their privileges. Claiming Moses as their authority, they relate an insidious and ridiculous story to ambush the Lord, whom they call "teacher," perhaps without much conviction (Lk 20:27).

As usual, Jesus answers in a bewildering way. Leaving aside a myopic and literal interpretation of the law, the Lord refers to a central text of the Jewish faith, one that is certainly more important than the text cited by the Sadducees. In fact, the third chapter of Exodus brings us the revelation of the name of God. We know that in the Jewish mentality the name expresses the very person. This is the dialogue in which God gives Moses the mission of liberating his people. In doing that, God is showing sensitivity to the oppression that the Jews are suffering in Egypt, and this attitude is framed by two statements: "I am the God of your father, the God of Abraham, the God of Isaac, and the God of Jacob" (Ex 3:6, quoted in Luke) and "I am who I am" (Ex 3:14). Jesus reveals the profound meaning of this communication to Moses: "He is God, not of the dead, but of the living" (Lk 20:37).

A God Who Liberates

The God of the ancestors of the Jewish people is Yahweh, the God of life, the one who is just with others. Faith in the resurrection is faith in a God who gives and wants to give life to all "for to him all of them are alive" (Lk 20:38). This is why he is a liberating God. Paul speaks of the God "who loved us and through grace gave us eternal comfort and good hope" (2 Thes 2:16). Comfort is the term used by second Isaiah to speak of liberation — a gift of grace which leads us to prayer and solidarity.

Faith and hope in the resurrection must be translated into a commitment to defend life. We know what this implies today in Peru where powers of death (the different types of violence present among us) seem to torture the people, especially the poorest and the oppressed. Faith in the resurrection does not take us out of history; on the contrary, it makes us incarnate ourselves in it with the conviction that its ultimate meaning is in life. This kind of hope gave courage to the Maccabees to resist the threats of the mighty of their time (2 Mc 7). Believing in the God of the living makes us reject the premature and unjust death inflicted upon so many of our contemporaries.

Thirty-Third Sunday

A. Can We Love without Taking Risks?
Prv 31:10–13, 19–20, 30–31; 1 Thes 5:1–6; Mt 25:14–30

In these days of the predominance of liberal or neoliberal economy, it would be tempting to take advantage of the theme of the talents (the talent had a great deal of value) to speak of money saved and invested, of wandering capital and secret bank accounts. But in fact the parable of the talents points to something else.

Two Attitudes

The parable tells us about two attitudes: of those who pass on what they have received from God and of those who keep for themselves what the Lord wanted to give to them. In addition, the focus of the parable is in the criticism of the second attitude. From the start, in the image of the absence of the "man, going on a journey" (v. 14), the responsibility of Christians in history is recalled. They are responsible for the proclamation of the gospel. In everyday life, with its good and bad moments, its tensions and conflicts, Jesus' disciples have to bear witness to life. That is the meaning of receiving the talents. This is why Saint Paul tells us that we have "to keep awake" (1 Thes 5:6). The first two slaves did just that. Moreover, their vigilance is translated into service and, thanks to their work, the Lord's gifts have produced fruits.

The first reading is taken from a classic text of Proverbs. In this passage, beyond the limits imposed by a particular vision of a woman's role, we find the praise of a generous behavior which naturally expresses love of others.

The Real Joy of the Lord

The attitude of the third slave in the parable is entirely different. Mean and fearful, he pretends to be on good terms with God without leaving his own world (v. 18). He thinks that a life of faith is something that happens only between himself and God — a God he considers demanding and harsh, more interested in punishment than in love (vv. 24–25). He does not understand the meaning of the gospel's demands, which he interprets as religious norms of exact and formal observance. Others, the people living around him, have no place in his Christian life. Moreover, his relationship with others could be dangerous for him; they might have taken him away from his intended path and prevented him from complying with what he sees as his obligations as a believer. This is why he prefers to take no risks and to give back to the Lord exactly what he has received. Thus, he feels more secure. Saint Paul would say that he is "asleep" (1 Thes 5:6).

The slave will soon know, and so will we, that his way will not lead him to light but to darkness (v. 30). In his narrow-mindedness, he can conceive only of a God in terms of rewards and punishments. On the contrary, the God of Jesus never tires of loving freely and of making demands. The grace of his love overflows the banks of our selfishness and false security. Faith is not something that we keep in a safe to protect it. Faith is life which is expressed in love and gift to our neighbor. In the gospels, being afraid is equivalent to having no faith. Therefore, how can we love without taking risks, without entering into the world of our country's dispossessed, who are struggling for their right to life? Our solidarity with them will lead us to unforeseen dangers and conflicts and perhaps to misunderstandings within our own family and our Christian community. However, the parable of the talents teaches us that the joy of the Lord (vv. 21 and 23), as well as our own joy, consists in a Christian life based on grace, courage, and concern for others rather than on formality, self-protection, and fear.

B. A Gospel of Hope
Dn 12:1–3; Heb 10:11–14, 18; Mk 13:24–32

Ordinary time is coming to a close. We are already preparing for the advent of the Lord.

End of the Temple or End of History?

The gospel text is taken from the most difficult chapter of Mark. It is often interpreted as announcing the end of the world. However, if we take the chapter as a whole, we will be able to see that we are dealing with the theme of meaning rather than chronology.

In response to the admiration for the temple of Jerusalem expressed by his disciples, Jesus announces its destruction (vv. 1–2). His followers then ask when that is going to take place and what the sign will be (v. 4). The entire text bears the imprint of that proclamation and that question. The Lord tells them that, like him, they will also be signs of contradiction (vv. 14–22). The disciples must be forewarned (v. 23). Here the temple represents the power of the privileged of the time, those who reject the proclamation of the kingdom and who will seek to kill Jesus and to eradicate his memory. They will not succeed. The Lord will come with power and majesty (vv. 24–27). His message will not be forgotten.

The temptation of the temple is permanent. It does not belong to one period of history or to the Jewish people alone. It is a risk which also threatens disciples, both the immediate and subsequent disciples like us. We too can transform the first fruits of the kingdom, the church, into a rich and powerful temple, a building evoking admiration and lending support to undue privileges. Jesus has come and he continues to come to put an end to this type of religion. His message is liberating because it calls us to serve rather than to dominate. Shortly before, Jesus said that he had come to serve rather than to be served (Mk 10:45). The temple means just the opposite. From that point of view, its destruction is not the end of history. It is an event that must be seen in the light of the kingdom and judged from the perspective of the Parousia, the return of the Lord.

Reading the Signs of the Times

We can read those signs only by analyzing events day by day (vv. 28–32). Attention to what is happening around us draws its inspiration from the conviction that the Lord's word is embodied in a history which seems to contradict it, but through which God is also speaking to us. If we maintain the gospel in a greedy and aseptic way, if we look for it where we had it hidden and wrapped up just for ourselves, we will not find it; it will have disappeared. There will be hard times, but if we do away with our impulse to make ourselves into a "temple" of privileges and pride, we will be ready to welcome salvation, the friendship of the Lord (Dn 12:1). God's life will lift us up from the dust of the earth (v. 2). Being on guard characterizes those who have hope, people who are attuned to the growth of the kingdom of God. In this way and with Christ, we will be offering our lives (Heb 10).

C. With Perseverance
Mal 4:1–2; 2 Thes 3:7–12; Lk 21:5–19

Before narrating Jesus' death and resurrection, Luke, like Mark, has Jesus give a farewell discourse.

Discernment in Difficult Times

Even though Luke's text is very close to Mark's, there are also a few significant differences. In Luke, Jesus addresses not only the disciples. His words are not limited to a privileged few or to close friends, as seems to be the case in Mark. Jesus' words also reach other people. The prophesy starts with the temple (vv. 5–6), but it moves beyond. The Lord warns those who will be his followers not to be deceived by impostors who, in some way, want to take their place. He asks them to be discerning in terms of the confusing events to come (vv. 8–11). They should be heartened by the conviction that "the end will not follow immediately" (v. 9).

Jesus' followers are going to be mistreated and persecuted (vv. 11–12). But this must be an opportunity to bear witness to the Lord's teaching (v. 13). We are well aware of that on a continent where this testimony has led to the surrender of lives. Luke looks at things from the point of view of victims of persecution. Moreover, Luke assures them that the Lord will assist his witnesses at that moment to enable them to resist and contradict their adversaries. The Lord will give them the necessary eloquence and wisdom to confront their opponents' accusations (vv. 14–15). In the book of Acts, Luke presents various similar cases among the first gospel proclaimers. Among those who will oppose Jesus' followers, there will be people who are very close to them, thus making that situation even more painful (v. 16).

Having Confidence

Foreseeing all these problems, which have been happening in the historical experience of Christians throughout the centuries, does not prevent Luke from emphasizing our reasons to hope. It stimulates him instead. Our text ends by reasserting a conviction: "Not a hair of your head will perish. By your endurance you will gain your souls" (vv. 18–19). The Lord will be with those who speak in his name. This is a call to constancy, to perseverance, and to steadfastness in hope. Thus, we will gain our lives, which is another way of translating the word expressed by the term "souls."

This implies that we give a testimony of an austere life which is not a burden on anyone. In this regard, Paul presents himself simply as "an example to imitate" (2 Thes 3:9). Simplicity of life, hope, and trust in the Lord will enable us to face difficult situations and to be discerning with the assurance that "the sun of righteousness shall rise, with healing wings" (Mal 4:2) and will enlighten us.

Jesus Christ, King of the Universe

A. Eternal Life
Ez 34:11–12, 15–17; 1 Cor 15:20–26, 28; Mt 25:31–46

At the end of ordinary time, the liturgy reminds us of the meaning of the reign of Jesus Christ.

From the Perspective of Insignificance

Jesus' preaching, started in the fifth chapter of Matthew with the beatitudes addressed to those who follow his teaching, concludes now by reminding us of what is essential in the conduct of the disciples. The Son of Man (Mt 25:31), the king (v. 34), will come to judge the nations. His kingdom is not a kingdom of power but of service: "The Son of Man came not to be served but to serve"

(Mt 20:28). This is the criterion for judgment. Entering into the kingdom, definitive life, eternal life presupposes that disciples have followed the path of the master in serving all people and especially those with the greatest need.

However, precisely because we are dealing with eternal life, it is not limited to what is beyond human history. It is not only future life, it is eternal life. That means life of all times, including the present. The demands of the kingdom lead to giving life now: giving food, something to drink, etc. These actions must express the grace that God has given us in giving his own life. Thus, the preferred addressees are the "least" and the most forgotten. Here Matthew uses the same term he uses to refer to Bethlehem (2:6), the insignificant city from which the Messiah comes. In this sense, all the poor and forgotten people are insignificant like Bethlehem, yet from them, the Lord comes to us. This is why the text is telling us that in serving the poor we are serving the Christ of our faith and that in solidarity with the neediest we recognize the humble kingship of the Son of Man. There is no other way to "inherit the kingdom" (25:34), that is to say being face to face with the Lord.

What Is Definitive

God's judgment is not confined to the realm of the individual. A few years back, in commenting on this text of Matthew, John Paul II recalled its "social dimension," stating that he was "referring to the total universal dimension of injustice and of evil." He concluded with these severe warnings: "in the light of Christ's words, the poor South will judge the opulent North. And poor people and poor nations — poor in different ways, not only lacking food but also deprived of freedom and of other human rights — will be judging those who snatch away their possessions, accumulating for themselves the imperialist monopoly of economic and political predominance at the expense of others" (Homily in Namao, Canada, September 17, 1984). The Lord and the poor of our country have much to say about the indifference, the frivolity, and the subtle cruelty of those who accumulate for themselves the goods they take away from others.

The Son of Man is king. He is also a shepherd, and he will look after his sheep (Ez 34). His reign of service is here and now an expression of his victory over death (1 Cor 15). Believing that God has communicated his own life to us does not take us out of history. On the contrary, it makes us assume it fully because what is definitive is judged in what is transitory.

B. The Alpha and the Omega
Dan 7:13–14; Rv 1:5–8; Jn 18:33–37

The liturgical year ends with this Sunday. The feast, formerly called Christ the King, has been renewed by the council to stress the universal rule of Jesus.

Authentic Kingship

The core of Jesus' message is the kingdom of God. The God of Jesus Christ is the God of the kingdom, the one who has a word and an involvement in human history from which the image of kingdom is taken. The God of the Bible cannot be separated from his plan, the kingdom. Central in the synoptic gospels, the theme of the kingdom does not present itself in the same way in John. In his gospel, the focus of the theme is on the kingship of Christ.

This is what we have in today's passage from John. Echoing the accusation of the Jews, Pilate asks Jesus: "Are you the King of the Jews?" (v. 33). The accused prepares his answer with a previous question which shakes the Roman official's ground: "Do you ask this on your own or did others tell you about me?" (v. 34). Pilate's arrogance does not intimidate Jesus, who then gives his own answer in the well-known words: "My kingdom is not from this world" (v. 36). At once, Jesus gives the reason: my kingdom does not use coercion, it is not imposed. The idea is repeated: "my kingdom is not from this world."

We can easily fall into the temptation of interpreting this statement as a reference to a kingdom on an exclusively religious and spiritual level, with little or no incidence in the temporal realm, in concrete history. However, such an interpretation does not correspond to the gospel as a whole. An earlier text from John can help us understand the present text. In chapter eight, in the midst of a harsh controversy with the Pharisees, Jesus tells them: "I am not of this world" (v. 23). The terms in the original Greek language are exactly the same. There is a distance and even a rupture, and Jesus wants to point it out. However, it is not between what is religious and temporal but rather between domination and service. Jesus' kingdom is unlike the one that Pilate knows, a kingdom of arbitrariness, privileges, and domination. Jesus' kingdom is a kingdom of love, justice, and service.

I Am a King

Pilate is astute and he is not misled. He does not see in Jesus' answer a denial of his kingship. He infers and insists: "So you are a king" (v. 37). The Lord accepts without hedging: "You say that I am a king. For this I came into the world": to inaugurate a world of peace and fellowship, of justice and respect for other people's rights, of love for God and for one another. This is his kingdom which comes into human history, enhancing it and leading it beyond itself, a kingdom which will have no end though it is present as of now; it is not only for the future, "his dominion is everlasting" (Dn 7:14). It is not limited to the past, to the present, or to the future. In the Lord's Prayer, we ask for this kingdom to come in its fullness.

Jesus bears witness to that truth. He gives testimony of the will to love of the Father whose reign "is everlasting" as the prophet Daniel announces (7:14). If we listen to the voice of Jesus, we belong to the truth (Jn 18:37), we are made to "be a kingdom" (Rv 1:6). Jesus and the kingdom he proclaims are the ultimate meaning of our lives, "the Alpha and the Omega" (v. 8), the beginning and the end.

C. Service, Not Domination
2 Sm 5:1–3; Col 1:12–20; Lk 23:35–43

Ordinary time ends with the feast of Jesus Christ, king of the universe. We are invited to reflect on the meaning of the kingdom.

The Kingdom of the Son

Jesus is condemned to death for claiming he is a king. This is what his accusers are saying and Jesus himself admits it to Pilate, the representative of the king (the Roman emperor) whose armies are occupying Palestine and oppressing its inhabitants (Lk 23:1–3). Jesus' status as king of the Jews is found in the inscription on the upper part of the cross (Lk 23:38). It is in stark contrast with the physical situation of the man nailed on the cross. Is this a king? Of what kingdom?

The people who had been listening to Jesus' preaching are looking at the crucified one in bewilderment and perhaps consternation. The officials (literally the leaders) who had been challenged by his teaching are scoffing at him now; they are enjoying their victory. The one who had presented himself as the Savior is not able to save himself. They were thinking that this would discredit him before the crowd (vv. 35–38). Once again, they had misunderstood. But we too run the risk of misunderstanding — affirming, for example, that Jesus admits he is the king of a purely spiritual realm without any connection with this world. The kingdom of God, which the Messiah announces, is a universal reality from which no one escapes. In a beautiful christological canticle, Paul tells us that "all things have been created through him and for him" (Col 1:16).

Here the radical opposition is not between what is spiritual and temporal, religious and historical. Rather, it is between the power of domination and the power of service. Jesus is not a king like this world's kings who dominate and mistreat those who are under them. Jesus does not use his power for his own benefit and this is precisely why he does not save himself. The Lord has come to teach us that all power (political, religious, or intellectual) is at the service of the oppressed and the destitute.

The Son of David

Service, not domination, is the great norm of the kingdom announced by the Lord. It is betrayed when we use whatever power we may have received in order to impose our ideas and to preserve our privileges, for example, when as church people we take advantage of our situation in society to turn a deaf ear to the rights of people who do not share our faith. An attitude of service presupposes sensitivity to listen to others. That testimony alone will open hearts and minds to the proclamation of the kingdom of Christ. The attitude of Jesus, who never used his power to his own advantage, broke the hardness of one of the criminals with whom he was crucified (Lk 23:40–41). The Lord's testimony made him understand of what kingdom Jesus was king: of a kingdom which, from now on, in this world and in society, must change our way of perceiving things and relating with others. It must inspire us to incarnate the great values of the reign of God in our history.

In fact, we must not forget that the one in whom the Lord has made the "fullness of God" (Col 1:19) dwell is the son of David (2 Sm 5:1–5), a man of our history and, as Luke reminds us (23:6), a Galilean — a member, therefore, of a despised people. From that situation, the Lord is calling us to a kingdom of solidarity; he is calling us to be with him (Lk 23:43).

Solemn Feasts

"Blessed is she who believed."
(Lk 1:45)

Saint Peter and Saint Paul

The Proclamation of the Message
Acts 12:1–11; 2 Tm 4:6–8, 17–18; Mt 16:13–19

The liturgy of the church likes to present the two great apostles Peter and Paul together. Their figures illuminate each other.

Recognizing Jesus

The so-called profession of faith of Peter is no doubt a central text in the gospels. During the liturgical year, we have already come across it in its different versions. Here it is presented as the starting point and the foundation of Peter's mission and, through him, the mission of all the followers of Jesus. The key question is to ask ourselves who the Lord is for us. It is the question that Jesus asks his disciples. Always eager, Peter speaks in the name of all: "You are the Messiah, the Son of the living God" (Mt 16:16). The expression which Matthew puts on Peter's lips is the development of the one used by Mark in the parallel passage (8:29). Christ and the Son of God point to the same reality: Jesus' messiahship. The reference to the living God occurs several times in Matthew. It reminds us that the biblical God intervenes in history to liberate and to give life, differently from gods who neither hear nor speak.

Matthew presents Peter with his merits and enthusiasm but also with his weaknesses. The last time Peter is mentioned, it is in reference to the fear he experiences which leads him to deny Jesus. The evangelist leaves him weeping "bitterly" when he becomes aware of his error and his cowardice (26:69–75). However, his repentance and his honesty make Peter embrace the road of discipleship again. The pillar of the church, as Paul calls him (Gal 2:9), is righteous and sinful at the same time. The Lord trusts him (Mt 16:19) and accompanies him in his mission of announcing the gospel (Acts 12:1–11).

The Good Fight

In a type of assessment of his life's journey as an apostle, sensing that "the time of his departure has come" (2 Tm 4:6), Paul considers that he "has finished the race" (v. 7). He has fought

273

an important fight and has kept the faith, and now he is waiting trustingly for "the crown of righteousness" (v. 8). The former persecutor of Christians had to work hard to be heard in the church, especially to make it understand his mission to non-Jews.

In a text from the letter to the Galatians, which is read on the vigil of this feast, Paul claims the rights inherent to the vocation he received. Unlike Peter, Paul was not among the first followers of the Lord. But his mission was directly entrusted to him "through a revelation of Jesus Christ" (1:12). Like the great prophets, Paul "was set apart before he was born" (v. 15) to proclaim the gospel "among the Gentiles" (v. 16) and the Lord stood by him to help him carry out that responsibility (2 Tm 4:17).

His awareness of being the apostle to the Gentiles led Paul to a confrontation with Peter. Differences form part of a disciple's mission. What is important is to dialogue as they both did in Jerusalem. There the tasks were divided up: some would go to the Jews and others to the Gentiles. However, Peter gives some advice to Paul and to those who are with him. They asked, Paul says, "that we remember the poor, which was actually what I was eager to do" (Gal 2:10). On that point, the two apostles agreed. We too should agree with them by doing the same and doing it eagerly.

Assumption

Everything Is Grace
Rv 11:19, 12:1–6, 10; 1 Cor 15:20–26; Lk 1:39–56

The saints are our models of Christian life. This is especially true of Mary because of the exceptional place she occupies in the history of salvation.

A Canticle of Thanksgiving

We find the first part of Luke's text in Advent (fourth Sunday, cycle C). What follows is taken from Mary's canticle which we call the Magnificat. Mary proclaims this song of thanksgiving not as an isolated person but as the daughter of a people. This is clearly Luke's intention.

With her people, Mary sings the greatness of God. The power of the Lord, revealed in history through his salvific deeds, is the source of profound rejoicing (v. 47). God's liberating actions come from the lowly and the oppressed (v. 48; the Greek word which we translate as "lowly" has a connotation of servitude and destitution). God looks on Mary with love which makes the young Jewish girl happy (blessed). The covenant between God and his people starts to be renewed in Mary. The joy which Mary is experiencing prepares her to proclaim the good news. At the source of the proclamation of the gospel, we always find a joyful experience of the Lord. This feeling expands her heart and prepares her, once again, to welcome the presence of the Lord.

Thus, Mary moves to the central point of her canticle, the proclamation of the holiness of God, "and holy is his name" (v. 49). God's mercy makes him welcoming and tender and it reaches out to everyone. It is also the foundation of what we celebrate on this feast of the Assumption. Everything comes from God and from his gratuitous love. This is the heart of biblical revelation.

Against Death

Preference for the poor and the oppressed runs through the entire Bible. Mary's song powerfully recalls this preference: "He has brought down the powerful from their thrones and lifted up the lowly; he has filled the hungry with good things and sent the rich away empty" (vv. 52–53). The text simply states what we read here and in the whole Bible. Attempts to soften it and to take away its historical bite simply ignore the biblical promises. Once more, we are in the presence of what is called a "messianic inversion." As Jesus will say, the last will be first. In Mary's song, the poor are identified in terms of a basic and cruel deprivation: hunger.

As we are well aware in these latitudes, hunger signifies premature and unjust death — unjust because it is the result of exclusion and deprivation, the result of sin. This complex reality helps us understand Paul's statement about the resurrection of Christ: "The last enemy to be destroyed is death" (1 Cor 15:26). The resurrection is the victory over death and over all that death implies. It is the affirmation of life. History, in the course of which the Son of God becomes incarnate, Mary, who carries him in her womb, and the church, which has to proclaim him (see the first reading from the book of Revelation): all are pregnant with life.

All of this becomes the subject of thanksgiving for Mary and for her people (Lk 1:54–55). The spiritual power of the Magnificat — from the perspective of a reality marked by poverty, we are especially sensitive to it — consists in making us see that the quest for justice must be placed within the framework of the grace of God's love. This is a demanding and profound synthesis at stake in which, as Mary's song reminds us, is our fidelity to Jesus' gospel.

Saint Rose of Lima

A Neighbor from Lima
Sir 3:17–24; Phil 3:8–14; Mt 13:31–35

Having a saint as a neighbor is a unique experience. It marks the devotion to Saint Rose among Peruvians.

From What Is Small

The city of Lima, where Rose was born and lived, was very small, between fifteen thousand and twenty thousand inhabitants. There were almost as many people of African origin as of Spanish origin. Indians also formed an important part (around 10 percent) of Lima's residents. Marginalization and discrimination of the different groups of poor certainly existed. In this atmosphere, Rose lived her Christian life as a lay woman, living the spirituality of the Dominican Third Order. She lived at home rather than being cloistered in one of the great monasteries of Lima.

Matthew's text presents two brief parables showing the kingdom growing from insignificant beginnings. The mustard seed "is the smallest of all the seeds," but it will grow into a great tree where the birds of the air will build their nests (v. 32). The lowliness of the kingdom and of those who are to proclaim it is an essential aspect of the gospel message, something which is not always appreciated by those who seek what is marvelous and miraculous. The text from Sirach also deals with humility and smallness (first reading). This is the attitude preferred by the Lord and also the way he becomes present in human history. Rose of Lima offers us a testimony of that simplicity. She was just one of many residents of Lima but she took very seriously the call to holiness which the gospel addresses to every Christian. Her life of faith was expressed through prayer and the service of others. The trait that her contemporaries and her biographers emphasize the most is her concern for the sick and the needy, especially for blacks and Indians.

The second and even shorter parable of Matthew left a profound imprint in our Christian memory: the kingdom is like the yeast which makes the flour rise and enables us to make bread. Likewise, the kingdom of life and of love gives meaning and direction to human history by transforming it into a place of encounter with God and one another. The presence of Rose — and of Martin de Porres — in the history of Lima, her love and her surrender to others, are manifestations of that yeast which must make our world more human and loving.

Christ Jesus Made Her His Own

The knowledge (or the love) of God must be the absolute value of our lives (Phil 3:8). It does not mean that other aspects of human existence are devoid of interest but that they must be relativized in the strict sense of the term: they have to be placed in relation with the absoluteness of the kingdom. In addition, the kingdom sheds light on all other dimensions and it makes them appear in all their value. Paul asserts this in his forceful and cutting style. In this way, he translates his experience, and without false pride he believes that "Christ Jesus has made me his own" (v. 12). Therefore, with trust and hope, Paul strains forward "to what lies ahead" (v. 13).

This is also the way that in Lima, the city she dearly loved, Rose lived the love of God which filled her life. For that very reason, she converted her life into serving the most needy among her neighbors. Christ also made her his own through his testimony and message. In turn, by going over the only bridge on the Rimac across to the barrio of the marginalized, Rose sought to find the face of the Lord in the faces of the poorest people of Lima in her time. Her life serves as an incentive for our own search.

All Saints

Disciples' Attitudes
Rv 7:2–4, 9–14; 1 Jn 3:1–3; Mt 5:1–12

The Matthean text of the beatitudes is undoubtedly one of the best-known texts in the gospels. The feast of "All Saints" is the feast of all Christians. In fact, being a disciple of Jesus implies striving to be holy as our heavenly Father is holy (Mt 5:48).

From One Kind of Poverty to Another

Blessed are the poor in spirit, says the Lord when he starts his proclamation of the kingdom of life in the so-called sermon on the mount. Matthew concludes the presentation of this proclamation in his twenty-fifth chapter (chapters 26 to 28 relate the passion, death, and resurrection of Christ) where he tells us that those who are sensitive to the needs of the poor will enter the kingdom. This is why we can say that this gospel situates Jesus' proclamation between two statements about the poor: spiritual poverty (at the beginning of chapter 5) and material poverty (at the end of chapter 25) in the words of frequently used expressions. This helps us to understand the meaning of the beatitudes.

The eight beatitudes speak to us of the fundamental attitudes of Jesus' disciples and of Christians. Disciples must totally trust God (poor in spirit); they must share the suffering of others (those who weep). Like the Lord (Mt 11:30), they must be kind to others (the meek). They must fervently want justice to reign in this world (those who hunger and thirst for righteousness). Moreover, disciples must bear in their hearts the poor (the needy) in history (the merciful). They must be consistent and upright in their lives (the pure in heart). They must do their best to establish peace as the outcome of justice (the peacemakers). All of this means that they will be opposed by those who refuse to recognize the rights of others (the persecuted for righteousness' sake).

The Gift of Filiation

The gift of the kingdom requires these options and convictions on the part of Christians. If we act in keeping with them, we will enter the kingdom of heaven whose meaning is expressed as consolation, land, fullness, mercy, the vision of God, and divine filiation. The substance of that behavior is presented in the twenty-fifth chapter: disciples are those who feed the hungry, give a drink to the thirsty, etc., in other words, those who are committed to the needy. The poor in spirit translate their love of God and of others by being in solidarity with the real poor in a material sense. In their actions for the poor, the marginalized, and the oppressed, they will encounter Jesus himself: "you did it to me." And encountering the Lord is a grace.

It is impossible to embrace the cause of the poor, whereby our fidelity to Christ is verified (see John Paul II, *On Human Work*, no. 8), without causing resistance and hostility, without going through "the great ordeal" (Rv 7:14). Receiving the grace of being children of God (1 Jn 3:1) involves creating authentic friendship and justice in our society.

The beatitudes point out the basic attitudes of Christians. They constitute the "Magna Carta" of Jesus' disciples. How are we to prevent this from being a dead letter to us, something that we throw in the bottom of a drawer and we forget to respond to? Without the attitudes indicated in the beatitudes we will not be able to keep alive the hope of seeing God "as he is" (1 Jn 3:2).

Immaculate Conception

Like Mary

Gn 3:9–15, 20; Eph 1:3–6, 11–12; Lk 1:26–38

The gospels center on Jesus, and Mary is portrayed in them as the believer par excellence, the model of our faith.

Hail, Full of Grace

The name of the son promised to Zechariah is John, which means "the Lord looks favorably" (as mentioned in Lk 1:66). In fact, the first two chapters of Luke recall the loving and saving presence of

God. In our text, the dialogue with Mary begins with an exhortation to rejoice (v. 28). In the Bible, rejoicing is a characteristic note of the fulfillment of God's promises. Since Mary receives God's favor, the expression "full of grace" spontaneously replaces her name. Thus, "rejoice, Mary" becomes "Greetings, favored one!" The Lord is at her side; she has "found favor with God" (v. 30). It all happens because of God's free and gratuitous love. Faith is the gift which inaugurates the dialogue. God puts his trust in Mary and, in turn, this makes her put her trust in God, converting her into a believer. Therefore, there is no foundation for fear, but there is reason for surrender (v. 30). Fear is precisely the opposite of trust in God. By looking favorably on Mary, God solicits her faith, and thanks to her response the young Jewish girl has a part in God's work.

What is announced will be the work of the Holy Spirit, and the power of the Most High will overshadow her (vv. 32 and 35). The gift of the incarnation takes place in history. It is the synthesis of the power of the Spirit and Mary's lowliness. Her son will be great and will be called "the Son of the Most High" (v. 32). Jesus' mission is marked by this responsibility, and in it God's great saving plan is accomplished (see Eph 1). Mary is like the new Eve (Gn 3:20), a name which seems to mean life, vitality, hence the expression "mother of the living." Because of all this, Mary's motherhood is more than a personal gift, it is a gift to all humankind through Mary. It is a charism in the strict sense of the word, a gift given to one person for the benefit of the community. Every gift we receive involves a task and a responsibility: we are Christians and we form a church in terms of others. This is why we have to bear witness to the love of God in all circumstances.

Mary, the Believer

Mary is aware of all the implications of her accepting God's will: "Here I am, the servant of the Lord; let it be with me according to your word" (v. 38). In the canticle of the Magnificat, Mary will again call herself servant. Luke has in mind the meaning of the Hebrew word which we translate by "servant." It means belonging to God rather than subordination or inferiority. Servants are those who announce the Lord's message, those who receive a mission (Acts 2:18). Belonging to God is expressed by our availability, by our welcoming his plan for our lives and our world. Mary does not ask for a sign as Zechariah had done (Lk 1:18). She shows her total confidence in the will of God. Mary makes God's will her own in her body and her faith. We must do the same.

The text of Ephesians shows us the deep meaning of human existence. We have come into this world to be daughters and sons of God (vv. 4–5). Being God's children is not something added from outside the human condition, instead it is its very raison d'être. The grace of God's love is the first and the last word. However, we cannot accept God's plan of love and peace if we do not incarnate it in our daily lives, if we do not get rid of our petty advantages, and if we do not take risks. Like Mary.

Index of Biblical References

OLD TESTAMENT

APOCRYPHA

NEW TESTAMENT